1979

University of St. Francis
GEN   070.4092 M394
Marzolf, Marion.
Up from the footnote :

3 0301 00053853 4

W9-ABR-425

UP FROM THE FOOTNOTE

* * *

UP FROM
THE
FOOTNOTE

* * *

A History of
Women Journalists

by
MARION MARZOLF

COMMUNICATION ARTS BOOKS

HASTINGS HOUSE, PUBLISHERS
New York 10016

LIBRARY
College of St. Francis
JOLIET, ILL.

Copyright © 1977, by Marion Tuttle Marzolf.

All rights reserved. No part of this publication may be reproduced, stored in a retrieval system, or transmitted, in any form or by any means, electronic, mechanical, photocopying, recording or otherwise, without the prior permission of the copyright owner or the publishers.

Library of Congress Cataloging in Publication Data

Marzolf, Marion.
 Up from the footnote.

 (Communication arts books)
 Includes bibliographies and index.
  1. Women journalists—United States. 2. Women journalists—Europe. I. Title.
 PN4872.M37   070.4'092'2 [B]   77-5398
 ISBN 0-8038-7502-9

Published simultaneously in Canada by
Saunders of Toronto, Ltd., Don Mills, Ontario

Printed in the United States of America
Designed by Al Lichtenberg

070.4092
M394

* * *

Contents

$14.45 associated collegiate Press

8-22-79

86755

Foreword

Brenda Starr in the comic strips, Rosalind Russell in the movies and Mary Tyler Moore on TV may be the public's image of the woman reporter. But the real thing, as I hope this book will begin to demonstrate, has been infinitely more interesting than the stereotype. She has been tough-minded, determined, aggressive, intelligent, independent and professional. But she has also been compassionate, hopeful, intuitive and warmly human.

The woman journalist has been forthright and engaging. She's gotten to the top when getting to the top wasn't easy and she's asked no quarter. Professionalism has been her code, and by it she's won the respect and admiration of her colleagues and bosses. She's often been the first woman to handle a specific job and often been alone in a field dominated by men.

Meeting these women journalists through their words and accomplishments, gleaned from hundreds of books, clippings, scholarly studies, popularized profiles, speeches, tapes, letters and interviews during a period of over four years has increased my affection for this fascinating profession.

It is my hope that readers will share a new sense of community and continuity with these pioneers who have so long been hidden from view. Women journalists have a rich history and tradition, but they are just beginning to discover it. This book highlights experiences and thoughts of many women in various journalistic jobs and stages of professional development. It is hoped that it will be useful to those who are already active in journalism and to those who are contemplating it as a life work.

* * *

Acknowledgments

This book has been in process, in one form or another, since 1972. The idea began when Professor Anne Firor Scott of Duke University lectured at the University of Michigan and told her audience that women "act as if they had no history."

I looked at the journalism history that I was teaching. Women were mentioned mostly in the footnotes in standard journalism history texts. I resolved to search for them and recover their lost history.

University of Michigan students in my first seminar helped gather names and experiences, and together we published a special issue of the student laboratory paper, *The Michigan Journalist,* and later a bibliography. Their enthusiasm spurred me on. My journalism faculty colleagues, especially Professors John D. Stevens, William E. Porter and Peter Clarke, encouraged my work, and for that I am most grateful.

Special and very deep thanks go to Dr. Ramona R. Rush, who shared my early plan for the book as a collection of articles including history, image and discrimination studies. She devoted much time and effort to a first draft that our editors wanted reworked into an historical overview. Other early and intended contributors, some of whose work was eventually adapted and used with their permission, also have my generous thanks for their efforts, encouragement and understanding. They are: Dr. William Bowman and Joann Lublin for their studies of contemporary professionals, Sally Quick and Joy Hart for their work on the feminist press, Darlene Stern for help on the bibliography, Dr. Maurine Beasley, for her work on early correspondents, and Dr. Matilda Butler-Paisley and Dr. Mary Ann Yodelis for their research.

Many students have contributed to the success of this venture through research which they willingly shared with me. Colleagues at other universities were frequently willing to read sections of the manuscript and offer criticism or share materials of their own with me. Their contributions are noted in the text and list of sources, but additional thanks are due to Professors Vernon Stone, Cathy Covert, Tom Reilly and Leland Stowe for their special assistance.

In the course of the research I have been warmly received by many professional women journalists who have willingly told me their stories. To each of them I will always be grateful not just for the help but also for the friendship. To Barbara Abel of the Milwaukee *Journal* and a NEH journalism fellow at the University of Michigan I owe a special debt of gratitude for an exacting and helpful reading of the final manuscript. It was a pleasure to interview Ishbel Ross, who wrote the first history of American women journalists and who greeted my work with warmth and enthusiasm.

The experience and strength gained through my work in Women in Communications, Inc. and the Association for Education in Journalism has been very important.

The constant support and encouragement so spontaneously given by my husband, Kingsbury, is precious beyond measure.

1

* * *

Widow Printer to Big City Reporter

IN COLONIAL AMERICA it was "quite a common thing for widows—especially of printers, innkeepers, and traders—to take up and carry on the husband's trade, and not uncommon for them to set up businesses of their own," observed Isaiah Thomas, himself a printer and the first historian of American journalism.

Printing in the Colonies

At one time there were as many as four colonial women printers operating in different parts of the country. The earliest was Dinah Nuthead in Maryland in 1696. Five, including Nuthead, were official printers before the War for Independence, and all but one of those also published a weekly newspaper.

Printing in the colonies was introduced in 1638 at Harvard University, and the first continuously published newspaper was established in 1704. Most early printers had to supplement their incomes by selling a variety of goods along with printed pamphlets, broadsides and commercial forms. The designation as an official printer assured regular government work.

So it was not an unimportant piece of cargo that was loaded

on the ship *John* bound for New England. A printing press and types accompanied the Reverend Jose Glover of Surrey, England, his wife, five children, numerous servants and a locksmith named Stephen Day and family. Glover died before the ship reached port, so it was Mistress Glover who bought the house in Cambridge and installed the first printing press in North America there in 1638. In the first two years her printer issued a broadsheet, an almanac and the *Bay Psalm Book*. Not long after, she was married to the president of Harvard College and she moved her printing press into the lean-to at his lodge. When she died, he managed the press.

By the start of the American Revolution at least 14 women had been printers in the colonies. Their names are usually forgotten in the histories of journalism; only occasionally are they footnoted. They deserve mention here because they are the "foremothers" of the generations of women in journalism.

They were: Elizabeth Timothy (South Carolina), Dinah Nuthead (Maryland), Sarah Updike Goddard (Rhode Island), Mary Katherine Goddard (Maryland), Anne Smith Franklin (Rhode Island), Cornelia Smith Bradford (New York), Anna Maul Zenger (New York), Clementina Rind (Virginia), Anne Hoof Green (Maryland), Mary Timothy Crouch (South Carolina), Pennelope Russell (Massachusetts), Mrs. H. Boyle (Virginia), Mrs. Nicholas Hasselbaugh (Maryland) and Margaret Green Draper (Massachusetts).

According to Susan Henry, her doctoral research at Syracuse University has convinced her that each of these women existed and was a printer. She and others found several other women associated with print shops or as owners or workers, including Sarah Packe and Eleanore Parks (Virginia), Cornelia Bradford and Jane Aitken (Philadelphia), Deborah Read Franklin and Mary Biddle (Pennsylvania), Joanna Perry (Boston), Elizabeth Holt and Ann Greenleaf (New York).

Printing families like the Franklins and the Goddards passed the craft on through wives and daughters as well as sons; all were trained to work in the family business when they were young. James Franklin, for example, taught his daughter to set type. Twice his widow, Anne, assumed management of the family newspaper and print shops. When

James died in 1735, she handled the Rhode Island paper, and when her son, James, Jr., died in 1762, she assumed control of his Newport *Mercury*, a Rhode Island paper, running it until her death in 1763. Her journalistic career spanned 23 years.

Isaiah Thomas often saw Anne and her daughters at work in the Franklin shop and recalled that the "daughters were correct and quick compositors at case; they were instructed by their father, whom they assisted." Thomas also thought they were sensible and amiable women. They worked at proofreading, copy editing, typesetting and occasionally at reporting.

Colonial women shared the hardships, but their lives were not recorded, said Arthur M. Schlesinger in *New Viewpoints in American History*, as he examined their status. Sometimes women inherited property, but legally women were the property of men. Most women could not read or write and the few that were educated were given training in manners, morals, social and household talents. They undoubtedly engaged in some discussion of current affairs in their homes, and as widow printers at least a few took active stands in the controversy with England.

Historians skip over these early women printer-editors, usually passing them off as accidents created by the early deaths of husbands or fathers. But how was it that at least some of them could carry on the demanding tasks of reading, writing, setting type, keeping books and managing a business? That story is still to be uncovered, but partial answers are starting to emerge in the new research.

✳ ✳ ✳

Elizabeth Timothy, editor of the *South Carolina Gazette* in Charleston for seven years following the death of her husband in 1738, was highly praised by Benjamin Franklin for her business sense. Franklin had helped Timothy establish himself as Charleston's official printer in 1731 for which Franklin received a third of the profits. Franklin complained about Timothy's poor financial accounting, but he praised the regularity and exactitude of widow Timothy's quarterly reports. He attributed her ability in this field to her having been "born and bred in Holland, where, as I have been informed, the knowledge of accounts makes a part of female education."

Franklin also said that the widow managed the business with "such success that she not only brought up reputably a family of children but at the expiration of the term was able to purchase of me the printing house and establish her son in it," as was intended in the original contract.

Elizabeth Timothy took over publication of the *Gazette* in order to carry on the family business and, although she published in her son's name, her first issue on January 4, 1739, carried the announcement that she was editing the paper. This established her, according to Ira Lee Baker's research, as America's first woman editor-publisher. She asked her readers "to continue their Favours and good Offices to this poor afflicted Widow and six small children and another hourly expected."

Her first newspapers carried little local news, said Baker, and the quality of the literary content also suffered at first. The *Gazette* relied more heavily than ever before on foreign and domestic news exchanges. She herself often wrote homilies and she carried essays that emulated those in English journals. She reprinted dramas, poetry and literary classics as well as printing the first efforts of new Southern writers. The *Gazette* remained four pages, approximately 8 by 13 inches in size, and type was at first set in two columns, later in three, during her editorship.

During her tenure the paper was not "political" and did not offend the authorities. When Elizabeth Timothy died in 1757, 11 years after turning the paper over to her son, she left substantial assets that reflected the shrewd business ability of the "poor afflicted widow." A plaque honoring her as the first woman newspaper publisher in the United States was presented to the South Carolina Press Association by Women in Communications, Inc., in 1975 at ceremonies in the printing museum at Charles Towne Landing, site of the first South Carolina colony.

* * *

The Goddards of Rhode Island made an unusual printing family because it was mother and daughter who carried a substantial part of the financial risk and practical editing and printing work of four papers associated with William Goddard, nominally and legally their owner. Sarah Goddard was born to a well-established Rhode Island family and was educated beyond what was customary for young women of her time. Her husband died in 1757.

She invested in a newspaper established by her son William in 1762. She and her daughter, Mary Katherine, helped run the Providence *Gazette and Country Journal* and assisted in the selling and printing of books, almanacs and legal forms that were part of the colonial printer's normal business. The business was not profitable enough for William, however, and in 1765 he moved to New York, suspending the paper and leaving the shop under the direction of his mother. She and her daughter continued to supply legal forms and almanacs and brought out at least one special issue of the paper in 1765 under the imprint of S. and W. Goddard. According to Nancy Chudacoff's research, that was the first time Sarah Goddard's name appeared in the business.

William returned and revived the paper in 1766, but soon left for Philadelphia. The women remained and Sarah Goddard and Company (Mary Katherine and a printer) ran the business from the summer of 1766. Their first book was written by a woman.

Although William Goddard still regarded himself as head of the business while he was establishing a new paper in Philadelphia, the *Pennsylvania Chronicle and Universal Advertiser*, his mother really ran the *Gazette* and his sister became an accomplished printer.

Mother and son were both ardent patriots and when Goddard was the first to print John Dickinson's "Letters from a Farmer in Pennsylvania to the Inhabitants of the British Colonies," his mother wrote suggesting that he print the "Farmer's" letters in a pamphlet and soon, because she thought they "appear to be the completest pieces ever wrote on the subject in America." She told him they were "universally admired in Providence."

Goddard's partners urged him to bring his mother to Philadelphia in the hope that she would have a calming influence on his temper. She wished to continue in Providence and only agreed to leave in 1768 because of "the more endearing ties of Nature which exist between a Parent and an only son. . . ."

In Philadelphia she was briefly allowed to run a small printing press, but this was removed when William's partners feared that mother and son might engage in competition on the side. When Goddard signed over to her son her remaining interest in her husband's estate, he agreed to support her from his Philadelphia business, and she continued to work with him until her death in 1770.

Mary Katherine also aided her brother, managing two of his newspapers. In 1733, when he decided to close the Philadelphia newspaper in order to found the first newspaper in Baltimore, his sister ran the *Chronicle* until the *Maryland Journal* had been established. And while Goddard was off establishing a new postal system, she ran the *Journal* for eight years. She started a paper mill in 1776 and on January 18, 1777, was first to print the Declaration of Independence with the names of all the signers.

Mary Katherine Goddard lived in a man's world, as Fred Farrar observed in his thesis on the colonial press, and when her brother returned in 1781, he took the paper away from her. They quarreled. She retained her job as postmistress and her bookshop, which she operated with profit until her retirement in 1810. According to Isaiah Thomas she did some "very good book printing."

✻   ✻   ✻

Clementina Rind only served as editor of the *Virginia Gazette* in Williamsburg for 13 months, but because she often spoke her mind on the rapidly deteriorating state of relations with England, she left an image of herself as an articulate observer of state affairs (said Norma Schneider in a study of the printer). She took over the paper in 1773 upon the death of her husband and petitioned to succeed him as public printer. She did receive a large part of the public business, including the printing contract for the post office.

Rind was a Whig, as her husband had been, and at first she tried to publish articles on both sides of an issue. In October, 1773, she published the controversial "Cato Letters" on liberty, representative government and freedom of expression, but she also reprinted an article urging the House of Burgesses to resist.

The pro-American views in her newspaper increased and she clearly expressed her anger over the tax on tea. When the British decided to close the port of Boston after the Boston Tea Party, Rind's paper was no longer impartial. She held up her edition for a day in order to publish the Virginia resolution opposing this British action as "an injury to American rights" and began to support the people in Boston. She reprinted articles from the North begging the colonies to send supplies to the besieged port. When it was suggested that colonies boycott all British goods, she published the names of each colony as it agreed to participate. She also published letters from London telling about the ill effects of the boycott.

When the Virginia governor warned against public meetings and signing of documents against the king or parliament, she published that as well as mention of "several letters from principle gentlemen in England . . . who wish us to continue firm in our opposition, as the only means of redress."

When she had been editor for a year, Rind ran a notice about her poor health, and commented on the importance of free exercise of the press "in all matters which serve not the ends of corruption and malevolence." She set forth her aim

> . . . to revive, at all times in her power, the spirit of this paper, by a due observance of material intelligence, and a proper attention to all pieces with which she may be favored from any of her correspondents with which, if they exceed not the bounds of her gazette, and are frought with either a decent of moral tendancey, shall have the proper arrangement.

When she died in 1774, the *Gazette* eulogized her as a lady

> . . . loved by the muses, and fair science too . . . and fortitude of mind combined with the softer graces of her sex . . .

to form a bright example of her life of editor, mistress, daughter, mother, wife.

✳ ✳ ✳

Not all printers, nor all women printers, were on the patriot side. As the war of words began to heat up, one who was pro-British had to flee Boston under the protection of the evacuating British troops. She was Margaret Draper, who had taken charge of the country's oldest newspaper, the *Massachusetts Gazette and Boston News-Letter,* as of mid-1774. She was the granddaughter of Bartholomew Green, an early printer and publisher of the Boston *News-Letter.* She married her cousin, Richard Draper, whose father had apprenticed under Green and had been taken into the business.

According to Susan Henry's research on the Drapers, little is known about Margaret Draper until she married. The paper was considered a Tory paper, but actually carried articles and letters on both sides of the issue, including John Dickinson's "Farmer" letters.

Under Margaret Draper the publication became less balanced and carried vehement defenses of the Intolerable Acts, attacks on the patriot press and warnings that rebellion would result in defeat. She was only able to publish irregularly following the battle of Lexington and Concord, and on March 6, 1776, she left for Halifax with departing British troops. She had taken in a young partner in mid-1775 and he started a newspaper in Nova Scotia. She fled to England and filed for government compensation for her losses, which she eventually received. She was in poor health when she arrived in England at nearly 50 years of age and her remaining days apparently included no printing work.

After the Revolution

Women continued to work in the printing offices in the late 1700's and the early 1800's, primarily in small printing establishments and for book publishers. They were not employed to any extent on the large city newspapers that flourished during the Civil War, apparently because much of the work was done under great pressure and at night. Bookbinding, however, did attract their talents, as did engraving, but the pay was low.

In Boston, for example, in 1831 there were 687 men in the allied printing trades, most of whom were paid $1.50 per day, and 395 women and 215 boys, most of whom were paid 50 cents, according to figures in *Women in Industry*.

Women were not encouraged to join the printing trade for several reasons: it had a long apprenticeship period, there was an abundance of male applicants and the unions were anti-women.

Hostility to women in the printing trade was vigorous enough in Philadelphia in 1832 to alarm the Typographical Society when it was rumored that a member was planning to employ women compositors and install a non-union foreman over them. The accused member felt "called upon" to write a letter to be spread upon the minutes of the Society "denying that he had ever intended to employ women." And there were similar incidents elsewhere.

The National Typographical Union in 1854 discussed the problem of women printers and resolved not to encourage employment of female compositors. It reaffirmed this in 1855 and continued to discuss the matter regularly. The number of women printers increased, nevertheless, as did the number of women in the big cities in need of work.

In 1869 women petitioned to form their own separate printers unions and one was organized in New York City in 1870. These efforts were not successful; women still maintained a lower wage scale and that made them dangerous competition for other unionized labor.

The printing firm of Gray and Green in New York City was an exception. An article in the New York *Daily Tribune* in 1869 announced the opening of a training school for women printers in which the company had taken 20 women and a dozen boys for the first class taught by two workwomen. This company employed 30 to 40 women compositors (among their

400 hands) including an experienced forewoman and was well satisfied with their work, so much so that they intended to pay the women the same wages as men for the same work.

In 1873 the unions voted to admit women to full membership in local unions and demanded the same pay for women printers as for men. In 1905 women accounted for around 20 per cent of all persons employed in printing and publishing—in 1890 women, by comparison, had been 14 per cent of the total—an increase in number from 19,026 to 37,614.

On the editorial side, a few women carried on the local family-owned newspapers at the turn of the century and into the early 1800's. Cornelia M. Walter took up her brother's former post as editor of the Boston *Transcript* in 1842 and Ann S. Stephens of the New York *Evening Express* was one of the pioneer women hired as an editorial writer and literary critic in 1837, jobs she held for 30 years. Author Lydia Marie Child, after editing a children's magazine, became editor in 1841 of the *Anti-Slavery Standard,* the journal of the American Anti-Slavery Society. During the years from 1841–1844 she also wrote a weekly letter to the Boston *Courier* covering New York City's literary, social, musical and dramatic life. The letters were published in book form. During these pre-Civil War years it was not unusual for women who were active in the cause of abolition, suffrage and temperance, like Sarah and Angelina Grimké, to write special articles for the newspapers. But career women journalists and editors were still rare.

A transplanted New Englander, Sarah Hillhouse, became the first woman publisher and editor in Georgia in 1803 when she assumed control of the Washington *Monitor* upon the death of her husband. She was 40 years old and had already buried three of her six children at the time. According to her son, she "immediately took the management of the paper and learned and practiced every mechanical service pertaining to the office." The circulation was about 800 when she took it over and the paper was smaller in size than a tabloid, running four columns of type.

General news emphasizing public issues, a touch of humor and even sensationalism added spice to her paper, said Wallace B. Eberhard in his analysis of her editorship, which lasted until 1811 or 1812 when her son assumed control. She clipped from other newspapers, as was customary, but she also wrote her own reports and opinions. She encouraged use of the *Monitor's* columns for political exchanges by local figures, sometimes under assumed names. She once carried a long article by ""Dorothy Distaff" under the headline "Female patriotism" which said that a "hundred thousand spinning wheels would be as effective as 10,000 of the best militia." She published copies of the state and federal laws in her newspaper and was considered to have a good business sense.

* * *

The early nineteenth century women publishers' names that came down as examples through history, on the other hand, were those who were outspoken and unconventional: Anne Royall, Victoria Woodhull and Jane Swisshelm. They were crusaders for social justice, female emancipation, abolition and the like and wrote in the sharp and biting style of their day, but they are usually recalled as being social oddities.

Anne Royall published her own paper in Washington, D.C., for 23 years, beginning in 1831, and she published ten highly praised travel volumes. She was a self-educated woman who was encouraged to love books. When her husband, a wealthy eccentric, died leaving his fortune to his children, she left New Orleans. She went to Washington in 1824 to request a pension from Royall's service in the War for Independence. She was 54. On the trip to the capital she took notes of the places and people she saw and published them: *Sketches of History, Life and Manners in the United States* in 1826. They were so popular that she wrote nine more, traveling and selling subscriptions to her books until 1831. Then she started her political newspaper in Washington. It was named *Paul Pry* at first. Later called the *Huntress,* it existed until 1854.

Her newspaper was full of sympathy for the underdog as she supported the causes of the Indians and the immigrants. She championed scientific research and free public education and she encouraged clean-up campaigns in the cities. But it was her reputation as a "common scold" that was remembered. Apparently a group of missionaries conducted services below her windows in an attempt to convert her and she shouted back at them. They brought suit, and under an old law she was found guilty of being a "public nuisance, common brawler and common scold" in 1829. Royall's literary reputation rests on the travel journals which historians consider a valuable first-hand source description of town and village life in early nineteenth-century America.

As Americans moved across the nation, pushing the line of the frontier westward, women shared the hardships of pioneer life with their men and helped to build the farms and villages and the newspapers of the West. Their names and deeds may be recorded in some state and county histories, but most of their stories are still awaiting discovery. One such woman was Mathilde Franziska Anneke, who established the *Deutsche Frauenzeitung* (German Woman's Journal) in Milwaukee in 1852, a paper devoted to feminist issues. Her hiring of women compositors so upset the local German printers that they formed the first typographical society in that city to protect printers against the encroachment of females. Anneke moved her publication to New York and Jersey City, where it was discontinued in 1854 or 1855. She was apparently the first woman publisher in Wisconsin.

Women's publications developed in the early 1800's and one of the earliest and most successful was *Godey's Lady's Book* of Philadelphia. Its noted editor, Sara Josepha Hale, is thought to have been the first to develop a magazine that specialized in women's interests. When she was asked to edit *Ladies' Magazine* in 1828 in Boston, she said that she would "promote the reputation of women" and make them "acquainted with their duties and privileges as women."

One of those duties was to become educated and to serve as teachers for the young, a new idea for women at the time. When Godey absorbed the two magazines in 1837, he asked her to edit the new *Lady's Book,* which she did until her retirement at age 90. (She died two years later in 1879.) The magazine reached a circulation of 150,000.

Hale published new American writers, who later became literary greats, along with coverage of fashion and household furnishings and her own articles on the domestic ideals and the advancement of women. For many years she worked to have Thanksgiving made a national holiday. Her campaign was successful in 1863. She opposed such radical women as Victoria Woodhull and Fanny Wright because she thought they were trying to destroy the very foundations of the American home with their advocacy of free love and abolition of marriage rites.

Other women's magazines and illustrated magazines in mid-nineteenth century America attracted the writing and editing talents of some women. A few originated their own publications. The *Lowell Offering,* started by the factory girls of Lowell, Massachusetts, in 1840, was filled with material written by this rather unique group of young women. Fanny Wright, a popular lecturer on women's issues, established a paper in 1829 called the *Sentinel* in New York and later one called *Man,* in which she presented her views on religious, political and social doctrines. After the Seneca Falls Convention of 1848, women increasingly raised their voices in the cause of abolition and equal rights and in abolitionist and feminist publications. (See Chapter 7.)

✳   ✳   ✳

In the cities only a few women were engaged in journalism; the most distinguished was Maragret Fuller. After editing *The Dial* literary magazine with Ralph Waldo Emerson, she was hired by Horace Greeley to write literary reviews and profiles for his New York *Tribune.*

Fuller hated to leave New England, but found that New York was "the point where American and European interests converge." It offered her a "richer and more varied exercise for thought and life" in 20 months than 20 years in another part of the United States. She met a wide variety of people, including the "literati" of the city.

Greeley hired Fuller in 1844 to write three articles a week for the daily edition of the *Tribune,* two on literary subjects and one on social matters. Many of these were used in the weekly and semi-weekly editions of the paper. He wanted to attract more women readers and hired her as literary editor with a view to concentrating on news about literature, the arts and social questions. She was free to select topics and approaches and she could cull items from the foreign press. Her book, *Woman in the Nineteenth Century*, was published by Greeley and his partner in 1845, and he frequently applauded her efforts in behalf of women's rights and admired her courage.

Fuller was outspoken as a critic and developed her own method of "general affirmation" coupled with "judicious use of severe criticism" in a spirit of telling the whole truth. She offended her friends sometimes but they couldn't fault her grounding in literary criticism. She did bring forward new writers and works of freshness.

In order to cover social issues, Fuller visited prisons and houses of correction and wrote about the city's remedial and corrective systems and about the immigrant population and their problems. She decided to tour Europe in 1845 and serve as a *Tribune* correspondent, probably the first American woman to serve as a foreign correspondent.

In London she met the intellectual set and first learned in detail about revolutionary plans for Italy. In Italy she collected material for a book on that country and set about writing it, became involved with the revolutionary movement, fell in love, married and bore a son. She reported the 1848 revolution in Italy for the *Tribune* and left Rome when all foreigners were ordered out in June, 1849. Fuller and her husband and son were drowned in a shipwreck off the coast of America in 1850 on the homeward journey.

✳   ✳   ✳

As women became involved in social and political issues swirling through American society in the years immediately preceding the Civil War, they were drawn to that center of political decision making, Washington, D.C. They were correspondents for some of the influential newspapers and magazines of the day and their reporting covered political and social commentary.

Jane Grey Swisshelm, an ardent abolitionist, was one of the

first. She had arranged to send a column on the question of disposition of lands taken in the Mexican War to Horace Greeley's *Tribune* in 1850. When she arrived in Washington, she found it was difficult to hear and see Congressional debate from the public galleries. She appealed to the Vice-President, Millard Fillmore, for a seat in the Senate Press Gallery.

The Vice-President was "much surprised and tried to dissuade me," she recalled in her autobiography, *Half A Century.* "The place would be very unpleasant for a lady, and would attract attention."

But he gave her a seat, which she occupied for only one day. Swisshelm left Washington hastily, fearing that Greeley would discharge her for a dispatch containing a scandalous rumor about Daniel Webster she had sent to her own Pittsburgh *Sunday Visiter,* an abolitionist publication she founded in 1847. She was quick to pick up rumors about those who opposed abolition and said she believed this bit of gossip. She was subjected to a storm of criticism for the item.

An early advocate of women's rights, Swisshelm declared that women, black and white, should have the opportunity to make use of their minds. Her columns on these issues were collected in 1853 in a book called *Letters to Country Girls.* In it she said that millions of women were condemned to menial drudgery that men would scorn and for it they earned one fourth the wages.

> They plough, harrow, reap, dig, make hay, rake, bind grain, thrash, chop wood, milk, churn, do anything that is hard work, physical labor, and who says anything against it? But let one presume to use her mental powers—let her aspire to turn editor, public speaker, doctor, lawyer—take up any profession or avocation which is deemed honorable and requires talent, and O! bring cologne, get a cambric kerchief and feather fan, unloose his corsets and take off his cravat! What a fainting fit Mr. Propriety has taken! Just to think that "one of the deah creathures"—the heavenly angels, should forsake the sphere—woman's sphere—to mix with the wicked strife of this wicked world!

Swisshelm's unhappy marriage forced her to leave her husband. She suffered a breakdown in 1856 and fought in the courts for her freedom. She then moved to Minnesota to be near her sister and started the St. Cloud *Visiter*. She was a staunch Republican and vigorously opposed the Democratic power structure in the town. One night her press and type were destroyed, but the townspeople rallied to support her. After a libel suit that put her out of business, she started a new paper, the St. Cloud *Democrat*. She pledged that she would discuss any subject she wished and the opposition ceased.

Swisshelm went to Washington on a lecture tour in 1863 to oppose leniency for the Sioux Indians accused of massacring white settlers. She was offered a clerkship in the Quartermaster General's office and accepted. She sold her frontier newspaper but continued to write for it. While waiting for her government job she volunteered to nurse wounded Union soldiers and was shocked at their treatment. She launched a drive to collect pickles, lemons and oranges, which it was believed would aid in fighting gangrene. "No well man or woman has a right to a glass of lemonade," she wrote to the *Tribune*.

She attacked the Lincoln administration, calling the president too soft-hearted toward Democrats, and with a new paper, *The Reconstructionist*, in 1865 continued her attacks on the government's policies toward the South. This led to Swisshelm's dismissal and she closed her paper in 1866 and retired to Pennsylvania to write her life story.

Abolition and the Civil War

According to research on the early Washington women correspondents by Maurine Beasley in her doctoral dissertation, Sara Jane Clarke, whose pen name was "Grace Greenwood," became the second Washington woman correspondent. She had written a popular series of letters in the New York *Home Journal* in the 1840's on suitably genteel topics, but in her support of abolition was considered a "strong minded woman."

Clarke's contributions to the abolitionist paper, the *National Era*, lost her her job as junior editor of *Godey's Lady's Book* because it offended Southern readers. She was promptly hired as an assistant at the *National Era*, and came to Washington in June, 1850, to work for that paper and correspond for the

Saturday Evening Post of Philadelphia. She apparently did not use the press gallery.

Another woman who wrote for the *Era* and corresponded for the Boston newspaper, the *Congregationalist,* was Mary Abigail Dodge. In the *Era* essays she signed herself "Gail Hamilton" but in the Boston paper her political articles were signed "Cunctare." She did not need gallery access because she met leading anti-slavery figures in her editor's home, where she was also the governess for his six children. She left Washington in 1860 but returned during Reconstruction.

During the Civil War there were at least three women Washington correspondents using the pen name "Miriam," but Mary Clemmer Ames and Emily ("Olivia") Edson Briggs were the foremost correspondents among women, according to Beasley. Ames was the highest paid newspaperwoman of her day, and was known for her column "Woman's Letter from Washington" in the *Independent,* an influential New York weekly. She attacked corruption in the Grant administration, exposing drunken Congressmen, and she championed woman suffrage and supported the newly emancipated black population. She maintained her image as a proper lady, too.

Ames criticized women correspondents who dared invade the reporter's galleries, but defended women's right to work when they lacked a male provider. The "true woman" belonged in the home, she said. She wrote book reviews, columns and advertising copy from 1869 to 1872 for the Brooklyn *Daily Union,* for which she received a salary of $5,000. She also published fiction, poetry and Washington recollections.

As "Olivia" Emily Edson Briggs focused on Washington personalities and social life, and between 1866 and 1882, according to Beasley, earned as much as $3,500 a year. She covered President Johnson's impeachement trial, but stayed out of the gallery because she felt women were unwelcome. She wrote for the Philadelphia *Press.*

The names of women correspondents eligible for the Capitol press galleries were first listed in the *Congressional Directory* in 1870. There were four, but by 1879 there were 20. That year the standing committee of correspondents ruled that no more than three reporters could be assigned to the galleries by any one

newspaper and barred part-time journalists. The women had
been part-time correspondents and the new rule barred them
along with 79 men. But at this point women were no longer a
rarity in the nation's capital as journalists, and some, like
Mary Dodge and Sara Clarke Lippincott, returned in the 1870's
and wrote articles, often political, for the New York *Times* and
the *Tribune*.

Following the Civil War women continued to blaze trails in
journalism. Ellen Browning Scripps, sister of James and Edward Scripps, worked with them on their Michigan and Ohio
newspapers, wrote a column and handled their feature syndicate. She was an ardent suffragist and temperance worker.
Other women were founding and editing weekly newspapers
in the Midwest and in the territories and working as reporters
and society editors on the dailies.

The Civil War brought new roles for women in the South,
and journalism was one field where some found work. But it
was still unusual in 1868 when Piney W. Forsythe took over
her father's Liberty (Mississippi) *Advocate*. Along with her
two sisters, who had been raised as printers, she successfully
ran the newspaper, but would not attend a convention of Mississippi editors "for fear they would stare at me."

In New Orleans, Eliza Jane Poitevent was to become an outstanding pioneer woman in Southern journalism. She began
her career by writing poems in the 1860's under the name of
"Pearl Rivers" and apparently by 1870 had joined the New
Orleans *Daily Picayune* as literary editor. In 1872 she married
the 64-year-old publisher, Alva Holbrook. When he died in
1876 she inherited the debt-ridden newspaper. Ignoring her
family's advice to come home, the 26-year-old woman began
instead a 20-year career as proprietor. Her business manager
was George Nicholson, who in 1878 became her second husband. Together they directed the paper, but she was the editorial force and innovator, according to a study by Lamar
Bridges.

The *Daily Picayune* remained conservative in appearance,
and followed a strict policy of avoiding sensationalism. Nothing was to be published that could not be read in the family
circle, said its owner-editor. Poitevent increased circulation

and financial stability of the paper by expanding the advertising and by appealing to that family circle with a growing array of features: cartoons, Sunday comics, illustrations, increased sports coverage, columns on household hints, health care, popular science, fashion and fiction. She wrote her own society column, and hired Elizabeth Meriwether Gilmer, who later became Dorothy Dix, the noted lovelorn columnist.

Eliza Holbrook Nicholson was a founder and first president of the Woman's National Press Association, located in New Orleans in 1885. The organization numbered around 300 members in New York, Boston, Philadelphia, St. Louis, Chicago and San Francisco. When foreign members were added two years later, the name was changed to the Woman's International Press Association and she was its president as well.

$$* \quad * \quad *$$

Free-lancing bright articles, travel impressions or essays on society and manners offered many early women writers an opportunity in the world of big city daily journalism in the last half of the nineteenth century. The growth of the popular press after the Civil War demanded ever more entertaining and imaginative copy and women wrote some of it. How much, it is difficult to tell, because articles were rarely signed and editors still resisted identifying female writers as such. Among the earliest of the travel writers was Nancy Johnson who toured Europe in 1857 and sent back social impressions to the New York *Times.*

In the late 1860's a few women had taken jobs as reporters on city papers in New York, Boston, Baltimore, Chicago and Philadelphia. The woman who did turn up at a newspaper office to write copy was such a novelty in the 1860's that she often became a celebrity herself for braving the dangers of city life. Since women often worked on morning newspapers, they were out late at night and the obligation to escort lady journalists home was considered a nuisance by editors.

"I wanted to be treated like a man," declared Sally Joy of the Boston *Post,* when she joined the staff shortly after the Civil War. She proceeded to earn her credentials as an independent professional woman and ignored the youthful escort assigned to accompany her to meetings that began at 7 p.m. She covered a suffrage convention in Vermont alone, the only woman reporter at the affair. Said a male reporter from the Boston *Herald,*

> She is pretty, piquante, and dresses charmingly . . . and she has made a reputation as a newspaper correspondent and reporter of which any man might be proud. And this is saying a good deal for a woman . . . she is as independent as she is self-supporting and she votes for woman's suffrage.

Sally Joy later became "Penelope Penfeather" of the Boston *Herald* and wrote a column on fashions and the home. She continued her writing after she married. She became the first president of the New England Woman's Press Association and helped found the General Federation of Women's Clubs.

An unusual pair of women publishers appeared briefly in 1870 with a 16-page paper that carried a mixture of sensation, woman's rights and free-love tracts, among other things. They were Victoria Woodhull and her sister Tennessee Claflin. After years of traveling and prophesying with their religious-mystic father, they started a brokerage house and the newspaper in New York City. They editorialized on social disease and prostitution and exposed scandals in New York society. In 1870 they announced Woodhull's candidacy for President, shocking their friends. In 1872 they broke the story of The Rev. Henry Ward Beecher's affair with his friend's wife and were arrested and charged with sending obscene literature (their description of the affair) through the mail. Although the sisters were not convicted, in May, 1873, they ceased publishing their journal and left for London.

"Women's Topics"

With a growing audience of women who could and did read and with burgeoning advertising in newspapers and magazines directed at those women shoppers, it seemed necessary to attract more women readers to the newspapers. Women's columns, society notes, fashion and household hints and cooking columns blossomed in the 1880's and 1890's along with the first syndication of such material.

Many of the earliest society writers were men, such as William Bininger, the New York *Herald's* society editor in the 1870's. But the new interest in women readers helped open the door a bit wider to women writers. It was obvious that women were best suited to write about the stuff that made up their lives. In 1880, for the first time, the U.S. Census recorded 288 women in editing and reporting jobs and by 1890 there were 600 more of them.

One of the first to observe what interested women of the late nineteenth century and to report on this was "Jennie June" Croly (Jane Cunningham). She published her first article in 1855 in the New York *Herald*. The "Jennie June" by-line soon became famous with her articles about parties, clothes and beauty, the topics that "brought spark to feminine gatherings." She apparently began the first syndicated fashion column and pioneered the use of duplicate exchange articles, an early form of syndication during the Civil War period. She suggested the founding in 1860 of *Demorest's Illustrated Magazine of Fashions* and edited it for 27 years, while working at a variety of New York daily newspapers.

She married David Croly, editor of the New York *World*, and followed him to the New York *Daily Graphic*. She became an assistant editor and drama critic for *Noah's Sunday Times* in 1862, headed the New York *World's* woman's department in 1862 and moved to the *Graphic* in 1872. She had three children but continued her professional career for 40 years.

Croly often worked late at night in the newsroom with other editors and reporters, and one admiring editor commented: "You go on so naturally and make so little fuss about your work that I sometimes forget you are a woman."

She replied, "There's no sex in labor." She believed that her work should be taken as the achievement of an individual, with no qualifications, no indulgences, no extenuations, simply because "I happen to be a woman working along the same lines as men."

Her columns in the 1870's on courtship, marriage, engagements, honeymoons and wifely duties were considered bold for their time and brought her national recognition. From her early efforts, and those of other writers of women's columns, came the pages of the 1890's and with them a measure of respectability for women journalists.

Croly was a pioneer in other ways, too. Her New York *Dispatch* column of 1859 was said to be the first newspaper column devoted exclusively to women. She was the first woman known to teach college-level journalism—at New Rutger's Institute for Young Ladies in New York in 1896. She was a founder of the New York Woman's Press Club and Sorosis, the first woman's club in America that started the women's club movement.

Syndication and Daring Subjects

"Jenny June" and "Fanny Fern"at the Philadelphia *Ledger*, Rebecca Harding Davis and Lucia G. Calhoun at the New York *Tribune*, and "Grace Greenwood" at the New York *Times* all aided in paving the way for women writers in the daily press. So did Midy (Maria) Morgan, an expert horsewoman who was the New York *Times'* livestock reporter from 1869 to 1892. But it was Samuel S. McClure who developed the successful method of syndication of topical articles and fiction by recognized writers and expanded the market for free-lance writers, many of them women. McClure sold articles to the magazines and newspapers in the 1880's and 1890's and introduced a syndicated woman's page in 1892.

Daily journalism in New York in the late 1880's was enlivened by Joseph Pulitzer, who successfully applied the crusading and independent journalism he had pioneered on the St. Louis *Post-Dispatch* to the big city New York *World*. Reports of sensational crimes and lengthy interviews with convicted criminals and unfaithful lovers filled the front pages along with daring travel adventures, humorous sketches and glimpses of unusual ways of life. Although stories of political graft and exposés were of prime importance to Pulitzer and got front page billing, the lighter and more entertaining copy occupied a large part of the 8 to 14 daily pages and most of the 32 pages on Sundays.

When Elizabeth ("Nellie Bly") Cochrane brazened her way into Pulitzer's office in 1887 for an interview, the paper was in the market for imaginative, fresh copy that would sell papers. Cochrane, who began her journalistic career at the Pittsburgh *Dispatch* in 1885 with a daring series on divorce, now proposed to feign insanity and do an exposé for Pulitzer on the treatment of the insane at the infamous Blackwell's Island asylum. The paper offered her a $25 advance and promised to get her released in a few days.

Cochrane was successful in her masquerade as a Spanish woman of good family who had lost her memory and her sanity. Once inside people still believed her insane even when she acted normally. She was horrified at conditions there, including abuse of inmates, poor sanitation and bad food. Many inmates apparently had been committed by families just to get them out of the way. Her stories filled a page and a half and led the Sunday feature section two weeks in a row. This was followed by an official investigation of the asylum and some improvements. It made Nellie Bly an overnight celebrity at age 22.

She followed up with a succession of stunt articles: mashers in Central Park, factory work, lobby rings, women's prison, fraudulent money-making schemes, a fake mesmerist. She joined Buffalo Bill's Wild West Show and wrote about it. People never knew where she'd be next, and they never recognized her when she did turn up.

Her greatest publicity stunt was a globe-circling tour by ship, train, burro, sampan, carriage and cart for the *World* to beat the record of Jules Verne's fictional hero, Captain Phileas Fogg. She made the journey in 72 days, 6 hours and 11 minutes, well ahead of the 80-day target. Her progress was reported in long, colorful dispatches, usually on the Sunday feature page, but when she raced by train across the American continent on the final leg of the trip in January, 1890, Nellie Bly became front-page news.

After her trip she received her own by-line column and began specializing in stories about social conditions and children. In 1895 she married a wealthy industrialist and when he died she tried to keep his business going. She returned to journalism and wrote a column on orphans for the New York *Journal* from 1919 to 1922. When she died the obituary in her paper called her "America's best reporter." Women reporters were no longer unique.

The urge to write for newspapers was not confined to the big cities. In Knoxville, Tennessee, for example, Pattie Boyd told the editor of the old Knoxville *Tribune* (later *Journal*): "All you write about is politics, politics. Why don't you have something to say about what people are doing and saying?"

So convincing was this 18-year-old girl that she walked away with a job as society editor, a position she held for 52 years. Her influence was so great that Knoxville called her a "social dictator," said June Adamson in her research on Tennessee women journalists. Boyd's pages gave women special status and she was blunt in refusing space to women of mediocre means and little cultural background. "But my deah," she would say, "you don't belong on the cover page."

Although she was active in women's clubs and worked to see that women got the vote in Tennessee, Boyd is primarily remembered for telling Knoxville society about its own doings. She prided herself on having written more than 30,000 wedding announcements without receiving a complaint. She wrote at home until 1911 when she began to "go to the office regularly." And she wrote in pencil until just a few years before retiring, when a new managing editor convinced her to try a typewriter. She never had or needed a by-line because all Knoxville knew that "Miss Pattie" was the voice behind "Gossip had it . . ."

Recognition of Women Journalists

Women journalists by 1889 had made such an impact on the profession that the *Journalist*, a professional journal in New York City, devoted its entire January 26 issue to profiles of 50 women editors and reporters, 10 of them black. The editor admitted his mistake in not devoting space to women workers in journalism previously and said he wished to disabuse the old fogies of the profession of the idea that a newspaperwoman is in any way less a woman because she earns her living by wielding a pencil instead of sewing on buttons for the "lords of creation."

These profiles included editors of women's magazines in New York, reporters and editors from Chicago and other midwestern towns and from the South. Many of the profiles made the point that these women were able journalists as well as charming and feminine women, wives and mothers.

Miriam Follin Leslie, who worked at her husband's side in creating *Frank Leslie's Illustrated Newspaper* and carried it on after his death "is a woman of business, the strict disciplinarian, critical judge and shrewd negotiator" during the day, said the article. At home she is a "woman of genuine sentiment and finer feelings" who lives in a dainty and tastefully decorated apartment and who could easily be mistaken for a "marquise of the *grand siècle*" in her elegant French silk attire.

The black woman in journalism, said the *Journalist's* editor, occupied a special place because the black man had not contested her every step toward recognition as they worked side by side on the plantations and continued this arrangement in other spheres. The editor continued,

> There is no better example than Mrs. N. F. Mossell, who began her journalistic career as a writer for the *Christian Recorder*. She soon wrote short stories and articles for several black journals and edited the woman's pages of the New York *Freeman*. Her style was clear, compact and convincing.

Mossell wrote on the woman question and on race for several Philadelphia publications.

Ida B. Wells-Barnett of Mississippi, who wrote under the by-line "Iola," was perhaps the best known of these early black women journalists who crusaded for equal rights. She began writing while still a student at Fisk University and continued during her early career as a teacher in Memphis. She became half-owner and editor of the Mississippi *Free Speech,* but after 1892, when that newspaper's plant was sacked, she devoted her energies to traveling, speaking and writing on racial injustice. In Chicago, where she located in the mid-1890's, she wrote for black and white publications, including Chicago's *Inter-Ocean,* and organized women's clubs and kindergartens.

8 6 7 5 5

LIBRARY
College of St. Francis
JOLIET, ILL.

Several of the black women journalists specialized in articles on or for children and women, and often their publications were those of religious organizations. Many of them free-lanced stories and articles to many black and white publications. Lillian Alberta Lewis, whose pen name was "Bert Islew," was a columnist for the Boston *Advocate* and was "recognized in all circles for her ability and works side by side with editors and reporters without an iota of distinction being made."

Press Associations

As early as 1885, women journalists began forming press clubs and associations in order to further their professionalism. For the most part they were not welcome in the male counterpart organizations. The New England Woman's Press Association and the Woman's National Press Association were formed in 1885. The Illinois Women's Press Association, formed in 1886, had 66 members by 1888. Several of these state groups would join in 1937 to form the National Federation of Press Women, Inc., which would grow to a membership of 4,000 in the 1970's.

New York women journalists suggested forming a Woman's Press Club for the "women writers who work hard and well" in 1889. It was to be a place to "meet for the general good and public and private gain, not a place for tea and tattle." The number of women in journalism more than doubled in the 1890's so that by 1900 there were 2,193 women reporters and editors, according to the U.S. Census, or 7.3 per cent of the profession, including magazine and book publishing.

Urbanization and industrialization, changing social attitudes about working women, new economic and legal status for women plus increased educational opportunities for them opened new horizons to women who wished to work outside the home in something other than nursing and teaching. The rapid growth of popular mass circulation magazines in the turn-of-the-century era, such as *Saturday Evening Post, The Ladies' Home Journal, Cosmopolitan, Collier's, Munsey's, McClure's* and *McCall's* greatly expanded the job market for women who found magazine work less pressured and more inviting than daily newspaper journalism. Magazines created a large free-lance market. Several women became outstanding editors and writers, especially on the women's magazines.

As photography became an important part of the American magazine in the late nineteenth century, the photojournalist made an appearance. At least one of these early popular news-and-magazine photographers was a woman, Frances Benjamin Johnston, whose work was published extensively in *Demorest's Family Magazine* between 1889 and 1893. The photographs covered a wide range from a series on the U.S. Mint and an investigative study of workers in the Pennsylvania coal fields to Mammoth cave, and the homes of presidents, Congressmen and diplomats. Her photographs of the American school system, exhibited in the Paris Exposition of 1900, included those of Hampton Institute in Virginia, which were later used for fund-raising for black education. She opened a portrait studio in the 1890's and continued to publish in popular magazines of the period, gradually specializing in architectural photography.

Changing Image

The Spanish-American War of 1898 offered another adventurous woman a new writing opportunity. While a few women wrote woman's-eye-view reports on the wounded or on nursing, Anna Benjamin was a professional war reporter for *Leslie's Illustrated Newspaper*. She wrote critically and intelligently on what she saw and kept herself out of the story, said Charles Brown in his study of her work. She covered preparations for the Cuban invasion from Tampa and Key West, Florida, and prepared to follow the expedition to Cuba.

"I know what you think," Benjamin told a British correspondent. "You think it ridiculous my being here; you are laughing at me wanting to go, that's the worst of being a woman. But just let me tell you, I'm going through to Cuba and not all the old generals in the Army are going to stop me."

They tried. But Benjamin was not daunted and she scooped many of her competitors by sending back some of the first dispatchs of Spanish defeats. She was 23 when she went to war, and the New York *Tribune* described her as "slight and girlish in appearance." After the war she covered the Philippine insurrection and then went on to report from Japan, China, Russia—crossing by the Trans-Siberian railroad—and Paris. She wrote for *Leslie's,* and *Tribune, Outlook* and *Atlantic Monthly.* She began work on a book in France, but died of a tumor in 1902 at age 27 before the book was finished.

Looking back at her own entry into American journalism during the early 1880's, Florence Finch Kelly described the problems facing these early women journalists. In Boston and Chicago there was one woman per paper to handle society and fashion news. In California in 1887 she found less prejudice against women, perhaps because of the youth of the community, but although women were offered newspaper jobs, none of the women who had undertaken them were doing work of "real consequence." Most "fluttered about with emotional articles of slight value." Kelly, who later reported for the New York *Sun* and wrote editorials for Philadelphia's *North American,* devoted her final 30 years in journalism as a book reviewer for the New York *Times,* helping set the standards for that department.

Although Kelly had once been refused a by-line because there was already a woman's by-line in the issue for that day, she believed that by the early 1890's many of the prejudices against women in newspaper offices had disappeared. In her autobiography, *Flowing Stream,* she anticipated a rosy future for the women journalists because the younger male editors were less prejudiced and women themselves had made an impressive record in nearly all kinds of newspaper work: reporting, feature writing, interviews, critical work, desk work and editorial writing.

✳ ✳ ✳

Times were changing, Foster Coates, a magazine writer and a city editor of the New York *Journal,* agreed in an 1892 article in *The Ladies' Home Journal.* Women were doing good work for the leading newspapers, editors told him, and it was pretty well established by this time that the "average woman possesses as much brains as the average man," he said.

> Woman can no longer be considered weak, shy and retiring, because physical culture has made her dashing, straight and strong. The young woman with a good constitution, who knows how to write good English and is willing to work hard has as good an opportunity as any man similarly equipped to succeed in journalism.

Attitudes were also changing about what these women might write. Formerly it was thought that they could only write fashion or society notes, said Coates, but journalism was beginning to require that men and women specialize. "It depended altogether on the taste and inclination of the writer what topic he or she should follow."

Chances for promotion for a woman were not very good, Coates added, unless she was "exceptionally talented." The "tendency" was still to place men in charge of important departments even in places where women were well paid as writers, but "this order of things should not last . . . will not endure if women themselves want to change it."

· SOURCES CONSULTED ·

Edith Abbott, *Women in Industry, A Study in American Economic History* (New York: D. Appleton & Co., 1918).

June Adamson, "South's Early Society Editor Rules as Social Dictator," *Editor and Publisher*, Nov. 11, 1972.

Ira Lee Baker, "Elizabeth Timothy: America's First Woman Editor," Unpublished M.S. thesis, University of Illinois, Urbana, Ill., 1963.

Maurine Beasley, "Pens and Petticoats: Early Women Washington Correspondents," *Journalism History*, Vol. 1, No. 4, Winter 1974–75.

Maurine Beasley, *The First Women Washington Correspondents* (Washington, D.C.: G. Washington University, 1976).

Lamar W. Bridges, letter to the author, and Eliza Jane Nicholson of the 'Picayune,' *Journalism History*, Vol. 2, No. 4, pp. 110–115.

Arthur W. Brown, *Margaret Fuller* (New York: Twayne Publishers, Inc., 1964).

Charles B. Brown, "A Woman's Odyssey: The War Correspondence of Anna Benjamin," *Journalism Quarterly*, Autumn 1969.

Nancy Fisher Chudacoff, "Woman in the News 1762–1770: Sarah Updike Goddard," *Rhode Island History*, Fall 1973.

Thomas Ewing Dabney, *One Hundred Great Years: The Story of the Times-Picayune From Its Founding to 1940* (New York: Greenwood Press, Publishers, 1944).

Elisabeth Dexter, *Colonial Women of Affairs* (New York: Houghton Mifflin Co., 1924).

Susan E. Dickinson, "Woman in Journalism," in *Woman's Work in America,* Annie Nathan Meyer, ed., (New York: Henry Holt and Company, 1891).

Carolyn Steward Dyer, "Mathilde Anneke, the *Frauenzeitung* and the German Bookprinters," unpublished paper, University of Wisconsin, School of Journalism, 1973.

Wallace B. Eberhard, "Sarah Porter Hillhouse: Setting the Record Straight," *Journalism History,* Vol. 1, No. 4, Winter 1974–75.

Frederick B. Farrar, unpublished M.A. thesis on the Colonial Press, History Department, Adelphi University, 1974.

Susan Henry, "Margaret Draper: Colonial Printer Who Challenged the Patriots," *Journalism History,* Vol. 1, No. 4, Winter 1974–75, and letter to the author.

George Juergens, *Joseph Pulitzer and the New York World* (New Jersey: Princeton University Press, 1966).

Johanna Johnston, *Mrs. Satan: The Incredible Saga of Victoria C. Woodhull* (New York: G. P. Putnam's Sons, 1967).

Florence Finch Kelly, *Flowing Stream* (New York: E. P. Dutton and Co., 1939).

Arthur J. Larsen, ed. *Crusader and Feminist: Letters of Jane Grey Swisshelm 1858–1865* (St. Paul: Minnesota Historical Society, 1934).

Peter Lyon, *Success Story: The Life and Times of S. S. McClure* (New York: Charles Scribner's Sons, 1963).

S. S. McClure, *My Autobiography* (New York: Frederick Ungar Publishing Co., 1963).

Samuel Eliot Morison, *The Intellectual Life of Colonial New England* (New York: New York University Press, 1956).

Mignon Rittenhouse, *The Amazing Nellie Bly* (New York: E. P. Dutton & Co., Inc. 1956).

Ishbel Ross, *Ladies of the Press* (New York: Harper & Brothers, 1936).

Arthur Meier Schlesinger, *New Viewpoints in American History,* (New York: The Macmillan Co., 1925).

Norma Schneider, "Clementina Rind: 'Editor, Daughter, Mother, Wife,'" *Journalism History,* Vol. 1, No. 4, Winter 1974–75.

Henry Ladd Smith, "The Beauteous Jennie June: Pioneer Woman Journalist," *Journalism Quarterly,* Vol. 40, Spring 1963.

Isaiah Thomas, *The History of Printing in America* (Worchester, Mass.: Isaiah Thomas Press, 1810).

Anne Tucker, (ed.) *The Woman's Eye* (New York: Alfred A. Knopf, 1975).

Edward S. Wallace, *Destiny and Glory* (New York: Coward-McCann, Inc., 1957).

Margaret R. Weiss, "The Formidable Frances B. Johnston," *Saturday Review,* August 23, 1975.

Roland E. Wolseley, *The Black Press, U.S.A.* (Ames: The Iowa State University Press, 1971).

"Women Journalists," The *Journalist*, January 26, 1889.

Richardson Wright, *Forgotten Ladies* (Philadelphia: J. B. Lippincott, 1928).

Mary Ann Yodelis, unpublished research on colonial printers, University of Wisconsin, School of Journalism.

2

* * *

Sob Sister to War Correspondent

THE WOMAN'S ANGLE was "played up" in several ways in turn-of-the-century American urban journalism. Women's pages and Sunday sections became standard features of most daily newspapers, and women's magazines experienced burgeoning growth in circulation and size.

"Stunt girl" reporters were joined by "sob sisters," who covered sensational crimes with an emotional intensity that brought a tear to the eye. The woman reader was courted by advertisers and editors as they realized her importance as major shopper.

In 1899 there were four times as many daily newspapers as in 1870 and the population in cities of 8,000 or more grew by 52 per cent from 1880 to 1899, a large part of it immigrants. Intense competition between big city publishers like Joseph Pulitzer and William Randolph Hearst in New York for the largest circulations also included competition for the best writers and reporters. A growing number of the journalists were college educated and women had become an integral part of the newsroom. There were 300 of them in the first decade of the century, said Ishbel Ross in *Ladies of the Press*

The first decade of the twentieth century did bring a number of women generally into writing and editing jobs: over 4,000 by 1910, double that of the previous decade. Al-

32

though their career paths were still fairly limited to women's pages, feature writing, magazine writing and editing, stunts, columns and sob sister reporting, some did hard news. Editors were likely to be less grudging than before in their praise as a *Journalist* editorial of 1894 demonstrated:

> What does it take to be a lady journalist? Hard work, dedication, high ideals, sympathy, perception, a dash of cynicism, faith, hope, charity, a relish for news . . . a buoyancy of nature.

Journalism offered the opportunity to meet a vast number of the brightest minds around, an absorbing life and an escape from "the tea cup world" of most women.

Sensationalism

Hearst, more than any other publisher, helped "put newspaperwomen on the map," said Ross.

> Hundreds of them have passed through his doorways, some to lose their jobs with staggering swiftness; others to build up big syndicate names and draw down the highest salaries in the profession. From the moment he entered newspaper work he dramatized them; got them to make news. They became the most spectacular, the most highly paid, the most dashing newspaperwomen in the country, if not necessarily the finest news writers.

The "yellow journals" relied heavily on sensationalism and sometimes faked stories about sex, scandal and crime. There was a growing market in the populous big cities for the colorful, emotional writing of the "yellow press." Women often had a knack for such writing. Some of them developed into personalities whose columns attracted and held readers by the tens of thousands.

The earliest and one of the best known was Winifred Black Bonfils or "Annie Laurie." She started at the San Francisco *Examiner* before William Randolph Hearst left for college in the East. Her first big story was to cover the local send-off for Elizabeth Bisland who was starting her race around the world against Nellie Bly in 1889. When she turned in the story the city editor looked at the elaborate and stilted writing and told

her it was a bad story. He gave her a practical lesson in popular journalism:

> We don't want fine writing in a newspaper. Remember
> that. There's a gripman on the Powell Street line—he takes
> his car out at three o'clock in the morning, and while he's
> waiting for the signals he opens the morning paper. It's still
> wet from the press and by the light of his grip he reads it.
> Think of him when you're writing a story. Don't write a
> single word he can't understand and wouldn't read.

Bonfils learned the lesson well and went on to develop a
technique of vivid, personal writing that was highly charged
with emotion. Stunts were "in" during those days, and one of
her first was to expose the bad treatment women got at the
receiving hospital. She dressed in shabby clothing and faked
an accident in order to get her personal experience story.

She went on to write inside stories about a leper colony.
She stowed away on a presidential train to get an exclusive interview with President Benjamin Harrison and disguised herself as a boy to get into Galveston, Texas, to cover a flood there
resulting from a tidal wave. She interviewed the flamboyant
personalities of the era, including Henry Stanley and Sara
Bernhardt, and she rarely missed a good murder trial in her 40
years with the *Examiner*.

Bonfils hand-picked her successor, Adela Rogers St. John,
who was to write for Hearst for 50 years. Bonfils seemed to be
describing herself when she wrote to Hearst that she had discovered her replacement, a young woman with "the keen zest
for life of a child, the cool courage of a man, and the subtlety
of a woman." A woman has a distinct advantage over a man in
reporting, said Bonfils, "if she has sense enough to balance
her qualities."

✳ ✳ ✳

Another young woman of this period was to illustrate a
somewhat different career path, from woman's page and stunt
girl, front page reporting to a distinguished career as editor of
Harper's Bazaar. She was Elizabeth Garver Jordan, who first
entered newspapering as editor of the new woman's page of

Peck's Milwaukee *Sun* after completing college, She stayed there for a year and apparently in 1890 took a cub reporter job at the New York *World.*

Jordan refused to take minor woman's page assignments and quickly became a top feature writer. Her first job was a series of articles on Long Island summer resorts that would please hotel proprietors and "stimulate advertising, local pride and *World* circulation," according to her book, *Three Rousing Cheers.* It wasn't long before she turned in a "model story" that was posted in the city room. It was "The Death of Number Nine," the story of a penniless mother of nine who carried her dying child to a hospital three miles away. The baby died enroute; the article asked for contributions for a proper burial.

Jordan carried out a series of stunts, the most spectacular of which was to explore the Virginia and Tenessee mountain country for human interest stories on local characters and moonshiner camps. She told about this and other journalistic experiences in a magazine article, "The Newspaper Woman's Story." When she left the *World* in 1899 she was editor of the Sunday edition's comic supplement and the Editorial Forum. She continued a career as magazine editor, literary adviser, book writer and a playwright for theatre and cinema.

Jordan used to "bedazzle compositors by showing up in immaculate shirt-waists and slinging type with an experienced hand," said Ross. On one hectic night an editor exclaimed to her, "Good God! What a job. Can you imagine anything worse?" "Oh yes," she laughed, waving her dummy pages. "To lose it."

But to Elizabeth Banks, a transplanted Wisconsinite who tried her luck with American "yellow journalism" after freelancing in London, the job posed moral issues. She was asked to dress appropriately for a walk along Broadway at night and allow herself to be arrested and sent to jail as a "disreputable character." She could then write about the experience and call attention to certain city laws that needed reform. Banks said that was "indecent." She refused, but she surprised her editor by telling him she would do any job that he would willingly ask his sister to do if she were employed on the paper.

Although Banks enjoyed the spirit of comradeship and good fellowship that prevailed on American newspaper staffs and had been well treated by her male colleagues, she returned to England to a more genteel life as a magazine writer. She left this advice for aspiring women journalists of her day in her book, *Autobiography of a Newspaper Girl:*

> Sometimes it has seemed to me that women who live the newspaper life, because, perhaps, their experience is wider and broader and takes in more than does that of the average woman, are often called upon to bear a little more heartache, and to show it less, than the average woman.

Yellow journalism was not a school that Elizabeth Banks would recommend indiscriminately to all aspiring young women journalists.

Advice Columns and "Sob Sisters"

Two women gained enormous readership with their advice columns in Hearst's *Journal*. They were "Beatrice Fairfax" and "Dorothy Dix." Their real names were Marie Manning and Elizabeth Meriwether Gilmer. Manning began her career at age 20 working for the New York *World* on space rates, paid by the column inch, as were most starting journalists at the turn of the century.

Manning took a job at the *Journal* because it promised the opportunity to do music criticism as well as the household page. She began the advice column one day in 1898 when the managing editor, Arthur Brisbane, showed her two letters from readers about their personal lives. Could the household page use them? She thought it could and suggested a column along those lines. She wrote the first letters herself, but soon she had an ample supply of letters from readers and answered as Beatrice Fairfax. Her style was specific and direct and the column continued long after she stopped writing it.

Hearst took Dorothy Dix away from New Orleans where her column, "Dorothy Dix Talks," had already gained some popularity in the New Orleans *Picayune*. When she joined the *Journal* in 1901 her first assignment was to follow Carrie Nation to

Nebraska on a saloon-smashing tour. Dix worked on many major stories including political conventions, vice investigations and murder trials. She maintained her column at the same time and later (1917) it became her sole effort.

Dix felt that her columns did some good, really helping people who needed it, but she thought the "sob sister" murder stories only boosted circulation.

The "sob sisters" attracted attention at the famous trial of Harry Thaw, who was accused of murdering the fashionable New York architect, Stanford White, who he believed was his wife's lover. Four women feature writers had front-row press seats at the Thaw trial in 1907. They were Dorothy Dix, Winifred Black Bonfils, Ada Patterson and Nixola Greeley-Smith. Ada Patterson had come to work for the New York *Amercian* from St. Louis, and Nixola Greeley-Smith was an outstanding interviewer for the *Sunday World*. Each of these women had been summoned to give a sympathetic and emotional report of this sensational trial with its beautiful young heroine, Evelyn Nesbit Thaw, "the girl in the red velvet swing." Another reporter gave them the name "sob sisters" in his own report of the trial and the term stuck.

Although Ishbel Ross explained that Greeley-Smith was not a regular "sob sister," her sympathetic account of Evelyn Thaw on the witness stand serves as a fine example of the style:

> Looking at her I almost fancied myself in the children's court. It did not seem possible that this pale child could be the grown-up cause of Stanford White's alleged drugging of her . . . sitting there listening to this baring of her besmirched child's soul I felt myself almost as great a criminal as she made him appear. . .

The portrait is more fully drawn in Mildred Gilman's novel, *Sob Sister*, much of which was drawn from the author's own exploits for Hearst's New York *Journal* in the 1920's and 1930's. Gilman, among other things, scooped other reporters on the Earle Peacox torch murder story. She climbed the back fence at the victim's home and entered with Peacox, thinking he was another local reporter.

Gilman heard the victim's family convince Peacox to go to the police, who had been searching for him, "to get it over with." They had no idea he was guilty. He confessed almost immediately that he had poured gasoline on his wife and set the body aflame after he had bludgeoned her for spurning and humiliating him. After he left, the family noticed Gilman who claimed to be a friend of the dead wife. She offered condolences and was ushered out, immediately phoning in her story and telling the city editor that Peacox was at the police station. In this way her paper was first to break the confession story with Gilman's on-the-scene background material.

Gilman worked on the *Journal* for over three years, and she covered a number of lurid murders. These were given great prominence in the papers in those days because "we had so little international news. We never dreamed that another war could be possible," she recalled. "We thought Hitler and Mussolini were laughable figureheads."

Asked why she undertook such exciting and often dangerous things for the *Journal*, Gilman said that an "early tendency to daring goes way back." She was raised in Grand Rapids, Michigan, "the second girl in a family that wanted boys and followed by a much-desired brother." So she learned to be competitive very early. Her mother was an early feminist and her godmother a suffragist who chained herself to the White House fence, bearing a placard, "Down with Kaiser Wilson." Gilman's mother gave her the impression that,

> I could do or be anything I wanted to if I tried hard enough. She taught me to write before I went to school and had me keep a diary from then on. My father, whom I adored, tried to turn me into a boy. He didn't succeed, but I did do daring things that would please him—picking up snakes, walking over the Rio Grande River in flood . . . The newspaper job continued all this. I loved it and wanted to keep it, and the turnover of sob sisters on the *Journal* was great.

The going rate for men and women reporters in 1928 was $60 a week, but Gilman received $100, perhaps because she came to the job as an accomplished novelist. She covered more exciting and sensational news stories than others who stayed longer, she recalled, and resigned at the top of her success, with mixed feelings, in the depth of the depression to free-lance and raise a family. She published *Sob Sister*, which was made into a popular movie.

The only assignment Gilman turned down at the *Journal* was the electrocution of the murderer, Henry Colin Close, with whom she had become friendly through his wife. She not only turned it down, Gilman said, but:

> I took sick leave and kept the children of Mrs. Close in my apartment with me so none of the press could find them. Also, Mrs. Close had the ashes of her husband sent to my apartment after his body was cremated . . . to protect herself from the press. I forgot to tell my husband to expect them and he was astonished to receive the small leaden box, express collect, while I was off on a story.
>
> I had an easy time getting stories in the old days because I looked innocent and blonde and blue-eyed, and no one suspected me of duplicity or of having too many brains. I never hurt any of the people I duped and helped many like Mrs. Close, who became my dear friend before changing her name and disappearing entirely.

Adela Rogers St. John, "sob sister" for Hearst, churned out thousands of words on all the emotion-laden trials of the pre-war era, including the Hauptmann trial for the Lindbergh baby kidnapping.

✳   ✳   ✳

Ishbel Ross, who knew and worked with these early twentieth-century newspaperwomen described the division between those who worked on the "yellow press" and later the sensational tabloids and the women who worked for the traditional and serious newspapers. She herself was in the latter category as a cityside reporter for the New York *Tribune*.

> We were drilled in the importance of good writing and objective reporting rather than frenzied scoops. Although no paper worth its salt has ever been indifferent to the exclusive story, the reporters at the *World* and for the Hearst papers had to turn in spice and color. The women there were in hot competition to get a good story or die. They had to show their feelings in their reporting.

Ross covered the sensational trials, too. She was routed out of bed at 3 a.m., she recalled, to handle the breaking story of the Lindbergh baby kidnapping and she followed the story to its sad finish. She covered another trial which was on the front pages for nearly two years during that era of speakeasies and gangsters.

"Pay was miserable," Ross recalled, "about $35 to $37 a week." Her husband, who was still on space rates at the New York *Times,* made thousands of dollars on one trial, she said. The space rate system ended not long after the Lindbergh trial.

Ross, who was highly praised by her city editor, Stanley Walker, for her outstanding performance and competence under deadline pressure, got her start in journalism in Canada on the Toronto *Daily News* as a new emigrée from Scotland during the World War I period.

The editor told her she could work in the library filing things. She might try a story "if the opportunity arose." Three months later they needed a reporter to interview Emmeline Pankhurst who was arriving in Canada. The other newspapers would send reporters to meet the train as it arrived in Toronto. Her assignment was to board it outside the city and get the story first.

At 3 a.m. on a snowy morning she got on the train and bided her time until 7 a.m. Then she knocked at the famous lady's drawing room door. The secretary who answered said an interview was impossible because Mrs. Pankhurst had laryngitis and was saving her voice for her speech. Ross recalled:

> I went back to my seat, thinking this was the end of my career. I thought it over and hit upon an ingenious scheme. I wrote a little note telling Mrs. Pankhurst that an interview with her meant my breaking into journalism. "You, who have done so much for womankind, can you let me down on this?"

Ross got the interview and felt somewhat sorry because the lady really did have laryngitis,but she got a marvelous interview. "I didn't know how good it was," recalled Ross, "until I saw it the following day spread over seven columns on the front page, with a headline and my by-line."

The next day she was given a staff assignment. "So, I guess

I owe my career to Mrs. Pankhurst," said Ross, "although I was never a great suffrage sympathizer," unlike several of her newspaper colleagues.

Investigative Reporting

Ida M. Tarbell was another serious writer whose talents were especially suited to muckraking magazine journalism of the pre-World War I period. She had already gained editing experience at the *Chautauquan*, where she had worked for seven years, when she found history and biography were her real loves. She went to France to study at the Sorbonne and she supported herself with her free-lance articles. She persuaded six editors to buy her articles at $6 each, but in 1893 she still had to pawn her coat and watch to cover expenses.

In Paris, Samuel S. McClure met her on his talent search for writers for his new *McClure's* magazine. Tarbell agreed to be a contributing editor and returned to the United States to work on the staff. She wrote about Madame Roland, Napoleon and Lincoln, but "The History of Standard Oil" was her most famous piece of journalism. It was in the best tradition of investigative reporting—exhaustive and painstaking research backed up every statement. Her writing had a clarity of vision that was sharpened but not distorted by righteous indignation at what she found. The best American traditions were being wasted by a business system that placed a premium on rascality and unfair advantage, she explained. And for the first time Americans learned of the corruption in the system that was creating a great gap between the very rich and the very poor.

It was not a pleasant task for Tarbell. She said in her autobiography *All In A Day's Work,*

> The more intimately I went into my subject, the more hateful it became to me. No achievement on earth could justify those methods, I felt. I had a great desire to end my task, hear no more of it.

She continued to look for the truth, wherever it led, and in so doing established herself as one of the all-time great women journalists. Her Standard Oil research several decades later was acclaimed by historians as substantially accurate in all but a few minor details. Tarbell continued to write books on business and on women. When she was ready to retire she was asked to do a study of business for a nine-volume history, and at 80 she wrote her autobiography.

Foreign Corresponding

Another aspect of serious, hard news reporting is foreign correspondence. Many young women reporters may have dreamed about this during the first World War, but only one, Peggy Hull, a Kansas farm girl, was accredited to the American Expeditionary Forces by the War Department. She arrived in Liverpool just four days after General Pershing and was in Paris when American troops paraded there for the first time on July 4, 1917.

She had reported American militia movements from El Paso in 1914 for her newspaper, the Cleveland *Plain Dealer*. It gave her a taste for "war reporting." When the U.S. entered the World War, Hull bombarded editors with requests to be sent to France on assignment. There were no takers, so she raised money to finance her own trip and a Texas newspaper editor helped get her overseas.

Some of her fellow journalists resented her presence, she said. They complained to Army officers. "But through the aid of big-hearted and broad-minded correspondents such as Floyd Gibbons, Ring W. Lardner, George Pattulo and Webb Miller, she managed to visit all the American camps in France."

Hull spent two months with General Peyton March's brigade, but had to return home to care for her sick mother in July, 1918. She heard about an expedition to Vladivostok, Siberia, and applied to go. General March was handling the arrangements, and he complimented her on her reporting from France.

> Your stories are the sort that give the people at home a real idea of what the American soldier is like and what he likes and dislikes. I'd like to see you go with the Siberian expedition. These men are likely to be lost sight of in view of

the big things that are happening in France. If you can get an
editor to send you, I'll accredit you.

For six weeks she asked editors for that assignment. Finally
she asked Newspaper Enterprise Association and got an
"O.K." Hull got her pass and special accreditation from General March.

Hull had a flair for drama and dressed to suit her assignment. Overseas she wore a trim officer's tunic, calf-length
skirt, polished boots, Sam Browne belt and campaign hat. She
went along on marches with the boys and at night rolled up in
her poncho and slept on the ground along with other correspondents and the troops. After reporting the Siberian story,
she went to China and worked on the Shanghai *Gazette.* Later
she turned up in Paris where she roomed with another American correspondent, Irene Kuhn, in the 1920's. Kuhn recalled,

> She was a small, slender brown-eyed blonde . . . as femi-
> nine as a kitten and she had a will of iron. She was also the
> kindest, most generous and compassionate human being I've
> ever known.

Political Writing

Impertinence and ambition got Zoë Beckley out of the usual
run of bright features for the New York *Mail* and into political
reporting. The publisher was passing her desk one day and
asked what she was doing. She told him she was writing a
dull piece for his paper while he was about to board a special
train with a crew of writers bound for the Bull Moose Convention in Chicago. A few minutes later he returned and asked
her if she could be ready to take that train. She was. One of
her colleagues advised her,

> Think of these delegates as utterly dependent upon you.
> Ask the old dames a question—any question—and they'll
> talk their heads off. Get the one best idea for your lead, then
> throw in a little palaver of your own for color, and pull the
> whole thing together at the end.

He promised to show her how to put the story on the wire.
To Beckley this was really newspapering and after the conven-

tion she stayed on hard news. She wrote war stories, toured
the U.S. and Europe and wrote a daily column. Eventually, she
turned to news and feature syndicate writing where she established her reputation as a crack interviewer and columnist.

Other women reporters were becoming prominent during
the World War I era. One of them was Emma Bugbee of the
New York *Tribune*. She was the *Tribune's* only woman hard-
news reporter, so she was much in demand for assignments
involving the progress of women in public life, according to
Ishbel Ross. Bugbee was a feminist by conviction and had
nursed the suffrage cause from infancy, being on hand for
every innovation—the first woman judge, the first woman
governor, the first woman registrar.

Ross observed, "When they fail or turn corrupt she is in-
credulous. When they do a good job she is quietly trium-
phant."

The Suffrage Movement Makes Page One

When the suffrage campaign was in its busiest years, Bugbee
and Eleanor Booth Simmons, who came to the *Tribune* from
the *Sun* in 1915, spent nearly full time on that story. Women
covered the day-to-day events and interviews, but when the
movement made page one, stories were covered by men. On
the eve of the last big parade, one of the women was dep-
utized to ask Ogden Reid if the women could handle the story
themselves. He agreed, and Simmons, Bugbee and three
helpers turned in nine columns of copy.

In 1914, a 150-mile suffrage march to Albany was planned
and Bugbee asked to go. At first her editor said she'd get too
cold, but she insisted. She joined the march and she got cold
and wet, but she had the company of several other women reporters, including Dorothy Dix, Ada Patterson, Zoë Beckley
and Martha Coman.

Stories about suffrage helped improve the status of women
reporters once they became big news, said Ross, and by 1915
the *Tribune* newswomen were brought downstairs into the city
room. Women's news became part of the general news schedule. Bugbee continued to cover the activities of suffrage work-

ers after Congress passed the Nineteenth Amendment in 1917, and she followed women candidates in their run for office. She later covered Eleanor Roosevelt whose openness with reporters and her newsmaking activities helped build the status of newswomen during the Roosevelt years.

Although "yellow journalism" with its stunts, advice columns and sob sisters exploited the novelty of lady reporters, it also expanded the range of subject matter that women were allowed to cover. Some of these women used that opportunity to press editors for full-time employment as news reporters. The suffragists provided good copy for some women reporters and international affairs attracted others.

Rheta Childe Dorr, a reporter for the New York *Mail* in 1917 walked into the city room one day and announced: "I'm going to Russia." The Czar had abdicated and Dorr, an avid student of the French Revolution, wanted to cover a revolution. She had convinced her editor that she could handle any story, so he agreed to send her. In Russia she joined the "woman's battalion of death'"on their training operations, interviewed the Czarina's sister and others in Rasputin's circle. Her newspaper reports were combined into a book, *Inside the Russian Revolution.*

Dorr also covered the suffrage struggle in America and the start of the women's clubs at about the turn of the century. She had a difficult time convincing her editor at the New York *Post* that the clubs were news. She asked to cover a New York State Federation of Women's Clubs Assembly in Brooklyn as a news story. The editor told her to do a funny piece about it.

"I can't do that," she protested. "This isn't funny. These women are organizing. Women all over the country are organizing and it isn't funny. It is serious. Perhaps it's the most serious thing you and I are facing in our lives. I simply won't ridicule it."

"Young woman," said her editor, "the first lesson a cub reporter has to learn is that he has no opinions. He writes what his superiors tell him to write and he writes it their way."

The other newspapers treated the meeting as news. The next day her editor asked her to report on "this damned nonsense over in Brooklyn." After that she was regularly assigned to the woman's movement in the United States and in Europe, and she wrote a book about Susan B. Anthony.

As Ishbel Ross recalled,

> Women reporters in those heady 1920's were individualists, just like their male colleagues. I don't believe that in the 1920's any of the press women thought that they might be important links in helping to raise the status of women. As always the papers merely mirrored the prevailing attitudes of the community as a whole, and highlighted the unusual person or development. Except for the women who conducted social service or investigative campaigns for their papers, they were singularly lacking in the social consciousness that pervades the 1970's.
>
> They were driven by ambition, or seduced by the charm and diversity of each day's labors. They were apt to be indifferent to the rewards and possibilities of their work. They were miserably paid. With no unions behind them, they worked endless hours—often around the clock—and sometimes seven days a week and holidays.

Ross thought that the newspapers' emphasis on murder trials and crime in the 1920's illustrates one of the chief differences between newspapers of that day and those of the 1970's.

> The papers in the 1920's were so strongly localized that court trials got reams of space and attention. Of course it was also the prohibition era when crime was as much discussed as the CIA is today. Now the front pages of the large papers seek to cover the world, and even the tabloids take in the international picture.
>
> The tabloids brought about the most dramatic change I personally witnessed in my reporting days. They meant a great deal to the women of the press, as the editors of the New York *Daily News*, the *Mirror* and *Graphic* played them up, gave them important assignments and featured their bylines. The new approach shook us all up and energized us on the more conservative papers. It was a continuation of the heady race between Hearst and Pulitzer to which we were all accustomed on Park Row. Stars rose and fell under the Hearst banner, but women reporters touched new levels of fame and fortune.

Astonish, Bemuse, Dazzle or Horrify

The New York *Daily News* started American tabloid publication on June 26, 1919, and one of its first of many female stars was Julia Harpman, fresh from covering the courts in Knoxville, Tennessee. She quickly learned the new ground rules of a tabloid—astonish, bemuse, dazzle or horrify the reader. She covered the sensational murder trials of the early 1920's, accompanied Gertrude Ederle in her swim across the English Channel, crashed into the ocean in a crippled seaplane, interviewed gangsters and their molls and was repeatedly threatened with death. In the opinion of Ishbel Ross,

> Her city editor believed in his female reporters and spurred them to daring feats. He was a hard driver, sincere, quick-tempered, inconsistent. He was quick to spot a good story and he whipped his reporters into pursuing every clue to a dead end.
>
> Harpman worked night and day, moving from place to place without much time for sleep or meals. She endured freezing and soaking that seem incredible in retrospect. She also was one of the finest reporters, men or women, that New York has produced. She soon had the star men on the most conservative papers trying to keep up with her. She had a great gift for nosing out unexpected facts.

In the sensational Hall-Mills murder story of 1922, Harpman was one of the first reporters on the scene in New Brunswick, N.J., after the rector Edward Hall and a choir singer were found dead—apparent suicides. She got a coherent story out of the so-called "pig-woman" who accused Mrs. Hall. The "pig-woman" witness made good news copy, but Mrs. Hall was acquitted.

When Harpman retired she was followed at the *Daily News* by Grace Robinson, who carried on the tradition of covering trials. She covered a reopening of the Hall-Mills case and her reports led the paper day after day. One of her more unusual assignments was to follow Greta Garbo on her voyage to Sweden and get an exclusive interview from that publicity-shy actress. She failed. She had to be content with an interview along with Swedish reporters when the ship neared port.

Robinson had better luck with the Prince of Wales, who also

tried to avoid the American press during his American visit. She tracked him to a polo field and approached him when one of his Scotland Yard men left his side for a moment. He was so surprised that he answered her questions before he realized she was with the press. Then he gave her a little lecture about privacy. It was another *News* reporter, Imogene Stanley, who crashed a party and succeeded in dancing with the prince. In the news reports she became the "beautiful mystery girl in the green dress," but she refused to file a gushing, personal story to her own paper about the affair. She wrote it straight.

Keen Competition

By the time Mary Margaret McBride (later famed on radio) completed journalism school at the University of Missouri and took her first New York newspaper job, competition among newspaperwomen was keen. McBride had worked on the Cleveland *Press* and at public relations before taking a job at the *Mail* as a "sob sister reporter." She covered fires, accidents, murder trials and any sad stories involving women.

McBride was somewhat awed by the competition. She felt that she herself was not a good reporter. She was just "proud of being one at all." She worked hard and enjoyed it but she found the fascination of newspaper work hard to explain. In her autobiography, *A Long Way From Missouri,* she said:

> People were frequently snooty and rude to you, and you were filled with fear of failing on your story. You might be a coward off the job, but even the puniest would push through fire lines, walk proudly into police cordons on an assignment. You could even make a murderer feel you were his best friend to get his story.

She was in direct competition with the other afternoon newspaperwomen and feared them. When Zoë Beckley returned from a long feature writing trip, McBride thought she would lose her daily feature assignment to Beckley. She didn't, and Beckley turned out to be friendly. McBride admired Ross and Bugbee at the *Tribune* for their forthright and reassuring characters, and she looked up to Harpman and Robinson for their ability to avoid becoming hard-boiled in their fearless

crime reporting. McBride found herself most comfortable
doing the radio chats with fascinating people which made her
famous.

Journalists were beginning to consider themselves professionals, and although most often the men did not want women
to associate with them in the professional journalists' clubs,
women also needed professional interchange. They formed
their own clubs. McBride was in at the start of the New York
Newspaper Women's Club, founded by Martha Coman in the
early 1920's. The Club replaced the informal daily gatherings
of women reporters covering the suffrage movement. When
the suffrage story ended, the women missed these meetings.
Coman invited eight of them to tea one Sunday afternoon to
discuss forming a club that would attract New York's leading
newspaperwomen. (The New York Woman's Press Club,
formed earlier by Jennie June Croly, accepted members from
all communications fields; both groups were active.)

Emma Bugbee found that the advent of woman suffrage and
the success of women in modern life still had not enhanced
woman's value as such in the news. As she said in 1928:

> Almost the contrary is true. So long as women were pro-
> testing against inequality, fighting and opposing the es-
> tablished order, they were news. When they succeeded and
> ceased to fight, they ceased to be news as a sex.
> Today they are news chiefly as individuals and women in
> politics have become submerged in the general stream. Nor
> are women reporters treated with derision as earlier. When
> they are assigned to cover major stories it is on the basis of
> reportorial ability and only occasionally because women are
> supposed to have a more intuitive understanding of the psy-
> chology of women involved in the story.

As examples she cited Ishbel Ross and Grace Robinson for
their balanced court reporting that included the picturesque
and emotional aspects of the testimony and the legal implica-
tions.

Sob-sister reporting was declining in the late 1920's but
feminine viewpoint features were still abundant and many top
women reporters made their names that way. Executive ability
was being discovered in women in journalism, Bugbee said,

and the most natural goal was fashion editor or women's page editor. There were other women editors: Mrs. William Brown Melony, editor of the *Herald Tribune's Sunday Magazine* and Irita Van Doren, its book editor. Competition was keen; the average big city newspaper with a staff of 30 to 50 men in the late 1920's would have three women reporters, most of them assigned to the women's page. And Bugbee emphasized:

> It is not fair to say that a woman is debarred by her sex from holding the highest reportorial positions, though the executive chairs are almost never offered to her in the metropolitan papers.
>
> Probably she is less likely to get even the reportorial plums than a man of similar ability would, but nothing is impossible in this extremely haphazard but essentially fairminded profession. No city editor will deny a capable woman a good story merely out of sex prejudice: neither will any city editor deny his paper the chance to print a good story because of any notions about gallantry or protecting the weaker sex that might interfere with his asking a woman to cover it.

Catharine Brody, writing in the *American Mercury* of 1926 found that her small town experience as telegraph page editor and her copyreading study was of no help at the New York *Globe* when she asked her editor for a job on the desk. He refused, not because she lacked experience, but because she was a "girl." She deplored newspaper editors' treatment of women as only capable of stunts or women's angle stories and the exploitation of women by the Hearst papers. Tabloids paid women well for their stories but were not interested in developing the talents of these women as good reporters. Her plea was to be taken seriously on one's own merit, not to be stereotyped. Brody found all too frequently that editors were like the man on the Chicago *Tribune* who said, "We have five women now; that's more than anywhere else, and we're full up with girls."

The Press Galleries

As women undertook political reporting and pressed on with serious journalistic work despite these obstacles, they reappeared in the Washington press galleries as correspondents. One of the first full-time professionals was Cora Rigby, who had worked for the New York *Herald* for 15 years before joining the *Christian Science Monitor.* In 1918 she was appointed Washington correspondent for that newspaper and headed the *Monitor's* bureau there for over seven years. Her male colleagues resented her at first, but they grew to admire her because she was "so unobtrusive in her manner and so capable in her reporting."

In those days women reporters were not admitted to the National Press Club sessions with distinguished visitors to the nation's capitol. But many women were then corresponding for newspapers and magazines from Washington and handling public relations for the suffrage campaign. In 1919 a small group of them got together to form a Women's National Press Club. The first meeting drew some 40 women, 28 of whom became charter members. Rigby was the second president and served from 1920 to 1928.

Ten women in 1919 were accredited to the House and Senate Press Galleries along with a hundred men. One was Elizabeth King of the New York *Evening Post,* that paper's only woman correspondent. She covered national politics, government, railroad regulations and engineering topics. She had served as the paper's only woman correspondent in Albany, and when she took her seat at the press table there the men tossed candy in her lap.

As an accredited member of the Congressional Press Gallery King covered the League of Nations debates in 1919, and her ability to take shorthand made it possible to scoop her male colleagues by dictating directly from her notes to the telegraph operator.

One of her predecessors in the gallery, Mrs. George F. Richards (signed "Richards,") was the only woman there in 1912. She had inherited her husband's gallery seat along with his chain of newspapers in New England. When the Women's National Press Club was formed in 1919, four of its members had gallery privileges: Elizabeth King, Cora Rigby, Winifred Mallon and Roberta Bradshaw.

The number of women in reporting and editing jobs once

again doubled in the 1920's, bringing the total to nearly 12,000 or 24 per cent of the profession, an increase of 7.2 per cent in one decade. Most of their jobs were still on the women's pages, magazines or in book publishing, but the "new woman" of 1920 with her voting rights and new equality seems to have set the tone for a generation of serious-minded young women who favored journalism careers. Many outstanding newspaperwomen matured in this decade.

Although the numbers of women in the profession continued to rise with each decade, so did the numbers of men (except during World War I), and the proportion of women in the field continued growing by about 4 per cent per decade (except for a 1 per cent increase in the depression 1930's). Not until the 1940's and the war years were opportunities again as good for women as they had been in the 1920's. In the 1940's women leaped forward with another doubling of their total numbers (to 28,595) in these jobs, a 7 per cent increase. By 1950 they held 32 per cent of the total editing and reporting jobs.

Qualities Required . . . and Recognized

As women took on more difficult and varied tasks in journalism a new professional standard emerged for them, and Ishbel Ross, whose boss described her as "one of the all-time great cityside reporters" described it:

> The woman reporter really has to be a paradox. She must be ruthless at work . . . gentle in private life . . . not too beguiling to dazzle the men and disrupt the work . . . comradely with the male reporters . . . able to take the noise and pressure and rough language of the city room without showing disapproval or breaking into tears under the strain of rough criticism. She must do her own work, asking no help or pampering, and make no excuses.

In addition she had to be twice as careful as a man in verifying facts and writing clearly in order to win over editors' skepticism about women's sloppiness and carelessness in their writing. "She had to be sensible, imaginative, and resourceful . . . neither hard-boiled nor a cutie . . . She would need stamina and self-control. She would have to be resourceful and good-natured but have enough perception to avoid being taken in." And, she still had to fight the men's suspicion that women will go to pieces under the strain of a big story on deadline. That was one attitude that would die hard, Ross thought, and would keep many able women from the chance to try deadline page-one stories.

But Ross herself and others proved that they were capable of working under such deadline pressure. One was Agness (Aggie) Underwood, who became city editor of the Los Angeles *Evening Herald-Express* in 1947. The public may have been surprised at her promotion, but to Underwood it was the logical outcome of 12 years of grinding hard work as a cityside reporter and police reporter in Los Angeles. Her specialty was covering crime and courts and she turned in scoop after scoop in competition-hungry years. Newspapering was her life and she knew she'd "be miserably unhappy is she should forego, or be crowded out of, her calling."

She wasn't, and her managing editor, John B. T. Campbell, paid her what she regarded the supreme compliment. He said, "Aggie Underwood . . . should have been a man. A rip-snorting, go-gettum reporter who goes through fire lines, trails killers . . . using anything from airplanes to mules to reach the spot that in the newspapers is marked with an arrow or an 'x', What a gal!"

Policemen often tried to keep her away from the murder sites, telling her "there's blood all over." But that never stopped her and they finally stopped saying that. She was a whiz at cranking out deadline copy, and when she became editor she had no problem wielding authority.

Although Underwood sounds hard-boiled, in her relations with other reporters she could frequently be sympathetic and motherly. Reason and understanding were the best tools in dealing with reporters, she said. But she was tough when she had to be. She worked from sunup until well past sunset (4:30 a.m. until 9 p.m. was normal). Neither her son nor her daughter ever expressed any desire to become newspaper reporters. They knew how hard she worked and how low the pay was.

*   *   *

Some of America's most prominent newswomen began their careers in the 1920's. Two of the most outstanding and most honored were Dorothy Thompson and Anne O'Hare McCormick. Thompson became the first American woman to head a news bureau in Europe, and McCormick became the first woman on the New York *Times'* editorial board. They shared an interest in politics and an ability to report political and social developments with keen insight. Both have been honored by their peers for their achievements and ranked with the best journalists of their day.

Dorothy Thompson left for Europe in 1919 with another young woman writer. Both had gained a little experience in writing in New York and shared a large zest for life and adventure. Thompson had worked for the suffrage movement and then in publishing. The two planned to travel in Europe and live on profits from their writing. They covered the Irish hunger strike in County Cork in 1920, sent interviews and travel impressions from Italy and Paris and intended to go to Germany and Moscow. When her friend decided to marry, Thompson decided to continue the trip. She persuaded the Philadelphia *Public Ledger*'s Paris bureau to let her be their correspondent in Austria.

In 1921 she went to Vienna where she quickly became a part of the intellectual set of writers and artists. With her vibrant personality and quick wit she made many friends and developed good news sources that led to a salaried position as the *Ledger*'s correspondent. She also wrote publicity for the Red Cross. In 1924 she became the bureau chief in Berlin for the *Ledger* and the New York *Evening Post*. She had married a charming European intellectual who stayed home writing history while she dashed about Vienna gathering news. They carried on an intense social life, despite Thompson's demanding work schedule.

Thompson's office was in the apartment's living room, where according to her biographer, Marion K. Sanders, "a steady stream of copy poured from her typewriter without benefit of secretaries."

To cover her large territory, she had to rely on part-time local correspondents, who were unaccustomed to digging for news. She herself hurried off to Prague, Sofia or Salonika when a coup or revolution seemed imminent, and on the basis of her performance in Vienna was offered the Berlin post.

The break-up of her marriage and a second marriage, this time with author Sinclair Lewis who followed her around Europe until she said "yes," are part of the Berlin years. She spent some adventurous writing years in Europe before returning to New York in 1928.

A few other women became American correspondents in the 1920's and 1930's. Martha Gellhorn, covered the Spanish Civil War for *Collier's* magazine. Sigrid Schultz, headed a Chicago *Tribune* overseas bureau, (Gellhorn revisited Spain after Franco's death in 1976 and wrote in *New York* magazine about the "uncrushed spirit of the people" and her recollections of the wartime days there with Ernest Hemingway, whom she later married.) So, Thompson was not pleased to be singled out by *Nation* magazine to write on the "extraordinary feat" of being a female foreign newspaper correspondent. It should be no cause for "jubiliation every time a woman becomes, for the first time, an iceman, a road surveyor or a senator."

Thompson objected to the American habit of regarding women as "news" and assigning those stories to women writers, thus sucking into this field the talents of all women who seek a career in newspaper writing. She herself had selected foreign correspondence in order to avoid having to report on nothing but groups of women.

Despite a troubled marriage, Thompson continued to write for magazines and newspapers as Lewis worked on his books. They were divorced in 1942. Some of her articles on women encouraged them to regard their roles as wives and mothers as having the utmost importance.

In 1936 she received a contract from the New York *Herald Tribune* for a regular column called "On the Record" to be syndicated three times a week to over 200 subscribers with a peak circulation of 8 million. Her column alternated with that of Walter Lippmann, and she was one of the few highly regarded political analysts of the 1930's and 1940's.

According to Winston Churchill, Thompson helped rouse the U.S. from its isolationism with her warnings about Nazi

Germany, for which she had been expelled from Germany in 1933. An early critic of the New Deal programs, she switched her support from Wendell Willkie to Franklin D. Roosevelt in 1940 when she feared that Willkie might become isolationist. For this she clashed with her staunch Republican editors, and so she accepted an offer to move to the Bell Syndicate and the New York *Post* in 1941.

In the late 1920's Thompson had been a strong champion of Zionism, but in the 1940's she became a critic of the partition of Palestine, the creation of the state of Israel, Jewish terrorism and the dispossession of Palestinian Arabs. This brought increasing public criticism, and the *Post* dropped her column in 1947. Several papers cancelled her column, which ceased in 1958 after 21 years. Her *Ladies' Home Journal* column, which was non-political, ran for 20 years, but by the late 50's she was thought by her critics to have lost her acute judgment of politics.

✳   ✳   ✳

Thompson was often called the "first lady of American journalism" in her many lecture tours around the country. That was an accolade she had to share with her friend and colleague Anne O'Hare McCormick, the *Times'* roving correspondent and editorial colunist. McCormick began writing for the *Times* in 1921 and continued until her death in 1954. She married a young engineer and importer from Dayton, Ohio, and they were traveling abroad when she started writing about what she saw and the people she met. She sent her dispatches to the *Times* and they were accepted. She was a rarity on the *Times* where official policy had barred women reporters in the city room until 1934, with only a few exceptions.

McCormick was given a column called "Abroad," which alternated with Arthur Krock's column. She was told to be the "freedom editor" and stand up and shout "whenever freedom is interfered with in any part of the world."

She received the Pulitzer Prize in 1937 for her distinguished foreign correspondence. She also received many awards and honorary degrees and was called the "most honored woman in American journalism."

McCormick's writing was clear, lively and illuminating, and the columns that have been preserved in collections display a vitality and freshness. She was often asked to write books, but she refused because she wanted to keep up with the news. She felt that her energies could be used more effectively if she wrote the news while people were interested. When she died, a colleague said, "She was a reporter and gloried in the title. She could not understand how anyone could be satisfied with less than the personal observation on the spot. The word reporter, we on this newspaper think, is a beautiful name."

Talent, Not Gender

Political reporting attracted other outstanding women reporters, among them Doris Fleeson and Ruth Finney. Doris Fleeson joined the New York *Daily News* in 1927 and began a Washington column for United Features syndicate in 1933. She told Leland Stowe's WUOM radio audience in the 1950's that she had decided to become a newspaper reporter while she attended the University of Kansas. She looked at William Allen White and Ed Howe and they seemed to lead such exciting and interesting lives, she said, that she "saw no reason why (she) should not do the same."

"Thinking has no sex," Fleeson declared. She found it difficult to understand why there was an apparent fear that a woman was taking something away from someone when she took a job on a newspaper. She lamented the lack of women at the top level in journalism and feared that if this continued the bright women would size up the field and look elsewhere. "We need a great flowering of mind and spirit on the part of men in the newspaper management," she added.

Ruth Finney got her taste for political reporting at the Sacramento *Star*. She came to Washington in 1924 as a correspondent for the Scripps-Howard papers of California and New Mexico. She quickly realized that the press gallery was a man's world and that all the important newsmaking beats had

been pre-empted. But a public utility bill was receiving super-
ficial coverage, so Finney dug into that subject and soon became a leading expert on it. She also wrote stories on the Federal Trade Commission, NRA, budgets, oil scandals, power
lobbies and unemployment. Thorough research and clarity of
writing were her trademarks.

Sylvia Porter opened the financial pages to women in the
1930's with her financial column for the New York *Post*. She
joined the newspaper staff full-time in 1942, but they continued to by-line her writing "S. F. Porter" until they were
certain the public had accepted her as an expert.

Porter told Stowe that she wanted to be a writer from the
earliest days she could remember and studied economics in
college in order to have a specialty that fascinated her. "The
good reporter develops early," she said, "and she will be accepted for her talents and ability by men and women."

She detected a decline in prejudice and bias toward newspaperwomen in the 1950's compared with the 1930's. Porter
thought it would continue to decline, but that part of that
would depend on "how good the girl was."

Finney observed that the field in the 1950's was open to
people with talent and believed that newspapering was less
prone to prejudice against women than some other professional fields.

> Women on editorial desks are rare, but they do exist. So
> do women editors, editorial and political writers. No excuses
> are accepted. If you don't know how to do the assignment,
> you find out—in a hurry. You succeed or find another way to
> earn a living. An inexhaustible interest in people and things
> and boundless enthusiasm for work were what it took to be a
> newspaperwoman.

Dorothy Kilgallen, daughter of a Hearst newspaperman,
seemed to fit that description exactly. She began as a cub reporter in 1931 with the New York *Evening Journal* and covered
every kind of story, including stunts and sob sister trials. Like
Nellie Bly she also went around the world, but in 1936 it took
only 24 days by air. Her colleagues thought of her as a hard-
working reporter, one who would stay with any story assigned
as long as necessary to cover it. Bob Considine recalled:

I worked with her on a lot of stories, spot news, trials, conventions, inaugurations, coronations, murders, funerals, United Nations, visitations of kings and clowns, and she'd always be first to the phone, had the cleanest first sentence, hit the heart of a story in a few swift strokes.

Eleanor Roosevelt was already a public figure when she entered the White House as first lady and she enjoyed excellent press relations. From the start she barred men, and that meant that the wire services and major newspapers had to be sure to have a newspaperwoman in Washington. Her Monday morning 11 o'clock press conferences were a tradition established in the first week. They usually attracted 20 to 30 reporters, including a few "regulars" such as Emma Bugbee, Bess Furman of the Associated Press, Genevieve Forbes Herrick of the Chicago *Tribune*, Lorena Hickock of the Associated Press, May Craig, who wrote a column for the Portland (Maine) *Press-Herald* and other Maine newspapers, and Marie Manning Gasch of INS (the original Beatrice Fairfax).

Of all Mrs. Roosevelt's regulars, May Craig was probably the best known. She was a regular on the NBC-TV program "Meet the Press" and for 30 years at presidential press conferences from Roosevelt to LBJ, where her hats and nettlesome questions made her a fixture. Her sharp mind and peppery persistence in getting answers to her questions led fellow reporters to characterize her as having a mind "sharp as cider vinegar and retentive as a lobster trap."

Craig was an activist in the struggle for women's rights. She had marched in a suffragist parade at the time of Woodrow Wilson's inauguration. She fought against the all-male National Press Club and stag meetings of the White House Correspondents' Association and for washroom facilities for women correspondents. She was the only woman journalist accompanying President Truman in 1947 to the International American Defense Conference in Brazil and in 1949 was the first woman correspondent allowed on a battleship at sea. Craig also reported the London buzz bomb raids, the Normandy campaign and the liberation of Paris during World War II, flew in the Berlin Airlift and covered the Korean truce talks.

Bess Furman came to Washington in the aftermath of the

1928 political campaign for the Omaha *Bee-News*. In Washington, she became an accredited AP bureau staffer, last on a list of 36 persons, she recalled in her book, *Washington By-Line*. That put her on the miscellaneous beat, picking up stories on the edges of government town and news of interest to women. She was an old hand at digging out features and handling breaking news by the time the Roosevelts arrived.

Eleanor Roosevelt's regular press conferences were symbolic of the change in social style that accompanied that family to the White House, Furman recalled. She "not only made news for, but friends with the women of the press." And it "happened naturally, one friendly gesture leading to another on a basis of day-by-day camaraderie."

The warmth of this association was outside the professional relationships, said Furman. It also was clear that reporters were supposed to ask any tough questions and to use any devices they could think of "to trap her into an appropriately newsworthy answer."

Furman left the AP in 1937 to establish a feature writing service with her sister and to allow both to spend more time with their families. During the war years she worked for Dorothy Ducas, head of the magazine section of the Office of War Information. By 1943, however, when a job as woman-interest writer for the New York *Times* in Washington opened up, she was ready to return to full-time newspapering. She was on the job when Mrs. Roosevelt gave her last press conference in 1945, when the first lady said that she believed the "12 Roosevelt years had marked significant changes, including a better position for women."

In the Thick of Things

Improvements were also taking place in the small towns and rural areas in the nation and women continued to expand their opportunities in journalism there as well as in the urban centers. Prejudice against women is just as ingrained if not more so in these small local settings, but women were often willing to accept low pay and long hours and serve with unyielding dedication in these newspaper offices. The record of their work is largely untold, but studies indicate that their numbers are fairly high. Dogged persistence and endurance characterize them as surely as their big city sisters.

One study of Tennessee women journalists by June Adamson turned up a publisher, telegraph editor and star reporter, among others. Edith O'Keefe Susong began her career as publisher of the Greenville *Sun* in 1916. She had two strikes against her when she started: she was a woman and a divorcee with two children to support. The stigma of divorce at that time was real; it was rarely mentioned in polite society. This strong and talented woman overcame that. She purchased a dying newspaper plant and built it into a going business that could be passed on to a grandson, first to have a journalism degree in the family.

Susong was forceful in her political beliefs but she always knew how far her readers would go and what they would do. She loved the work and said, "What is more exciting and more challenging than to be always in the thick of things and a chronicler of current history as it happens?"

A woman working in a man's world was Lucy Curtis Templeton, probably the first telegraph editor in the South when she accepted that job in 1910 at the Knoxville *News-Sentinel.* She had persuaded the publisher to let her work at the paper as a proofreader in 1904 when she finished college. At that time the paper employed a society editor and two women in the business department. She was the first woman in the back shop and the printers resented her at first. Gradually she won their respect and even their affection.

Templeton had been working only a few weeks when someone asked "if I supposed I could handle the telegraph copy for a few days." She said that she could, but she had never handled telegraph copy nor written a headline. "Someone made me a style sheet and wished me well," she recalled. "At times I was tempted to steal downstairs and never come back."

The paper came out and she felt extremely proud of her handiwork. She remained on the desk for two or three weeks before returning to read proof. After that she was given several copyreading jobs, and when she returned to the newspaper widowed after only three years of marriage, she became telegraph editor. She held that job for many of her 57 years in the business.

Templeton got out an "extra" announcing the start of World War I. She had to look around for type large enough for that headline and finally removed it from a toothpaste ad, she recalled. She said she felt sorry for people who were glad to leave their work.

> When I leave my work . . . I have the feeling when I depart that I leave the pulse of the community behind me . . . to me the composing room is the heart of the newspaper plant, the sound of the metal dropping into the slots . . . the race against time, the quiet wave and courtesy of the men, the smell of tobacco and ink, all make up the atmosphere that is so much the breath of life . . .

This was an enthusiasm that was shared by Nellie Kenyon, a reporter at the Chattanooga *News,* who was the first to dig up the complete background story of the Scopes "monkey trial." Her story detailing the careful planning of this test case was picked up by newspapers around the country. She covered the state house beat for over 40 years and once reported that the governor had a secret tape recorder hidden under his desk. She'd been given a tip that she'd "find something interesting under his desk."

So Kenyon joined a tour of school children and dropped her purse, spilling the contents. As she picked up her things, she also picked up her story. The governor was recording conversations with visitors and using a foot pedal to activate the machine. The governor admitted it to her and she rushed back with the story.

Colleagues called her persistent. Her philosophy was to get the story no matter what the obstacles, and her sharp eyes often led her to see what others missed. She covered the trials of James Hoffa, ex-president of the Teamsters Union and Al Capone's departure for prison, and she interviewed presidents and covered routine state house news.

Kenyon believed that women in business were handicapped by aging, particularly after they passed 40, but she maintained that she was "never discriminated against as a woman except in salary."

When she found out that the male reporters were being paid more than she was, she marched into the managing editor's office and asked him whether he thought she was a good a reporter as any man on his staff. He said that she was. Then she asked him why she wasn't paid the same. The next week she got a raise.

"Men will turn against women reporters who use their femininity or sex to get the news," Kenyon warned. When she first started in newspaper work, women were scarce and not particularly welcome, but they gained respect by producing good work, she said. "Listen—that's the main thing," she told young reporters, "get the facts . . . be persistent . . . curious and have integrity."

Women Publishers

Women continued to publish newspapers and in 1937 there were at least 300 women publishers in a field of 12,000 American dailies and weeklies. Often they were wives, widows or daughters of publishing families, but that does not diminish their effectiveness or dedication to journalism. A well-known example is Eleanor Medill (Cissy) Patterson of the Chicago *Tribune* Medills, who pestered Hearst into letting her edit his Washington *Times-Herald* in the 1930's. She finally bought it. Her cousin Alicia Patterson founded *Newsday* on Long Island in 1940. Dorothy Schiff became vice-president and treasurer of the New York *Post* in 1942 and managed the paper after her husband retired.

Occasionally big city newswomen went to the small towns to run their own papers. Two women from New York, Grace Hamilton and Nina Babcock, for example, bought the Cedar Springs (Michigan) *Weekly Clipper* in 1933 and gradually won that town's affection and esteem.

One woman publisher who took a direct hand in running her newspaper's affairs was Helen Rogers Reid. She had been active in the New York State Woman's Suffrage party, and after the vote for women was won, she took a post as advertising solicitor for the New York *Tribune*, her husband's paper. She met Odgen Reid in her first post-college job as his mother's social secretary when the family was in London during Whitelaw Reid's tenure as ambassador. They married in 1911 after Ogden had been working on the family newspaper for three years. When she assumed a role at the newspaper in 1918, the other employees hardly knew what to expect. But Helen Reid was a serious professional woman. Her voice was soon heard in managing the newspaper's affairs. She increased the advertising revenue and put the paper on a solid footing.

Reid believed that the modern woman should have husband, children and job, but she expected no favors for herself from men. She discouraged polite courtesies, preferring to be treated as an individual around the office. She encouraged her staff to record the advancement of women in any field, and she expanded the women's pages to cover homemaking and domestic science more fully. She backed fresh air fund campaigns that sent children from the city to the country each summer.

Reid re-introduced features for the family, including food, fashion and bedtime stories. She believed the ideal newspaper should serve all members of the family. She also encouraged the patronage of women because they did 80 per cent of the nation's buying. The *Tribune* extended many opportunities to women journalists, and several departments, including the *Sunday Magazine,* were headed by women. No post was too difficult for a capable woman, thought Reid, who ran the paper after her husband died in 1947 and refused many offers to sell.

Discussing the role of women in journalism, Reid told an audience that because newspapers were an all-round institution they needed a woman's point of view:

> There are a lot of prejudices against newspaperwomen and the future is not a rosy one. Women have not projected their imaginations toward positions. Ability is still rated as a natural masculine characteristic and is considered an exception among women. A woman should work harder to establish the idea that a good piece of work is only a normal piece of work. . .

Journalism does make high demands on body and spirit, and it disillusions those who are attracted to it for reasons of glamour and adventure. The image of the dashing reporter always turning in a scoop and being celebrated as the "toast of the town" is in large part a creation of stage and screen, popular fiction and the comics. Brenda Starr never really writes her stories, she lives them. The reality of journalism is just as challenging as the illusion, however, but in another way.

Irene Corbally Kuhn entered daily journalism in the 1920's as a reporter on the Syracuse *Herald*. She was on the staff of the Chicago *Tribune's Paris Edition* and was one of the early woman correspondents in the Far East. After working on the staff of *The China Press* in Shanghai, she returned to New York to the New York *World-Telegram* where she had her share of scoops and sensational interviews. She was in her 40's when she decided to give up daily reporting for a varied career as author, broadcaster and syndicated columnist. She said:

> The newspaper person's job entails a terrifying responsibility. Human happiness and destiny are in his hands so often . . . to shatter or direct with a few lines set up in print and exposed to the world. It is a responsiblity that is carried best by the insensitive soul, the unimaginative man or woman who sees only the facts and records them, indifferent to the turmoil breaking around him. But insensitive, unimaginative men and women are the ones editors don't want. For while news stories must be written objectively, a reporter must have the capacity to get excited over news: to feel intensely the repercussions of good and evil. Without an echo in his own heart to the beat of life around him his writing is wooden.
>
> It is difficult not to be cynical when one has the inside track on everything, and it is harder to hold one's philosophy in the newspaper business than elsewhere, for the wear and tear on one's spirit and inner life are continuous. We are always in conflict with the things in which we firmly believe, as all normal people do—justice, decency, courage, honor—and the continuous cancellation of these beliefs everywhere.

The newspaper person is most often sentimental underneath a gruff exterior, she explained, and many live vicariously and rapidly without time "to sit down and examine the significance of events in relation to the world and oneself." She quit to do just that, she said in her autobiographical *Assigned to Adventure*. She did not regret a minute of her career. "To live close to reality is really to live," she concluded.

Women Photojournalists

The camera became a powerful tool of communications during the 1930's in the hands of two women who made outstanding contributions to photojournalism, Margaret Bourke-White and Dorothea Lange, both of whom brought little-explored corners of the world to public attention through their lenses.

Bourke-White, who had fallen in love with the natural beauty and powerful expression of American industrial buildings, was trying to capture the essence of a steel mill on film when she received a wire from Henry Luce asking her to come to New York at *Time's* expense. *Time* magazine was five years old and seemed to run only portraits on its cover, so she couldn't imagine why it might be interested in her photographs. She nearly ignored the summons, but decided to take the trip to cultivate additional sources for her architectural and landscape photography.

When she met the editors she learned the reason for their interest in her work. They had seen her industrial photographs which had been published in a few trade journals and in Cleveland publications. Her work was perfect for the new magazine of business that they were planning. They wanted a photographer who could interpret modern industrial civilization in a fresh, new way. She recalled in her autobiography, *Portrait of Myself:*

> It seemed miraculous to me that these editors and I should meet and join our forces at just this time—I with my dream of portraying industry in photographs, and they with their new magazine destined to hold just such photographs.

She entered into the project with the characteristic enthusiasm she always displayed for her work. Despite the stock market crash, *Fortune* came out in February, 1930, and Bourke-White had prepared the striking cover. A few years later when *Life* magazine was introduced, her photographs once again were featured on the cover and inside. Her story of Fort Peck Dam in Montana was called a human document of a new American frontier by the editors and her cover picture of the dam made that first issue on November 23, 1936, memorable.

Bourke-White's autobiography conveys a sense of excitement, joy of life, spirit of adventure and readiness for each day. She loved the swift pace of *Life* assignments, she said, with

> . . . The exhilaration of stepping over the threshold into a new land . . . a stiff deadline to meet, all the better. You said "yes" to the challenge and shaped up the story accordingly, and found joy and a sense of accomplishment in so doing.

There were only four photographers at first for *Life* and they were kept feverishly busy. She had put in two stiff years learning her craft in Columbus, developing a personal style and studying camera techniques, developing and printing from an experienced professional there. When the big break came she was ready. That was part of her luck, she thought.

Bourke-White's career included photographing her favored industrial subjects as well as people the world over including sharecroppers in the South, dust bowl farmers, people in Russia, Africa, India and Korea. She went on several wartime assignments as the first woman accredited war photographer during World War II. One of those was a bombing raid. This indomitable spirit carried her through painful last years as a victim of Parkinson's disease. She stopped *Life* assignments as of 1957, and her magnificent collection of photographs finally came to rest in Syracuse University after her death in 1971.

Dorothea Lange had studied photography and had taken photographs for pleasure and for clients in San Francisco for several years, but the depression pulled her work in a new direction. She and her artist husband had taken separate studios, and as she looked out on the street below she saw streams of the newly-unemployed men drifting in search of work. She was struck by the discrepancy of photographing the upper-crust clientele of the city and the scenes unfolding on the street. In the spring of 1934 she made her first street photographs, including the "White Angel Breadline," one of her most famous. She continued taking pictures of men sleeping in the parks, May Day demonstrations and strikes.

At Lange's first exhibition of these photographs in 1934 a social economist, Paul Taylor, saw the work and used one of the photographs to illustrate an article he had written. She accompanied him on several field trips to migrant camps in California where she photographed people for his federally-funded study. This work led to her assignment with the Resettlement Administration (later the Farm Security Administration) which formed a team that collected some 270,000 photographs from 1935 to 1942 in order to provide a sociological document of the tragic history of the Oklahoma dust bowl and its dispossessed people.

Lange used her photography as a way of exploring social phenomena and suggesting solutions, observed Karin Ohrn in her doctoral study of this photographer. Lange liked talking with people she photographed because it gave them a chance to meet on common ground, she said. Then she used their own words as the basis for her captions. The captions should add something to an audience's image, not just repeat the obvious, Lange believed.

Lange continued her documentary photography of groups of people, including old religious communities like the Shakers, Hutterites and Amish. She documented the internment of the Japanese-Americans during World War II and she worked for the Office of War Information during the war. Little of Lange's work was made available to a wide audience, during her lifetime said Ohrn, because she was interested in doing in-depth documentation, social change over extended periods of time, which was not suitable to the content of the popular magazines. Further, Lange wanted control over selection and layout of her photographs and regarded herself as a "chronicler" rather than as a photojournalist. She often worked with her second husband, Paul Taylor, on these social documentations, and wrote:

> Documentary photography records the social scene of our time. It mirrors the present and documents for the future. Its focus is man in his relation to mankind . . . Documentary photography stands on its own merits and has validity by itself.

Toward the end of her life in the 1950's and 1960's Lange arranged several exhibits of her work and published a photographic essay called *The American Country Woman* which included photographs from her work over the years.

World War II

The second World War took many men away from newspaper jobs and women filled the gaps on the city desks as copy editors. Some set type and ran presses. A few became foreign correspondents, serving with distinction. By 1943 women made up 50 per cent of the staffs of many newspapers in small cities and this trend was expected to continue.

More and more women filled these jobs. The United Press bureau in Washington, which had only had one woman reporter before the war had increased that number to 11 on beats, and several others worked in its office. Senate and House Galleries accredited 98 women compared to 30 six years earlier. Women covered nearly everything—police, government bureaus, State Department, Interior—but the 37 women White House correspondents were not among the nearly 400 accredited correspondents who attended the annual dinner of the Correspondents' Association in 1944. Led by May Craig, president of the Women's National Press Club, the women filed a formal protest.

A small group of women served as correspondents during the war, including Betty Wason (on radio), Lee Carson for INS, Ann Stringer for the UP, Helen Kirkpatrick for the Chicago *Daily News*, Tania Long and Sonia Tomara for the New York *Herald Tribune*. The war brought them to the front zone and they roughed it as bravely as any soldier and turned in their share of scoops, according to one of their colleagues, Chicago *Daily News* correspondent Leland Stowe.

At the top of that list was Sigrid Schultz, correspondent-in-chief for Central Europe for the Chicago *Tribune* for 15 years since 1926. She was the Berlin correspondent for Mutual Broadcasting and for the *Tribune* from 1938 to 1941. A native Chicagoan, Schultz was educated in America and continued her studies at the International Law School in Berlin and at the Sorbonne in Paris. She was an expert on military strategy and armaments and began her journalistic career without any prior training. She just followed instructions contained in letters and cables from her editor. She was called the "Dragon from Chicago" after she thwarted Goering's propaganda men in an attempt to plant spy documents in her apartment, part of a plan to harass correspondents and make an example of her.

Helen Kirkpatrick was the only woman on the Chicago *Daily News* foreign staff, and she and Tania Long were the only women reporting in London during the 1941 bombing of that city. Kirkpatrick had studied European history and was in Geneva to work on the staff of the Foreign Policy Association, writing for its publication. She met foreign correspondents in that job and occasionally helped them out with a story, which led to assignments for the *Herald Tribune* and a regular job with the Chicago *Daily News* in 1939. She was considered a shrewd analyst of world affairs and had an amazing ability to get inside stories on international events. Eight days before the blitzkrieg in the west she cabled exclusive information that the King of Belgium had advised the American government that his country expected to be the next victim of the Nazis.

Her London colleague, Tania Long, of the New York *Herald Tribune* had been a correspondent in Berlin, Copenhagen and Paris before she arrived in London where her vivid description of London's aerial bombings made front page news back home. Her hotel took two direct hits but she escaped injury.

Sonia Tomara, who fled Russia during the Russian revolution, also reported for the *Herald Tribune*. She started as a secretary to the foreign editor of a French newspaper, and because of his frequent absences, often took charge of the desk herself. She was soon plunged into international political reporting as well as financial affairs, which led to writing a weekly financial review for the *Herald Tribune* and to an assignment in its Paris bureau. She asked for an American assignment in 1937 but returned to Europe in 1939, to be met a week later by bombs raining on Warsaw.

"I was deadly scared," she admitted. "It's not glamorous to write eyewitness stories about the collapse of an heroic Polish capital or about the heart-rending sufferings of Polish refugees."

The Home Front

Most of the newswomen, of course, stayed on the home front and covered beats of increasing responsibility and importance. One who was no novice at hard news reporting when the war started was Miriam Ottenberg, who joined the Washington *Star* in 1937 as its first woman reporter to cover a whole range of stories, from police to White House. She had completed her studies in journalism at the University of Wisconsin and she wanted to be a police reporter. She thought that police reporting was the "closest thing to real reporting—no handouts to help you, no real friendly sources and, especially relevant, police reporting deals with *people* rather than things."

The *Star* had placed one or two women briefly in the newsroom before Ottenberg arrived, but their stories were primarily on topics of interest to women and these women were soon moved into the women's department. Ottenberg observed:

> In those early days I did human interest features and handled public service campaigns like the Community Chest and the *Star*'s annual Christmas campaign. What I wrote were sob stories to raise funds.
>
> Since I was the only girl in the newsroom until the war, if they wanted a story that required an impersonation (I was a ham actress as every good investigative reporter should be) I did it. . . . By the time the war came, I was covering every major murder and in those days, a murder was covered by several top reporters.
>
> An apocryphal joke about me was that I asked the city editor, when he was dispatching me on a murder story, "Do you want me to cover it or solve it?"

During the war Ottenberg was assigned to cover the draft, manpower and civil defense at all levels. "If a good murder came along, I did that, too," because by that time most of the men had gone to war, and the majority of the women in the newsroom had little experience. When the war ended she moved into the demobilization beat, and there she discovered that the Navy was trying to hold the younger men regardless of how long they had served and was releasing the older men.

Her story caused quite a stir and the Navy had to change to a fairer system. "It is an example of the reporter turning investigator as the need occurred," she pointed out.

A war does not create a newspaperwoman, observed Genevieve P. Herrick, Washington correspondent for the Chicago *Tribune*. It does give her greater opportunities and wider fields of journalistic activity. Herrick had started her own career in the final days of the first World War. Although she got the job because there were more openings with men away, she kept it because she did a good job. When the war ended, the men did come back, but to better jobs, though they did not edge Herrick out of her own job.

She foresaw that the same would happen at the end of World War II. "There would be a general reshuffling to a peacetime basis," she thought. Many of the women who had been hired to fill in during the emergency would leave, some because they wanted to, others to go back to their homes with returned soldier husbands, others to marry. But many others who had been acceptable in an emergency weren't really very good, and they knew it and would leave. Others, trained in wartime, would remain:

> Inez Robb in North Africa and Ruth Cowan of the AP were both doing unusual jobs, but they did good work in peacetime as well as wartime. The unusual woman is likely always to have unusual assignments, and the woman journalist was making the most of her wartime opportunities.

· SOURCES CONSULTED ·

June N. Adamson, "Selected Women in Tennessee Newspaper Journalism," Unpublished M.A. thesis, University of Tennessee, Knoxville, 1971.

Elizabeth Banks, *Autobiography of a Newspaper Girl* (London: Methuen & Co., 1902).

Margaret Bourke-White, *Portrait of Myself* (New York: Simon and Schuster, 1963).

Doris E. Fleischman, ed., *An Outline of Careers for Women: A Practical Guide to Achievement* (New York: Doubleday Doran and Co., Inc., 1928).

Bess Furman, *Washington By-Line: The Personal History of a Newspaperwoman* (New York: Alfred AL Knopf, 1949).

Irene Kuhn, *Assigned To Adventure* (London: George G. Harrap & Co., Ltd., 1938).

Mildred and Milton Lewis, *Famous Modern Newspaper Writers* (New York: Dodd, Mead & Co., 1963).

Nancy Madison Lewis, " A Century of Wisconsin Women Journalists," Unpublished M.A. thesis, University of Wisconsin-Madison, 1947.

Mary Margaret McBride, *A Long Way from Missouri* (New York: G. P. Putnams, 1959).

Margaret Inman Meaders, "Ida Minerva Tarbell, Journalist and Historian, 1857–1944," Unpublished M.A. thesis, University of Wisconsin, Madison, 1946.

Karin Ohrn, "Dorothea Lange: The Making of a Documentary Photographer," working title for doctoral research dissertation at Indiana University, unpublished.

Ishbel Ross, *Ladies of the Press* (New York: Harper & Brothers, 1936).

Marion K. Sanders, *Dorothy Thompson: A Legend in Her Time* (Boston: Houghton Mifflin Co., 1973).

Marion T. Sheehan, *The World at Home: Selections from the Writings of Anne O'Hare McCormick* (New York: Alfred A. Knopf, 1956).

Ida Tarbell, *All in the Day's Work* (New York: Macmillan Co., 1939).

Agnes Underwood, *Newspaperwoman* (New York: Harper & Brothers, 1949).

Professor Leland Stowe, University of Michigan, Department of Journalism, lecture notes for foreign correspondence course and radio tape on women in journalism, "News in 20th Century America," for WUOM in 1950's.

Personal letters to the author from Ishbel Ross, Miriam Ottenberg and Mildred Gilman Wohlforth, and interview with Ishbel Ross.

3

* * *

The Post World War II Pioneers

PEACE RETURNED and the reshuffling of jobs and lives took place as anticipated. Many women dropped out of the job market, having contributed their emergency effort, but others remained. Women reporters who stayed on in this post-war era were less noticed than their predecessors of the early twentieth century. Women had earned their standing as professionals and by and large newspapers no longer insisted on stunt girl antics. Women who had been teen-agers during the war and completed college as the war ended could see before them several outstanding women journalists who had climbed the professional ladder in the 1930's and 1940's.

The number of women editors and reporters in the entire field of newspaper, magazine and book publishing had increased by 7 per cent during the 1940's, and a slow increase continued into the 1950's so that by 1960 women claimed 36.6 per cent of all these jobs. The field was considerably larger, too. Magazines were still healthy but television was threatening. Growing advertising and public relations industries snapped up large supplies of talented writers. But something *was* different in the city rooms. Once again you could count the number of women in the newsroom on one hand and their beats were likely to be education, health, welfare or features.

Women were being returned to their peacetime roles—writing about women's interests, family and the home. It seemed to take more determination than ever to hang on to a hard news beat or to convince editors that women could do those jobs. The wartime lesson that "women could do anything" had contained an unspoken but powerful tag end—"in an emergency."

One woman's experience illustrates the point with brutal clarity. During World War II Dorothy Jurney was "acting city editor" for the Washington *News.* At the end of the war she was told that she could not be considered for that position permanently because she was a woman. In fact, she was asked to train her replacement, which she did, before taking a job as woman's editor at the Miami *Herald.*

"1949 . . . Newspaper-bent? It's a bad year for it," concluded *Mademoiselle's* job editor after a survey of 27 daily newspaper editors and 15 journalism schools.

> Four years ago, before the men came back you could have had a crack at a beginning job, even on a big-city daily, and it might have led into the metropolitan reporting most women aim for when they enter journalism. But the girls who started then and have been handling straight news now find themselves shifted to departments with a women's angle, and when they drop out of news jobs, men replace them.

One such woman was Margaret Allison, who wrote features ranging from rent control to the circus for the Minneapolis *Tribune* city staff, but was moved to the woman's page at the *Star* after the war.

The women entering the 1949 job market who did get jobs were being hired as society and women's page writers, or in related work in publicity, advertising, radio, magazines or specialized publications for the most part. Only a few were hired as general reporters. Editors told *Mademoiselle* that they were hiring about twice as many men as women in the beginning jobs. Women were paid less, about $40.50 a week—$8.50 less than usually offered men.

The old reasons were back, too. Editors said they hired men as general reporters because "assignments take them where 'I wouldn't want any lady relative of mine to go at night.' " Men were preferred for sports, politics, business, labor, agriculture, finance, copy and rewrite.

> Women get married and quit just about the time they're any good to you . . . women expect special consideration . . . women lack the all-round grasp of affairs it takes to operate on these jobs . . . women lack evenness of temperament, dependability, stability, quickness, range, understanding, knowledge, insight.

Prepare for Special Jobs

The advice directed to women in journalism schools was to prepare for the special jobs where being a woman was no disadvantage or might even be an advantage—women's departments and specialized publications. But if a young woman was really set on covering hard news, it was obvious that from then on it was going to take education plus reporting experience plus the kind of determination that would prove to editors that "this young woman really did eat, drink and sleep newspaper," as they said real newsmen did.

These became the two typical paths for women in journalism in the 1950's and beyond, and the common refrain from women in the hard news path, was "you have to work twice as hard as a man" to prove yourself.

One of the new generation was Marguerite (Maggie) Higgins. Her ambition—war correspondent. She finished her M.A. at Columbia University's Graduate School of Journalism in 1942 and went to work for the New York *Herald Tribune,* where she had been a campus stringer. She pestered editors to send her to cover the war. Getting nowhere, she went directly to Helen Rogers Reid with her plea. Higgins' reputation for dogged determination and thoroughness in her reporting helped convince the publisher. In August, 1944, she was sent overseas as a correspondent and she covered the wind-up of the war. In her book, *News is a Singular Thing,* she said:

> Having no laurels to rest on, I became a cyclone of energy. I was a ruthless city editor with myself. Each day I read every single French paper, as well as Agence France Presse, the French wire service. Then I would assign myself to check the validity of every major news development. Because of

the strict discipline of my city desk training, it never occurred to me to send out a story asserting, "Such and such is happening, according to the French press." I went to the ministry or individual involved, and probed until I found out to my own satisfaction precisely what the facts were.

Higgins was one of the first group of reporters to cover the U.S. capture of the Dachau concentration camp, and she turned in an eyewitness account. She covered the Nürnberg war trials, and became the *Herald Tribune*'s Berlin bureau chief in 1945. She was clearly aware of her disadvantage in being a young woman. Officials expected her to be dumb or sly or both, she said. She had hoped for the Berlin appointment but it was unexpected.

> . . . I was wearing a chip on my shoulder about the unlikelihood of my paper's picking a female to run an established newspaper bureau . . . I have since observed that many minorities—including women correspondents—have a tendency to wear chips on their shoulders and these frequently consist of taking the attitude that you are bound to be gypped out of an appointment or a promotion solely on the grounds that you are a woman, or a Jew, or a Negro. This attitude offers great and comforting opportunities of fooling yourself because it prevents your facing up to the fact that just possibly the reason you aren't going to receive a certain promotion is that your talents aren't up to it.

But Higgins' talents were certainly up to it. She went on to head the *Herald Tribune*'s Tokyo bureau and to turn in Pulitzer Prize reporting during the Korean War. She met discrimination head on. An Army colonel ordered her to leave the front in Korea one time. "You'll have to go back, young lady," he said. "You can't stay here. There may be trouble." "Trouble is news," she responded, "and the gathering of news is my job." Still, it was weeks before she was accepted on an equal basis with male reporters. Her fierce competition spurred some of them on to even greater reporting, it was thought. She married an officer she met through her work.

In 1963 Higgins began writing a column for *Newsday* and she covered the early days of the war in Vietnam, taking a hard anti-Communist line. A tropical disease she contracted there ended her life in 1966, at age 45. Colleagues admired her excellent reporting, envied her fantastic luck and griped about her willingness to trade on her femininity. But in all, they respected her as a journalist. Said Chicago *Daily News* correspondent, Peter Lisagor,

> Marguerite was one of the most feminine people in our business; most seem to get hard and masculine in their manner and approach. Marguerite, for all of her deep competitive instincts remained an extremely feminine woman. Often people believed the myth about her rather than the reality. Actually, as strong as she was and as independent and unafraid of life as she was, she would easily be afraid of, say, a mouse as anyone else would be. . . .

One of the best places to get experience and test the ability to work under constant pressure is with the wire services. In the late 1940's and 1950's there was usually at least one woman at a bureau. In Detroit in 1957, Gael Greene was one of them. She enjoyed the variety in wire service reporting and didn't mind rising at 4 a.m. to do the morning news for radio stations in the state. Her boss refused to put her on the night shift, and she did mind that a little. She really didn't want to work nights, she said, but she did hate "not being allowed to because she was a woman."

On her college newspaper the rallying cry had been, "Anything he can do, she can do better," and she carried that into her job, at first.

"Occasionally," Greene said, "I overdid it." Gradually she learned that in Detroit, at least at that time, there were some jobs that women could not do equally well. It was a disadvantage to be a woman reporter and dig for news in the automotive industry, which was all-male. She also felt at a disadvantage in handling sports, murders and disasters.

"Would you walk up to a corpse, recently liquidated, and lift his wallet to get his identity before the police arrive, like old Murphy here?" her city editor asked her. She said that she would, but wondered how she could tell because she had never been given the opportunity.

On the other hand, Greene found that bureau chiefs liked having a woman on the staff to do human interest stories and features because "women see things differently, things a man sometimes doesn't see at all."

The Era of "Togetherness"

The 1950's were called quiet times. College women looked ahead to bright and cheerful roles in families where togetherness was once again attainable and prized. The move to the suburbs was on. *Life* magazine had sounded a warning note in 1947, however, with its special feature on the "American Woman's Dilemma." The article dealt with the confusion and frustration created by conflict between traditional ideas on woman's place and woman's increasing involvement in roles outside the home.

Figures would show that the pace of female employment quickened during the postwar years so that by 1960 twice as many women were at work as in 1940, and fully 40 per cent of all women over age 16 held a job. The median age of women workers became 41 and the percentage of working wives had doubled from 15 per cent in 1940 to 30 per cent in 1960. The importance of these figures would not be fully realized until the women's liberation movement of the 1970's.

In journalism were women whose stars would rise in the 1960's and 1970's: Helen Thomas of United Press International, Elsie Carper of the Washington *Post*, Dorothy Jurney of the Miami *Herald*, Kathleen Teltsch and Betsy Wade of the New York *Times*, Carol Sutton of the Louisville *Courier-Journal* and Miriam Ottenberg and Mary McGrory of the Washington *Star*, to mention a few.

Mary McGrory had been writing bright copy for the *Star*'s book pages for six years before her big moment arrived. She was really interested in politics and on her days off would go to the Hill and write a few profiles and features.

One day in 1954 the national editor said, "Say, Mary, aren't you ever going to get married? Because if you're not, we'd like you to come out into the news room. We'd like to have you give color and humor and charm to the news columns."

Her first assignment was covering the Army-McCarthy

hearings. McGrory was petrified, she recalled in a *Ms.* interview. But it was the beginning of her career as a witty and irreverent observer of the political scene. By the 1970's her columns were syndicated in 40 newspapers, she had won numerous awards and was considered Washington's top woman reporter.

✳ ✳ ✳

In the late 1940's, Miriam Ottenberg started covering Congressional investigations. That led her to investigation of Washington crime and the administration of justice, "which in turn led to a Congressional investigation of Washington crime, a new police chief and such a pronounced curb in crime that it was going down here while it was going up all over the country," she recalled.

During the 1950's Ottenberg's investigations for the Washington *Star* dealt with the administration of justice, but by the late 1950's she had moved more and more into consumer fraud.

> Investigative reporting demands a lot of patience, going through endless records, not accepting the absence of complaints as meaning there aren't any complaints. For example, I had heard that in the early days of the wig craze here, women were being sold wigs which were worthless for as much as $400. I was tipped that some of the guys who had been driven out of the used car business as a result of my used car investigation had moved over to the wig business.
>
> But there were no complaints that I could find from the usual sources—like the Better Business Bureau. I figured that if the wigs were as bad as I had heard, the women who bought them on the installment plan probably were refusing to pay and if that happened, the bad guys might be threatening to sue them.
>
> So I went to the court records and sure enough, I found a number of my old "friends" suing local women. I called the women whose names appeared on the court papers and I had my complainants—lots of them. In a way, that was the most spectacular of successes. The story appeared on a Sunday in 1963 on page one. It was accompanied by a picture of a girl in a wig and a picture of a Yak, because one of my complainants had found that her "natural hair" wig was Yak hair.

On Monday, women started cancelling their orders for wigs and by mid-week, the bad guys were going out of business. It had one bad effect. One of the ex-used-car promoters, turned wig entrepreneur, switched to narcotics and another went back to his old game—the numbers.

There have been relatively few women in investigative reporting, although Ottenberg thinks they are quite effective at it.

A woman has many advantages as an investigative reporter. She can give the impression of being more sympathetic, whether she is or not, and this is effective in consumer fraud interviews. Men are less likely to brush her off with a rude answer (although they can be pretty rude—and threatening, too—when the stories start appearing).

I think women may have a larger bump of curiosity than men and that's a must. And what else is needed? An ability to get indignant, a true feeling of caring what happens to people, compassion without sentimentality, a willingness to work around the clock if necessary and patience, patience, patience.

Ottenberg's investigative work was not particularly dangerous, but when she did get into "somewhat sticky situations" her city editor "very sensibly arranged for a man to go with me as both protector and witness."

Few reporters, male or female, were doing investigative reporting in 1960 when Ottenberg won a Pulitzer prize for her exposé of the baby broker racket. At the first American Press Institute seminar on investigative reporting in 1963, only a few of about thirty reporters attending had ever done much investigative reporting up to that time. In Washington, Clark Mollenhoff, a Pulitzer prize winner, was one. Vance Trimble of Scripps-Howard, who won his Pulitzer the same year Ottenberg did, did some investigative reporting, but not full-time.

Ottenberg thinks that would-be investigative reporters should get their training "where your legwork is as important if not more important than your brainwork." And she warned against scorning covering the police.

It's still a great training ground and so is city hall.

Become a trained, meticuously accurate, objective reporter before you try becoming an investigative reporter. Don't

ever substitute your theories for basic facts. If you're wrong
once on your facts, your effectiveness is destroyed and you
have to build your credibility all over again.

The *Star*, Ottenberg said, had a good record on hiring and
promoting women reporters on general assignment after originally dragging its feet. It became the only newspaper in the
country with three women Pulitzer Prize winners: Ottenberg
in 1960, Mary Lou Forbes in 1968 and McGrory in 1975.
Forbes, who began at the *Star* as a 16-year-old copy girl during
World War II, rose through the ranks—reporter, assistant state
editor, state editor—to metropolitan editor where she bosses
all the reporters covering the metropolitan area. Her Pulitzer
was for deadline coverage of integration in Virginia.

A Wider Range of Choices

Women in journalism in 1975, Ottenberg thought, had far
greater opportunities than in 1937.

> The women's pages have become men-and-women's fea-
> ture pages . . . women get to cover the same things as men
> . . . women have a much wider range of choices than they
> had before . . . (The woman journalist) is respected as a
> fellow craftsman rather than solely as a woman.
> But one word of caution: To the extent she loses her femi-
> ninity, her effectiveness also diminishes. Men like to talk to
> women, at least they did in the past. Often, they find them
> more understanding, more sympathetic. And that's a big
> plus for a woman reporter—investigative or not.

Small town weeklies in postwar America also offered opportunities to women who wanted to combine writing, editing
and management. (Women were editor-publishers of 704
weeklies in 1941.) Betty Keen left the wire services to take an
associate editorship of the *Clear Creek Mining Journal* in Idaho
Springs, Colorado, and called it the job of her life. In 1951, she
won the Federation of Press Women's award for the best story
in a weekly. Frances Jones, age 24, would have agreed with
her. She had purchased the Lumpink County, (Georgia) *Dah-
lonega Nugget* in 1946. In less than a year she had increased
circulation from 376 to 1,000, raised advertising rates from two

cents to 38 cents per column inch and had put the shop in working order. She enjoyed keeping the mellow flavor of small-town gossip.

Occasionally, owning a small weekly put one in conflict with the community. Hazel Brannon Smith, owner of four weekly newspapers in Mississippi in the 1960's, was one of those who fought in the classic battle for freedom of speech and equality in support of the civil rights movement in the South. She opposed the formation of White Citizens' Councils in her town and was nearly put out of business for it. In 1964 she won a Pulitzer Prize for her efforts and a fund was raised to help her continue publishing.

✳ ✳ ✳

Photojournalism was a rewarding and stimulating profession in the 1940's and 1950's when big magazines and Sunday supplements provided a large market for photo stories. Ten top photographers named in 1959 included photojournalists Margaret Bourke-White and Lisa Larsen at *Life* and free-lancer Ruth Orkin, whose photo essays appeared in most of the mass magazines, including *Life, Look, Collier's* and the women's magazines. Orkin became something of a pioneer with 35mm. color photography, which many editors wouldn't even look at when she first began to show them. In March, 1950, she saw her first 35mm. color cover on *The Ladies' Home Journal.* Orkin was admired for her "instinctive and natural" photographs, especially of children and domestic scenes.

The demise of the big magazines coincided with raising her family and temporarily removed Orkin from active photojournalism. "It's really impossible to work as a photo essayist and raise children, too," she declared. "To work one must have concentrated periods of time plus the flexibility to follow the story, the people and the light. You can't always be worried about getting baby sitters."

Orkin's views were echoed by other photojournalists, including Charlotte Brooks of *Look* and free-lancers Suzanne Szasz and Esther Bubley, who sold to *Life, Look* and the women's magazines. All were interviewed by Margaret K. Morgan for a master's thesis in 1964. The photojournalists felt that their job demanded so much energy and preoccupation with other people that it "favored men or women who had few distractions." There was only one woman press photographer among the 150 on metropolitan dailies in 1949, for example, and although 55 per cent of the amateur photographers in the country were women, only 8 per cent of the members of the American Society of Magazine Photographers in 1960 were women.

Few of the women photojournalists said they were able to organize their lives well enough to attend to both photography and family. It helped to have a sympathetic husband, they agreed. Editors, on the other hand, were positive about the women photojournalists. They liked having a woman photographer—"she puts people at ease and helps them relax better than a man can," said one.

To survive, they all agreed, the woman photojournalist had to have the same technical ability as any man in the field, a good business sense, a driving ambition for a career, an all-consuming interest in people and curiosity about the world.

Mary Ellen Mark was one of those women who had been able to move from *Life* and *Look* to the more highly specialized photographic markets of the 1970's, such as *Ms., Esquire, Rolling Stone, Time* and *Newsweek*. Photography is very isolating, she said, and sometimes regretted being "married to my camera." Her work is praised by editors for its perception and insight. She usually transforms anonymous people into revealing statements about the nature of mankind and the quality of life around the world. Her photography has taken her from the rebellion in Ireland to the re-creation of Hollywood in its heyday.

In the field of architectural criticism another pioneer began writing in the New York *Times Magazine* in the 1960's. Destined to become America's foremost architectural critic, Ada Louise Huxtable showed an early determination to explore and analyze architecture for its cultural impact as well as its artistic qualities. In 1963, assistant managing editor Clifton Daniel asked her to do a regular column for the *Times*. At first she demurred, but when he told her he would have to ask someone else if she would not do it, she agreed.

In her work as critic, Huxtable believes in taking clear and forthright stands on social and design issues after making long and serious study. "The *Times* is a powerful platform," she says, "and that's a tremendous responsibility. But a critic must have informed opinions and express them." The *Times* evidently agrees; she was promoted to its editorial board.

To be an architectural critic today, Huxtable says, requires a great deal of study in several fields—architectural and art history, environmental affairs, economics, sociology, philosophy of criticism, urban planning and so on. She tells that to young aspirants, and adds: "Once you have accomplished that, you still have to persuade a newspaper editor to hire you, because most editors don't think that architecture is important."

Foreign Correspondents

Less than four per cent of the American foreign correspondents in Western Europe during the 1950's were women. Editors believed that women stay in journalism only until marriage and that women correspondents could not enjoy the confidence of European government officials, Theodore Kruglak found in a 1965 study. Those women who did get sent abroad had a hard time getting out of domestic and feature subjects into political news.

But there were a few of them, including Aline Mosby of the UPI, who served in Brussels, London, Moscow and Paris and Claire Sterling, who started as a cub reporter on *The Reporter* magazine in 1949 and persuaded the editor to send her to Rome as the Mediterranean and African correspondent. She was one of the ablest women journalists anywhere, said Leland Stowe of the Chicago *Daily News*. Others included Flora Lewis, who free-lanced for the New York *Times Sunday Magazine* and later served as a columnist on *Newsday*, Margaret Parton who was stationed in India for the New York *Herald Tribune*, Charlotte Ebener who covered the Mideast and Asia and Laura Bergquist of *Look* in Castro's Cuba.

The *Christian Science Monitor* sent Helen Zotos to Greece on a special assignment and she stayed to cover the civil war for the Associated Press. Her investigation of the 1948 murder of CBS news correspondent George Polk uncovered a Communist plot to create friction between the U.S. and the Greek royal government. She returned to the United States and worked as a UN correspondent in the early 1950's.

But by 1968 there were fewer women foreign correspondents than there had been in the 1930's. The New York *Times* had Gloria Emerson in Paris and UPI had Joan Deppa there; both were doing mostly features until the student riots gave them opportunities for hard news reporting. The *Christian Science Monitor* had Charlotte Saikowski in Russia. *Newsweek* had sent Liz Peer to Paris, and the Chicago *Daily News* had assigned Georgie Anne Geyer to South America. There were few others until the Vietnam war.

Georgette ("Dickey") Meyer Chapelle got her start in photojournalism during World War II and had covered trouble spots around the world for 27 years, but she became best known for her Vietnamese work. When she was killed by a booby-trap mine on one of her assignments there in 1965, an editor said: "She never tolerated favors in the field because of her sex, and personal integrity forced her to write only stories she had 'eyeballed' instead of merely accepting official government handouts."

Chapelle was a frankly controversial character with a love of adventure, an ability to empathize with the underdog—particularly the enlisted man—and a tendency to talk like a "tough guy." Her work took all her time, and marriage to a competing photographer couldn't take the strain of her "need for recognition and a place in journalism," as she put it.

Chapelle believed in trying to be objective with her photographs, but sometimes she found there were "no two sides to the story" and then she conveyed the emotional impact as she saw it. She received the Overseas Press Club's award for "reporting requiring exceptional courage and enterprise."

The Vietnam press corps included several women over the years: Chapelle, Margaret Kilgore, Liz Trotta, Beverley Deepe, Cathy Leroy, Linda Grant Martin, Frances FitzGerald, Esther Clark, Michel Ray, Denby Fawcett, Jurate Kazickas, Anne Morrissey, Karen Peterson and Gloria Emerson, but only a few of their by-lines were well known. Kate Webb (Australian born) of the UPI and Elizabeth Pond of the *Christian Science*

Monitor were each captured and held in Cambodia for some weeks during their tours of duty.

The attitudes of editors and the military had changed very little over the years. "Vietnam is no place for a woman . . . Why, for Christ's sake, didn't they send a man out here," spluttered a major to Gloria Emerson of the New York *Times* when she arrived.

A male colleague told Liz Trotta of NBC, who was about to leave for Vietnam, "Well, if you give it all you've got, you may do as well as the worst guy we have out there."

"Nothing in my previous background—and I had been a reporter for more than 10 years—really prepared me for South Vietnam," declared political reporter Margaret Kilgore of her 18-month assignment for UPI in 1970–71. Nothing "prepared" her for the

> . . . midnight rocket attacks, for hundreds of children and soldiers crying and dying in the hospitals, for pretty bar girls openly selling their bodies to the highest bidder, for the first hit, the first dead soldier or the stacks of Vietnamese bodies.
>
> The correspondent assigned to this war must be a political reporter, an expert on tactics, more familiar than many soldiers with a vast assortment of weaponry, a linguist, diplomat, administrator, daredevil, and one of the most suspicious, cautious people on earth.

Access to the battlefields was often a problem, Kilgore explained, and once she and her colleagues were dropped from a helicopter ten feet into the swamp below when enemy fire made it impossible for the helicopter to land.

At the time Kilgore served in Vietnam the press corps had been reduced from 700 to 200 and there were three other women, Emerson, Webb and Pond. During this most recent war editors still worried about sending women into danger zones, even when they were willing to try them as foreign correspondents.

Said Elizabeth Pond of the *Christian Science Monitor:*

> You have to keep working and supporting yourself until someone notices your work. This takes an enormous amount of time and energy and it best happens when you are young, exactly the period in life when most women are starting families and devoting much of their time to that. It is a rare indi-

vidual who can combine the two successfully until later in life. By then it is often difficult to break into the conservative patterns of established newspapers.

What does it take to be a correspondent? Pond said she agreed with an editor who told her it took

> . . . the thorough research of a scholar, so the reporter doesn't go off half-cocked on something without full knowledge, the skill of an artist in communicating and the instinct of an alley cat—for survival, garbage and gut fights.

But it's one of the most fascinating jobs journalism has to offer, Pond says. "You are not specialized. You get a chance to put the jigsaw puzzle together. You do the spot news, the features, the immediate perspective and the explanation. Then it's up to the historians and the experts to find the long-term trends."

Pond has reported in Vietnam, Czechoslovakia, Japan and the Soviet Union for the *Monitor*. Her first overseas reporting was done on her own during 1964–1965 free-lance trip in Eastern Europe after completing her graduate education in Soviet studies at Harvard. She had worked as a copy girl and clerk at the *Monitor*, and rejoined the staff in 1965 as a sub editor for European copy.

Because she knew the *Monitor* would not assign her there as a regular correspondent, she asked for a leave of absence to go to Vietnam in 1967. The *Monitor* decided to send her as a special correspondent for half a year. She wrote about urban politics and the impact of the war on village life. She took another leave to go to Prague in 1968, and she won an Alicia Patterson Fellowship in order to return to Saigon in 1969–1970. It was in 1970 that she and two other journalists who were looking at Cambodian villages strayed into insurgent territory, then were captured and held in Cambodia for five weeks.

After her release that same year the *Monitor* made her bureau chief in Tokyo and transferred her to Moscow for a two-year stay in 1974. She was the *Monitor's* second woman foreign correspondent. Charlotte Saikowski preceded her in both Tokyo and Moscow. (Saikowski became the *Monitor's* first woman among the top editors as editor of the editorial page.)

Each country requires somewhat different preparation and working methods, Pond explained. That is part of the fascination she finds in this work. For some countries there is a wealth of background information in books and scholarly journals, but for others the journalist has to rely almost entirely on personal contacts in the country. It helps to know the language, but an interpreter is still necessary for interviews and scanning the daily foreign papers.

A reporter has to be a sensitive observer of the culture and learn how to interpret and understand what is being seen and heard. Pond sharpens her cultural perceptions by constant daily contact with ordinary people as well as official and expert sources. She doesn't remain only in the big cities, but gets out to the countryside and villages. And she continually checks her observations with native sources. After perhaps half a year the correspondent begins to feel at home with the traditions and manners of the new society. "As a correspondent you have to keep putting people, (sources) together to get all sides. Gradually you learn the special interests and strengths and weaknesses of each source."

Foreign correspondence requires a combination of toughness and sensitivity, but Pond is not sure whether women have any special advantage or not in this field. She doesn't think that women are any more creative than men. "Society does allow women more freedom to operate to use their feelings," she says. That can be a plus, sometimes. But, according to Pond, the most important talents for a correspondent are perceiving and then communicating the dynamics of the country being covered.

Jurate Kazickas, who corresponded for the AP in the Middle East and Vietnam, explained that she had been one of three women journalists in Cairo in January, 1974. U.S. military officials in Vietnam treated her with "benevolent paternalism," she thought, more often thinking of her as an entertaining dinner partner than as a journalist capable of covering "terribly dangerous" stories.

There were some advantages in being a woman in a male-dominated foreign press corps, Kazickas told a meeting of the Sigma Delta Chi Deadline Club in New York City. In her travels she found many human interest stories ignored by her male colleagues. These stories rounded out and humanized the general overseas coverage she thought. Frequently she was the only woman at the press conference and found that she was highly visible and likely to get her questions answered because of that. "Feminine wiles are sometimes an extra benefit," she added, recommending using "whatever advantages you have to get a story."

The number of foreign correspondents working for the American media continued on a downward trend in 1975. The Overseas Press Club reported a drop of 28 per cent since 1970. Of the 676 full-time correspondents, 69 or 10.2 per cent were women, but 33 of those were foreign nationals. By far the largest number of the women worked in the Western Hemisphere—mostly in Canada and Puerto Rico. So the glamorous-sounding job of foreign correspondent appeared harder than ever to reach in the recession-struck 1970's.

Making Waves

Black women journalists could often be found in the 1950's and 1960's as society and religion reporters on the black weekly newspapers in the nation's urban areas and on religious and children's publications. Few were on the established press and few were national or foreign correspondents.

One who was had a doctorate from Boston University. She was Marguerite Cartwright, United Nations reporter and international affairs columnist for the Pittsburgh *Courier,* and a stringer for the Chicago *Sun-Times.* She covered the 1951 Zagreb Conference in Yugoslavia, where she interviewed President Tito. She attended many UN meetings and served as a liaison officer for the UN Department of Public Information before joining the faculty of Hunter College.

Ethel Payne joined the John Sengstacke newspapers in 1953 after graduating from the Medill School of Journalism at Northwestern University. She was the Washington correspondent for this successful chain of nine black weeklies in the East and Midwest. She covered the 1955 Bandung Conference, reported on black troops in Vietnam in 1966, covered the Nigerian Civil War in 1969 and accompanied the Secretary of

State and President Nixon on world trips. In 1973 she left Washington to return to Chicago to become associate editor of the Sengstacke newspapers.

The black press was born in a spirit of protest, said Payne, and it has continued to exist because "We have grave social problems." The greatest gift Americans could give themselves, she added, was to start talking to each other—on a one-to-one basis. Payne was working on projects to do that through a series of town meetings in Chicago and a citizens' coalition to work with police in combatting crime. Protest, crusade and social concern are at the heart of her weekly column which takes blacks and whites to task for not living up to their responsibilities and demands accountability from the nation's leaders.

"I've always had a crusading spirit," Payne explained. "If we can feel that we have at least made a dent, we can feel that we will at least live in less fear," she said of her latest crusade against crime. Newspapers have an important role in this, she added, to explain the issues—jobs, housing, employment and the criminal justice system.

Newspapering was a tradition in the Garland family although Phyl Garland nearly hated it by the time she completed Northwestern in 1957. She wanted to write, but not journalism. Her mother, Hazel Garland (later, editor-in-chief of the *New Pittsburgh Courier*) was women's editor of the *Courier* and got her an appointment with the editor. She was assigned to write a history of the black press for an anniversary issue. "I first saw the history of my people, as I looked through the back files and books," she recalled. "It turned me into a journalist." And it gained her a full-time position on the newspaper.

Although she had criticized *Ebony* for "not making waves" Garland accepted a job there in 1966 to edit and write, and some of her articles were among those that began to "make waves"—civil rights, black liberation, natural hair styles, plus interviews with black political leaders and musicians. In the fall of 1971 she started teaching, first at State University of New York, later at Columbia University's Graduate School of Journalism. She combined that with free-lancing.

Elizabeth Murphy Moss, vice-president and treasurer of the

Afro-American Company, publishers of the *Afro-American* chain of black weekly newspapers, began her career at the age of 11 on the family paper in Baltimore. She was a reporter and editor during World War II and went to England as a foreign correspondent to do a series on black troops. Although she is a trustee and member of the board of directors of her company, she still writes a weekly column, "If You Ask Me," under her pen name, Bettye M. Moss.

Standards vs. Statistics

To a large degree Helen Rogers Reid's standards have become the accepted ones for contemporary newspaperwomen. In their professional organizations and in their own jobs, the objective of postwar women journalists was to become professional journalists. Standards and opportunities for men and women in journalism should be the same, they believed.

The 1970's feminist movement showed them all too clearly that this was not always the case. Old prejudices remained: unequal pay, slower promotions, clustering in certain jobs and not others. It also showed that women had not been as energetic as they might have been in pressing for increased responsibility and better jobs. Women writers and editors in the 1970 census numbered 59,360, but they held few management positions. In newsrooms, women held 17,000 of the 69,500 jobs in 1970.

"The plain-Jane truth is that the communications media do not treat women with dignity, with equality, nor even with what best serves the employer," declared Ralph Otwell, managing editor of the Chicago *Sun-Times.* He was speaking at a 1971 regional conference of Sigma Delta Chi (Society of Professional Journalists), which that year had opened its membership to women.

Recognition of discrimination against women in media jobs grew rapidly following widely reported protests in 1970 at *The Ladies' Home Journal, Time, Newsweek* and the Washington *Post.* Print and broadcast newswomen, sometimes with the aid of local feminist groups, issued protests, filed discrimination charges and license renewal challenges.

The early 1970's were years of awareness, action and frustration, much talk and some accomplishment for professional newswomen. Their numbers slowly increased in the formerly sex-segregated jobs in the profession. They were doing sports writing, police reporting, environmental reporting, political reporting, science, financial and editorial writing as of 1974, and 10 per cent of the city editors and 12 per cent of the investigative reporters were women, said Helen K. Copley, chairman and chief executive of the Copley Newspapers. Copley estimated that there were 26,000 women in the nation's newsrooms in 1974. At the Copley Newspapers, for example, the percentage of women journalists had risen from 18 to 34 per cent in ten years.

"Women were considered second-class citizens in the newsroom until recently," agreed Marian Heiskell, a member of the New York *Times* board of directors in 1974. The reasons were partly protective, she explained, and it was "taken for granted that reporting was a man's world." But she added:

> It is only fair to say that women generally acquiesced in and accepted these ground rules. They were far less career-minded than they are today and less liberated in their willingness to be exposed to the seamy side of life.
> An examination of job applications from women for news jobs at the *Times* extending back over a fairly long period of time, reveals that the great majority specified that they wanted 9 to 5 jobs. How far can you expect to get on a metropolitan staff with this kind of requirement?

Many were successful, in spite of that, Heiskell added and predicted that the number of women in the newsroom would be larger in 1976. Leading news executives, she said, had found out that women were "just damned good" and they intended to develop more of them for key jobs.

Women in news media jobs were paid less and were segregated into certain job categories and geographical markets, William Bowman learned through his doctoral research survey which used a random sample of 1,340 journalists in 1970. Women were paid on the average of $4,540 less per year for doing what was considered essentially the same work, Bowman said, citing the mean annual salary for women in news jobs at $7,015 and for men $11,555. Nearly 70 per cent of the women in the sample had incomes of less than $10,000 while nearly 70 per cent of the men made more than that.

Women in newspaper work tended to be working in the small and medium markets and they often entered journalism after jobs in other fields. They tended to work in feminine beats or for women's pages. Women were rare in political, government, sports, business, finance and labor beats, Bowman said. When they reached middle-management, they were usually women's or society editors. The system, he concluded, channeled them into certain types of jobs when they were hired and there was little likelihood of a career ladder to the top.

Although the women surveyed recognized the discrimination, they were still more satisfied with their jobs than men. Women, Bowman concluded, manage to derive enjoyment from their work roles and from family roles. Where work becomes primary for women, often at the larger, more competitive news organizations, they sound more like their male colleagues with regard to dissatisfaction about the job.

Bowman's 1970 survey indicated that women held the following percentages of total news jobs: 20.3 in all reporting and editing jobs; 30.4 in news magazines; 21.1 in weekly newspapers; 22.4 in daily newspapers; 10.7 in radio and TV; 13 in wire service.

Some but not extensive discrimination existed in American newsrooms, Joann Lublin concluded in her 1971 study at Stanford. That was in hiring, job status, promotability and to a lesser extent in salary. Numerous jobs and beats were still linked to traditional sex roles, she observed, and advancement into management was limited by executives' conventional beliefs about women's performance capability.

News executives and newswomen (she surveyed about 300 in a national sample) concluded that the "women who had the same qualifications as a man would neither advance as quickly nor ever earn as many top positions on their publications."

Although the situation was not entirely rosy, Lublin thought that things were changing and that, once the recession began to ease, women and minorities would get first crack at more and more reporting jobs. And if their bosses had held their positions for less than a decade, it would be likely that women would receive equal treatment and opportunities, because these younger editors had less stereotyped attitudes about beat assignments.

Attitudes seemed to be changing for young reporters, too. A small, in-depth study of young Michigan reporters in 1975 indicated that in situations where both husband and wife were working journalists they were also sharing household responsibilities more than would be typical in a traditional marriage. These couples expected complications when children arrived, but it was clear that they were both thinking and planning for that eventuality in some new ways. These young men and women between the ages of 22 and 34 also tended to have similar professional goals.

Management and the Women's Challenges

In media management, however, the picture was still bleak in the 1970's. About two per cent of the management jobs on Newspaper Guild newspapers were held by women. The American Society of Newspaper Editors, whose members manage news staffs and determine policy, found only 7 of their 749 members were women. In 1972 ASNE located 59 potential new women members, but in 1974, *Editor and Publisher* was able to list only 16 women publishers in newspapers, several of whom were appointed in the 1970's.

Hiring, pay, equal assignments and promotions were the issues raised by women journalists in the 1970's, but their cases also sharply critized the "mindless doll" image projected through the media treatment of women in news, entertainment and advertising. Underlying the specific charges was the larger issue—the nation was under-utilizing one of its valuable resources, a talent pool of educated and trained women.

Militant feminists stormed the offices of *The Ladies' Home Journal* in March, 1970, to dramatize their objections to the sexist content of magazines directed at women. The *Journal* "projected a destructive image of women," they said. Their dramatic sit-in and confrontation with editor John Mack Carter caught media attention, and newspapers and news magazines soon carried photos of Carter surrounded by the sign-holding women. The *Journal* later published a special section edited by the women.

By 1974 the *Journal* and other women's magazines had altered their magazine content to add positive articles about professional women and to discuss current issues such as day care, abortion, rape laws, credit laws and the Equal Rights Amendment. Social research showed that women, including blue collar working women, had also changed their attitudes and were more career-minded and interested in self-improvement than they had been a decade earlier.

Newswomen could scarcely be expected to report on sit-ins, marches, lawsuits and demonstrations without examining their own work situations. In March, 1970, 46 of the women researchers and reporters and the one woman writer at *Newsweek* charged that magazine with a violation of Title VII of the Civil Rights Act of 1964. The complaint, filed with the Federal Equal Employment Opportunity Commission (EEOC), was the first of its kind. Women "are systematically discriminated against in both hiring and promotion and are forced to assume a subsidiary role simply because they are women," said the complaint.

The challenge was purposely filed the day *Newsweek* went on the stands with a cover story on "Women in Revolt," a story about the women's movement. The long-standing practice of hiring women as researchers and men as writers, even though they might have equal job and educational qualifications, was the major target of the suit. Of the 36 researchers, only one was a male. Of the 52 writers only one was a female.

"We think it especially important that so highly visible and ostensibly open-minded an institution should not be permitted to continue a blatant policy of discrimination against women," the complaint read.

The signers sent a separate letter to Katharine Graham, president of the Washington Post Company which publishes *Newsweek*. They deplored what they called "the day-to-day atmosphere that discourages women as professional journalists," but they added that they continued to feel "committed" to *Newsweek* and wanted "very much to contribute to making it a better magazine."

Osborn Elliott, *Newsweek*'s editor-in-chief, responded by saying that most of his researchers were women "because of a newsmagazine tradition going back almost 50 years." He added that a change in that tradition "has been under active consideration."

Newsweek had more than a dozen women among its foreign and domestic correspondents, he said, and management stood ready "to meet with any or all grievances they might have."

The complaint was withdrawn in August, 1970, when the management signed a memo promising "substantial changes," but in May, 1972, finding things virtually unchanged, 51 women filed a second EEOC complaint. That was withdrawn when a settlement was signed in June, 1973.

The Memorandum of Understanding that Elliott and the Women's Committee signed then said that one-third of all domestic reporters and one-third of all persons hired or trans-ferred onto the staff of foreign correspondents would be women by the end of 1974, one-third of all writers would be women, one-third of all researchers would be men and there would be one woman senior editor by the end of 1975. *Newsweek* agreed to provide training programs in writing and re-porting and establish an arbitration procedure.

The tradition of women as researchers but not writers had been broken during World War II, but from 1960 to 1973 no women were hired at *Newsweek* as writers. In the winter of 1970 there was one woman writer on the staff, but by mid-1975 there were 13 women writers out of a total of 40 and the research staff was one-third male. Lynn Young was the first woman to reach the senior editorship—in August, 1975. She had been with the magazine for ten years and a general editor since 1974.

Newsweek's senior editors were pleased with the progress that had been made. Said one of them, *Newsweek* "is proud of being the first to change this old tradition."

Women at *Time*, Inc. made a similar list of charges in May, 1970, and filed with the New York State Division of Human Rights. The group of women represented 35 per cent of the professional women employed by the company's magazine and book divisions. The number of women as editors, writers and correspondents "has risen steadily over the past few years," said *Time* management, but a preliminary hearing indicated that there was "probable cause" for the complaint. The company reached a settlement in February, 1971. During the period of conciliation, a few researchers were promoted to jobs as editors, two women became associate editors and two more became assistant picture editors. In March, 1972, *Time* also featured the women's status in America. The feature was put together by 19 women writers, correspondents and reporter-researchers (a new title) with senior editor Ruth Brine.

From Researchers to Writers

Time as the first news magazine, founded in 1923, started the news researcher job and its female tradition. At first the *Time* operation was largely clipping and rewriting and a group of young women were hired to do the clipping and library work. For many years Content Peckham directed the department. As *Time* grew the job enlarged. Marylois P. Vega, present chief of research, arrived at *Time* in 1942 with an education in economics and business and experience as an investment analyst in Wall Street. She became a researcher in the Nation section. In addition to checking final copy for accuracy, she explained, researchers dig for raw material, background and interviews for the writers who put the story together. *Time* regards the researcher role as vital in obtaining the depth of coverage desired on such a wide variety of issues.

During the 1940's there were few bureaus, and researchers like Vega also had opportunities to do field work on some stories. There were a few women writers at that time, but researching was considered exclusively a female job. In 1967 or 1968 Vega was looking for a map room researcher, someone with a degree in cartography or geography. After a long search they came up with two male candidates, both of whom "nearly ran from the room" when they learned there were no other males in that job. About 1970, that attitude started to change and men applied without being sought out, but as of 1975 there were only four men out of 48 researchers.

After the women's protest, *Time* established a tryout system for researchers who were interested in correspondence or writing jobs. "It is my feeling," Vega said, "that *Time* was not really so prejudiced, but that we had not done much to push or encourage women to seek writing jobs. It's also partly up to the employee," she added.

Some researchers have let their editors know of their writing interests and some were promoted over the years. Ruth Galvin, former chief in the Boston bureau, started as a researcher in the 1940's as did that bureau's new chief, Sandra Burton. One college graduate was hired directly as a writer because of the impressive list of story suggestions she sent in, two others were taken from *Life* and one from the Washington *Post* within the last decade, Vega explained. As of 1975, four correspondents in the New York bureau had been researchers, but three of those had been in the tryout program. The Newspaper Guild contract with Time, Inc., in 1976 included an affirmative action program and an attempt to set numerical goals for key jobs.

Things have improved at *Time,* and as one of the top male editors explained,

> The women have changed, and we have, too. Women today are more sure of their own authority and status now. They know their jobs demand time and energy, but if they are wives and mothers they also know how to handle that with more ease. It makes it a little easier for us when they do ask for writing jobs.

Newspaper women also registered complaints. The Washington *Post*'s newswomen challenged their own and other local dailies for discrimination against women. Their statement in May, 1970, asked the *Post* to hire more women in the news and editorial departments, to promote them to decision-making positions and to end discriminatory practices in the assignment and play of stories. They objected to the placement of stories about women's rights on the women's page "dumping ground" and charged that Washington newspaper editors denied them many assignments because of their sex. They also complained about degrading references to women in the local newspapers' stories and headlines and against the sterotyping that this reinforces.

The *Post*'s executive editor, Benjamin C. Bradlee, replied that the copy desks were being made aware of the sensitivity on these issues, and editors began to delete sexist language. In his June 3rd reply, Bradlee said the policy of the *Post* was to make the

> . . . equality and dignity of women completely and instinc- tively meaningful. This policy begins in the newsroom with hiring practices and follows naturally through assignment and promotion practices. We will use all our resources to combat discrimination against women reporters and photog- raphers in this city and elsewhere.

Two years later the women filed another complaint, this time charging that they were "losing ground at a time when more women are graduating from journalism schools and ap- plying for jobs" at the *Post* than ever before. Women made up 15 per cent of the news and editorial staff in June, 1970 (43 of 287), but in April, 1972 they made up only 13.6 per cent (40 of 294).

"The *Post*'s news department has expanded rapidly over the past 16 years," they charged "but the number of women has hardly increased at all." In June, 1956, for example, the metro- politan and national staffs consisted of 29 men and 7 women; in April, 1972, there were 65 men and 10 women.

The women singled out two other related problems: women, particularly on the metropolitan staff, were assigned less frequently than men to hard news and analysis stories, and stories that directly affect women, such as day care centers and women's rights, were considered of marginal value in the news sections. They charged:

> There seems to be a negative feeling on the part of some male editors about the professional capabilities of women re- porters and photographers just because they are women. In some instances reporters and photographers have not been sent out on potentially front page stories "to protect them" even though they had asked to go.

They asked for an affirmative action program—not a quota system—that would improve the present ratio of men to women on the paper, give equal opportunity for news assignments to women, examine pay policies, promote more women to decision-making jobs and apply equal standards in hiring, assigning and promoting women regardless of marital status.

By the end of May, 1972, the *Post* responded with a memo outlining an affirmative action program, including equal policies for hiring and promotion. The women called the response inadequate, and the following year in July, 1973, the EEOC opened an investigation in the matter. The percentage of newswomen had risen in 1973 to 16.3 (54 of 331 editors, reporters, photographers and artists). Some key promotions had been made: Elsie Carper and Mary Lou Beatty to assistant managing editors, Meg Greenfield to deputy editorial page editor and Joanne Omang to Latin American correspondent. The *Post* also appointed its first woman sports writer and had added two women photographers and a female suburban editor, for example. Over half the 25-person staff in "Style," the former women's section, was female.

"Tokenism is Over"

The EEOC concluded in June, 1974, that the *Post* did *not* show a pattern of discrimination in its recruitment, interviewing or hiring practices in the news department, but it found "probable cause" to believe that the *Post* did discriminate against women employees in making story assignments and in promotional opportunities.

In its April 24 settlement that year with the striking Newspaper Guild, the *Post* established an affirmative action committee on fair employment practices and promised to look into the feasibility of a day care center.

There is "no discrimination in assignments in the guise of personal protection," declared Elsie Carper in an interview. Women are not asked to do "women's news," and men and women have some area of choice in assignments. Sexist descriptions in news stories are flatly prohibited, she said. The *Post* uses Ms., Mrs. or Miss, according to the individual's preference, but it has not been able to decide to drop the title in second references for women as it does for men.

"Tokenism is over," declared Carper, the *Post*'s editor in charge of personnel matters, as she looked back over 1973. "This paper and some others feel that there should be more women in newspaper work and more women in positions to make contributions to content and exercise news judgment on stories."

The *Post* had a flood of applications from men and women after the Watergate exposé. From mid-1972 to mid-1973, for example, 1,233 people applied for newsroom jobs, 503 of them women. The *Post* interviewed 367 men and 224 women and hired 23 men and 12 women to full-time editorial positions, Carper said.

"Opportunities are much better for women today than when I first started," she recalled. Experienced women are getting long overdue promotions and women are being hired for new positions. "Editors are seeking input from varied backgrounds and views of life today because they believe that will make better newspapers."

Carper advised young women who want to be reporters not to get sidetracked on women's pages, unless that was what they really wanted. "The old-style women's pages are on their way out," she predicted. "Women should prepare right now—by taking the right college courses—to cover the government and not the governor's wife."

The best place to begin is on a small daily where "you see your work in print and can continually polish your talents," she said. On a large newspaper, competition is so keen that beginners are often overlooked and given stories that do not regularly make the paper. She thinks it is far better to come to a big paper with some experience.

The Guild's Program

Newswomen at the larger dailies were among the first to discuss discriminatory policies with their editors early in the 1970's, but what happened there was repeated in smaller newsrooms around the country. In November, 1970, the

American Newspaper Guild held a special Chicago conference on sex discrimination. Discrimination against women "is a pervasive reality in journalism" and an inherent part of the profession, the Guild charged. The 118 women delegates adopted a 30-point human rights package aimed at improving the rights of women and minorities in journalism—in hiring, advancement, pay, professional assignments and social welfare. About 40 per cent of the Guild's membership is female, one third of them in editorial jobs. The Guild decided to press its program through its locals and as of 1974 started a special drive to eliminate wage and other discriminatory clauses from all contracts, first by refusing to sign discriminatory clauses and then by legal means.

"Wiping out pay differentials for female reporters," announced the Guild in March, 1974, "is proceeding at the fastest pace in Guild history." In two years 19 contracts were adjusted to give equal pay to general reporters and women's department reporters (17 remained unchanged). Only eight contracts had been made equal in the previous 12 years, even though the pay differences ranged from $40 to $80 a month.

Local guilds were active after 1970 in initiating and backing complaints of discriminatory practices against women and minorities in several cities, and in 1973 the first contract was signed that treated maternity as a disability that deserved sick pay and provided paternity leave. Some guilds were pressing for child care facilities at places of employment, and the percentage of women employees in some newsrooms rose between 1972 and 1974: at the L.A. *Times* from 12 to 22 per cent and at the *Wall Street Journal* from 7 to 13 per cent, for example.

The wire services, which have nearly 3,000 employees, were criticized for their employment policies. The Associated Press, which had only two women among its 75 domestic correspondents, was charged with discrimination by its Guild. United Press International, with 1,400 employees started an affirmative action plan in 1971 and increased the percentage of women from 11 to 15 per cent in two-and-a-half years. They encouraged women to try for management positions and had a handful of correspondents and bureau managers who were women: Helen Thomas, Margaret Kilgore, Joan Deppa, Char-

lotte Moulton, Kate Webb, Aline Mosby, Lucinda Franks, Gay
Pauley and Barbara Frye. UPI's first woman chief of a major
bureau was Marguerite Davis who headed the Chicago bureau
in 1942.

"Stag" Restrictions

Pressure for equal treatment did open a few social and professional doors in the 1970's. The Women's National Press
Club voted to admit men in December, 1970, and elected two
men to its governing body the following year. It was renamed
the Washington Press Club. The all-male National Press Club,
which grudgingly had allowed women reporters to sit in the
balcony for the newsmaking luncheons with VIP's, finally decided to admit women in 1971. It quickly accepted 24 new
women members.

Washington's prestigious Gridiron Club, founded in 1908,
continued its "stag only" membership policy until November,
1974, when it voted to accept women members. The first was
Helen Thomas, UPI White House bureau chief. Women had
picketed the club's annual dinner in 1971, and a few women
were invited guests at the 1972 banquet. The club's first vote
in 1974 rejected the proposal to admit women by 26 to 18.

After lengthy discussions, Sigma Delta Chi, later called The
Society of Professional Journalists/Sigma Delta Chi, opened
membership to women (1971). In 1974, Val Hymes, Washington correspondent for Westinghouse TV stations became the
first woman professional to join the SPJ/SDX national board.
She was nominated for the post of national treasurer in 1976.

Theta Sigma Phi, was renamed Women in Communications, Inc. and opened to male members who support
WICI goals in 1972. Gradually, local press clubs and organizations were opened to women members. The Milwaukee Press
Club, oldest in the nation, admitted women in 1971.

Under the leadership of Marjorie Paxon from 1963 to 1967
Theta Sigma Phi stepped up its professional activities and
shed its sorority rituals. Paxon who started as a wire service
reporter in 1944 and later moved into editing women's pages,
became assistant managing editor of the Idaho *Statesman* in

1976. She and her successors encouraged TSP to take stands on freedom of the press, affirmative action, and equal rights issues. The organization supported the Equal Rights Amendment and particpated in International Women's Year, 1975.

In 1973, TSP/WICI began a joint program with Delta Sigma Theta, Inc., to encourage careers in journalism for minorities. Media Women, a group of black women in media, organized in New York and a few other cities, and New York media women formed an action-oriented Media Women's Association.

Despite several professional advances for media women, including serving as Pulitzer Prize jurors for the first time in 1972, there were still times when women were barred from press conferences by "stag" restrictions. Sports reporting for press and broadcast was one of the toughest specialty fields for women to enter, but here, too, press boxes were challenged and won, starting in the early 1970's. In 1974 there were at least 25 women working for the national media as sportwriters and another five or so in broadcasting. Their greatest problems were convincing editors and their colleagues that they could get and understand the story. Athletes, however, were quite willing to be interviewed by women reporters. "We love sports and we love our jobs," said Jackie Lapin who held sports department internships at the Detroit *Free Press* and the Washington *Post* before becoming a free-lance sportswriter in California.

Pressure to hire racial minorities, although strong in the 1960's had abated some in the 1970's, and both black journalists and editors were concerned about the small amount of progress that had been made. Charlayne Hunter, chief of the New York *Times'* Harlem bureau, voiced her dismay in 1975 over the closing of the minority journalism program at Columbia University and the declining financial aid available. Individual newspapers and groups were continuing programs to hire and train minorities and universities were trying to attract minorities to journalism.

The Columbia program was revived in 1976 aided by a developmental grant from the Gannett Newspaper Foundation, and it was moved to the University of California in Berkeley as the Summer Program for Minority Students. The Berkeley program was initially limited to 15 apprentice students for print media courses, whereas the Columbia Michele Clark program had included electronic journalism. The Clark program in seven years from 1968 to 1974, placed 225 minority journalists, roughly one-fifth of all non-whites working in the field in 1975, in print and broadcast newsrooms. Minority journalists still only constituted one per cent of the 38,000 news professionals on general circulation newspapers and three per cent of broadcast news staffs in 1975.

The women's movement in the 1970's appeared to be making progress, with the aid of affirmative action programs and legal suits, and it caused some women to analyze their own professional roles.

"I began to want to affect policy," said Lois Wille, who had been a reporter at the Chicago *Daily News* since 1957. "I realized that no one at the paper thought of me as part of the decision-making process."

Following the 1972 Democractic convention, Wille and other women at the *News* went in to complain about the lack of women reporters in political reporting. Within a few months Willie had been named assistant city editor in charge of special projects and was putting out a special monthly section called "Plus."

The Women's Movement on the Front Pages

Once again the women's movement offered some women the opportunity for good front page stories. Marcia Dubrow, first women general news reporter for Reuters in North America, said she got the women's beat in the 1970's "because no man would touch it."

But she would take a quintuplet story and ask the mother how she felt about having such a large number of kids that she couldn't afford. "I dropped all the baby talk and sought out women as experts."

Some of her stories led to investigative articles on organizations behind the anti-abortion campaign and the ERA and to stories on CIA and FBI spying on NOW. Not all of her stories made it past the desk, she said, but each one made the men consider the particular issue.

"Who wants to read about rape, abortion, child care, cancer?" an editor would ask. "Women do," she'd say, "and some men."

As she covered more and more of these subjects, Dubrow noticed a polarization developing in her office—an "us versus them" feeling. "When this happens," she declared,

> . . . we all lose. To avoid it I kept the issues objective and would not get lured into a debate on women or ideology. I talked straight news value and audience interest. For example: ERA is among the most important civil rights amendments of the century.
>
> I learned that you do not fight every fight. You pick and choose where to expend your emotional energies and professional effort. If you get angry when the editor questions your story on women's issues, you've lost the battle, because to him you become one more over-emotional woman.

She stressed the importance of having newswomen write and get these stories into the newspapers.

✳ ✳ ✳

As women moved into the fields that have been dominated by males, each developed a strategy for dealing with sources and colleagues to suit her personality and the times. Eileen Shanahan, the New York *Times'* distinguished business and labor reporter, said she "comes on like Gangbusters when she is dealing with a new public official."

Shanahan does more than the usual amount of homework before the interview and lets the expert know right away that she knows his field. "As soon as he learns that you've got brains, he has to take you seriously."

With colleagues, she makes sure that she always pays her share of the expenses and always has a supply of dollar bills on hand to make this relatively easy. She also advocated picking up the check whenever a male reporter would do so when lunching with a news source. "It's all part of establishing yourself as a professional journalist."

Sometimes Shanahan succeeds so well that a source will say, "You think like a man." Occasionally she quips back, "Yes, I know. I'm having an off day; I'll be myself tomorrow."

Police reporting has long been a masculine stronghold, but Toni House is one of several breaking down that barrier. She had been a local reporter at the Washington *Star* for four-and-a-half years before she was given the police beat in 1973.

"I happen to think police reporting is important because the general attitude of the police affects people's daily lives," she said. But police are distrustful of the press and she had trouble establishing rapport. House briefed herself on all the important issues and problems and would go into an office and make the policeman talk to her in an intelligent manner for ten minutes before she would leave.

"I wore them down. I was not going to go away; I was very serious. I wanted them to know that I was acting as a representative of the public in their domain. Now we've established a happy working relationship."

Another pioneer field is the copy desk. Betsy Wade broke into that at the *Times* in 1957, but by 1975 there were still only 10 women among the 75 copy editors there, and she works for some of her own former students.

When she took the job the editor said, "I have always been sure women would be good on the desk. I've been waiting for you for 16 years. You'd better be good."

Wade discovered that most copy editors considered newspaperwomen to be blatherheads. She found that to some she was an "amusing mascot," to others poison, and some just ignored her. She worked in the women's department for a year-and-a-half before being assigned to the city desk for good. Gradually the situation began to ease, and when the men began to swear normally around her she no longer felt so much in the way.

Editors began to hire more women to work on the desk when they had trouble filling the copy editing jobs with men in the late 1960's; they gradually realized that women were both competent at the job and not as sensitive to their profane outbursts as they had imagined. The job has some obvious advantages for women—regular hours—and that is still something that most women with families seek. The pay is usually better than that of a reporter.

Share the Wealth

Newswomen in some American newsrooms are beginning to help one another, remarked Eileen Shanahan. "There may still be some 'Queen Bees' around, but that's diminishing. As more and more women get into positions of authority and experience, they will help out new women coming along," she predicted.

For women who started out in the 1940's and 1950's it was more likely to be a man who helped with tips on how to do the reporting job. "I get great enjoyment out of helping the younger women coming along," Shanahan added.

That help is gratefully received, as one young woman put it.

> For years I toiled my solitary way, feeling that the problems I faced were individual and probably freakish. Now I learn that I was never alone, but only felt alone. Now the newspaper sisters discuss their problems, solutions and challenges, and we all derive great help and support from this. There is a growth through solidarity that is not imaginable until you've tried it.

"Women are also coming into their own as legitimate observers of political trends," said Helen Thomas, chief of the UPI White House bureau. She has chalked up several firsts in her field: first woman assigned to the White House on a permanent basis by a wire service, first woman member of the Gridiron Club, first woman president of the White House Correspondents' Association, first Woman of the Year for Communications.

When Helen Thomas started in 1943, there were opportunities because men were away. She first took a job as a copy girl at the Washington *Daily News,* working up to cub reporter before moving to the United Press. Her job was to file city news and write local radio news. She also wrote a personalities column. Then she covered the Justice Department and finally the White House.

Thomas describes her experiences in covering four Presidents—Kennedy, Johnson, Nixon and Ford—in her book, *Dateline: White House*. Her tough-minded news sense is tempered with compassion for the human beings who become presidents and their families, and this allows her to tell that story with grace and insight.

"I believe in tokenism," Thomas said. "Getting your foot in the door is the first step, but there have to be more and more women in jobs and in public office." That change started in the 1960's with a trend toward upward mobility for women. The women's liberation movement contributed greatly to the recognition of women's talents, she said. "Before that we were relegated to women's angles."

Thomas thinks journalism is the greatest profession on earth. "There is an element of learning every day and of participating in the real world, of keeping people informed and making democracy work. Journalists must put the spotlight on public officials and bring the American people in on the dialogue. "Too often public officials have too little faith in the intelligence of the American people," she said. "They only want the people to be in on the landings. They should be in on the take-offs, too."

The atmosphere in Washington has changed since Watergate, Thomas said, and officials know that they have to be more candid. "Journalists will have to keep up the pressure," she added. "We have to keep asking, 'Is it right? Will the people support it?' We have to keep after them until they answer our questions."

Perhaps one of the most encouraging developments in the long view was the promotion in the mid-1970's of several women to top management policy-making jobs: Christy Bulkeley to editor and publisher of *The Saratogian* (Saratoga Springs, New York); Carol Sutton to managing editor of the Louisville *Courier-Journal;* Judith Brown to executive vice-president and editor of the New Britain (Connecticut) *Herald;* Charlotte Curtis to associate editor in charge of the New York *Times'* Op/Ed page. And several women were promoted to positions as city editor, including Sally Jo Restivo at the Meriden (Connecticut) *Journal,* Marcia McQuern at the Riverside (California) *Press-Enterprise* and Beverly Hall at the Lansing (Michigan)

State Journal. Of the 26,000 women in newsrooms in 1975, it was estimated by ASNE that 226 were news editors, city editors, associate editors and publishers. Said Restivo,

> Getting there is only half the battle for women climbing the newspaper ladder from reporter to editor. Putting up with snide, cute and other tantrum-tempting remarks and attitudes is the toughest half. What male editor has to explain every time he answers the phone, 'Yes this really is the city editor . . . I'm not anyone's secretary'?

She quickly established her authority after being promoted in May, 1972, by giving vent to her fiery temper when necessary. Restivo thinks one of the best ways to break down the old sex-defined roles in the newsroom is to bring more women into the city room without a lot of fanfare and to expect them to do the best possible job.

> No woman should have to prove her ability to any further extreme than a man does to get a promotion. But she should not expect any doors to open either just because she is a minority.

Jean S. Taylor, Los Angeles *Times* associate editor, was recently named to the American Society of Newspaper Editors' committee on women's rights. She commented on the new trend in cityside promotions.

> The traditional way women on newspapers have advanced is by becoming women's editor. This turns out to be a dead end because bright young men, at the same time, are usually rewarded with junior editorships on the city desk of an urban daily. When smaller papers—in state capitals, for instance—start looking for management people, that's where they go. After these young men have proved their worth on the smaller papers, gotten promoted to managing editor or editor, they often come back to a higher level position on the city papers. The bright young woman, meantime, is still the women's editor.

✳ ✳ ✳

But part of the reason was that women did not fight sooner and harder against these traditional male attitudes, said Dorothy Jurney. When she was at the Miami *Herald,* her editors asked her about her goals in the newspaper business. Having been told at the Washington *News* that she could not be considered for the city editor's position because she was a woman, Jurney replied to her Miami editor "with a mealy-mouthed 'to do the best I can at whatever I am assigned.' "

She learned much later that they had been considering her for city editor but decided that "she didn't show any ambition."

Some years later Knight newspapers promoted Jurney to assistant managing editor at the Detroit *Free Press* and then asked her to take over the features departments at the Philadelphia *Inquirer* at that same rank. She accepted. "Women must be ready to accept these opportunities," she said, because they come with the equal treatment.

Beverly Hall said,

> Editing a family section is good experience. It gives you a chance to see how well you can direct a group of people and it offers great opportunities to display your creativity, news judgment and innovativeness. Managements today are looking for talent in these sections as well as on city side. As news coverage becomes more featurized in treatment, as it has on local newspapers, these sections offer excellent training.

Hall, who married the managing editor of her paper, the Lansing *State Journal,* said that balancing their work roles was the couple's greatest difficulty. They find it hard to stop thinking about the paper when they should be relaxing. On the other hand, they think that the intensity of their shared interests has been good for the paper.

Since both are strong individuals they often disagree at staff meetings. The employees know that they are not a "think-alike" team and "we reinforce the fact that we are two individuals, each responsible for our own actions and our own jobs." They have had no serious problems with employees, added her husband, Ben Burns. (Burns later moved to the Detroit *News* and his wife began law school courses.)

One problem newspapers have found in their attempts to promote women is that although many women are qualified, they express hesitancy to give up the niches they have carved out with hard work on reporting beats and start again at the bottom of the editing hierarchy. Another problem has been the editors' belief that women would expect special consideration.

"Women as well as men must resolve their family responsibilities privately," said Jurney, "before taking on new career responsibilities."

✳ ✳ ✳

The big step forward has been that, by mid-decade, some women were actually being given the chances to make such decisions. Some of them found they enjoyed management more than they had expected.

"It's where you change the things you don't like," declared Christy Bulkeley. She has changed the way of covering political campaigns and placed a "people emphasis throughout the paper, not just on the family page."

Publishers tell her that they are looking for women to promote into managerial jobs, and women tell her they are not being asked about their ambitions, Bulkeley said. "I tell the publishers to take a closer look at what women are doing outside the office. Many are working hard after hours in voluntary organizations using their management capacities."

And to the women she says, "Let management know that you are interested in moving up. Don't be intimidated. A woman has to "beat the pants off men" to get to a top position, she added, and one "who makes it to the top and fails to produce is going to make it sixteen times harder for other, perhaps more capable women, to overcome discrimination," she warned. Bulkeley gained confidence in her own managerial skills through her work in Women in Communications, Inc., and she found that she approached her position as publisher in much the same way she had as a reporter—asking questions and reading reports in order to find out what was going on. She also "treats all her staff at the *Saratogian* as she wishes people had treated her." She keeps them informed, asks for information and suggestions and lets them know her responses.

It's difficult to accurately measure women's progress in journalism because "we don't know what the situation was five or ten years ago," Bulkeley said, but recalled that she had to convince her editors at the Rochester (New York) *Times-Union* where she started in 1964 that she was interested in city government news by going to meetings in her spare time. When the male government reporter left, she was ready to step into the job.

"Women have to prove they can get the story. Then it is possible for them to move up through the ranks and be recognized for their ability and achievements, she said. Bulkeley was promoted to editorial page editor and then to publisher of the *Saratogian* in 1974.

* * *

Some newspaper groups have offered management training seminars to men and women for many years, and they have noticed that the number of women in those courses has noticeably increased since 1970. Katharine Graham told a group of industrialists, early in the 1970's:

> Management can't meet the challenge of discrimination against women by just promoting one or two women to highly visible jobs while the rest of the corporate structure remains a male preserve.
>
> Nor can we meet the challenge by taking any number of similarly isolated steps—electing one woman who is usually very attractive and over-qualified to a board of directors, promoting one woman to a management position with a long, impressive title and no influence at all, naming one female vice-president with real authority while the rest of the women in the organization are secretaries and keypunch operators without hope of advancement.

Instead, Graham challenged them to examine "how the ordinary woman fares." From the evidence it appeared to her that women concentrated in the same old jobs, jobs with low pay and low aspirations, a "caste system" which was still very much a fact of business life. "Management has to reform the system, and that involves changing basic attitudes, habits and policies," she charged.

> Even when we learn to think in terms of equal opportu-
> nities for women and discard outmoded negative attitudes
> toward career women we face another problem of adjusting
> women's life patterns into the time-frame of business, which
> is pegged to ten or twenty years of steady work and regular
> promotions with no provisions for five or ten years of ab-
> sence to bring up a family.
>
> It is not easy to create more flexible work patterns, but
> some way will have to be found to offer real opportunities to
> women who do want to take time out for families.

Graham's own company was working on this, but she
added that "we do not believe we have done nearly enough
. . . and many of us in management are still in the process of
discovering how stubborn and subtle many of our difficulties
are."

✳ ✳ ✳

Talk of improvements was tempered in 1974 and 1975 as rising inflation and unemployment, and hiring freezes gripped
newspapers as well as other businesses. It looks as though the
"gains that had been made were not going to be solid as long
as the economic situation is depressed," speculated Charlotte
Curtis, associate editor of the New York *Times.*

"Opportunities are few for the same economic reasons. . . .
There is a serious shortage of women in middle management
of newspapers as well as at the top management. This, of
course, is deplorable," she continued.

Curtis could look back on her own 27-year career for inspiration. She started as an intern at the Columbus *Citizen-Journal*
at age 19 and worked summers until completing college. Then
she began full-time newspaper work. She came to the *Times* in
1961 and became women's editor in 1966 where she drew
praises for her refreshing and penetrating coverage of issues
and life styles.

> Journalism *is* for women. . . . If I were very young and
> really wanted to go into the business, I'd prepare for it, try
> for a newspaper job and keep trying, and figure out some-
> where else to earn my living until I battered down some-
> body's door.

"We are at a turning point," L.A. *Times* columnist Georgie Ann Geyer told a national meeting of women journalists in the fall of 1976.

"The doors are open, and women no longer need to try to be men in doing their professional jobs as journalists," she said. "We can be ourselves." Conditions had changed dramatically during the 20 years in which she had been a reporter, foreign correspondent and columnist.

Geyer said it was now time to face what it means to be a woman journalist working alongside men with their support in covering the news. She suggested that it was time to recognize the differences between women and men, to examine women's values and make a place for them in the total coverage of news and human affairs.

This was no call to retreat to the "women's angle" segregation of the past, but a forthright challenge to women journalists to go beyond breaking down the barriers and enlarge the definition of news by "balancing out male values with their own. A spirit of cooperation, of humane and supportive values, instead of the old aggressive values of the frontier, may be just what is needed in the urban world in which we live," Geyer proposed, voicing an optimism that was slowly emerging at the end of the nation's Bicentennial year.

· SOURCES CONSULTED ·

William W. Bowman, "Distaff Journalists: Women as a Minority Group in the News Media" Unpublished Ph.D. dissertation, Department of Sociology, University of Illinois, Chicago Circle, 1974.

Frederick Ellis, "Dickey Chapelle: A Reporter and Her Work," Unpublished M.A. thesis, University of Wisconsin, 1968.

Marguerite Higgins, *News Is a Singular Thing* (Garden City: Doubleday and Co., 1955).

Marguerite Higgins, *War In Korea: The Report of a Woman Combat Correspondent* (New York: Doubleday & Co., Inc., 1951).

Carol Hutcheson, "Sex Roles, Work Roles, And the Status of Women in Journalism," Unpublished Senior Honors Thesis, University of Michigan, 1975.

Thedore E. Kruglak, *The Foreign Correspondents: A Study of the Men and Women*

Reporting for the American Information Media in Western Europe, (Geneva: Librarie E. Droz, 1955).

Carolyn M. Lenz, "Newspaperwomen on Metropolitan Dailies: An Historical Survey and Case Study," Unpublished M.A. thesis, University of Wisconsin, 1972.

Kathleen Kearney Lewis, "Maggie Higgins" Unpublished M.A. thesis, Univ. of Maryland, 1973.

Joann Lublin, "Discrimination Against Women in the Newsroom," Unpublished M.A. thesis, Stanford University, 1971.

Mary Ellen Mark and Annie Leibovitz, *The Photojournalist* (New York: Thomas Y. Crowell Co., Inc., 1974).

Margaret Knox Morgan, "Women in Photojournalism," Unpublished M.A. thesis, University of Missouri, 1963.

Personal letters to the author from Miriam Ottenberg, Dorothy Jurney, Charlotte Curtis, Betsy Wade, Helen Copley, Katharine Graham, Carol Sutton and Lois Wille.

Personal interviews with Christy Bulkeley, Elsie Carper, Joan Deppa, Marcia Dubrow, Osborn Elliott, Phyl Garland, Beverly Hall, Toni House, Dorothy Jurney, Joann Lublin, Ethyl Payne, Elizabeth Pond, Eileen Shanahan, Helen Thomas, Marylois P. Vega, Ada Louise Huxtable and Lynn Young.

4

* * *

Women Share
the Golden Voice

"HOW WOULD YOU LIKE a job in radio?"

"Radio," replied the young woman, "what's that?"

The man handed her a box called a crystal set and told her to take it home and listen to it. It was 1922. The station, WDAP in the Drake Hotel in Chicago, became WGN, and the woman, Myrtle Stahl, was to spend the next 40 years there in radio programming and administration.

When she started in October as an assistant to the owner her first job was to open the two barrels of mail that had accumulated since the station had started broadcasting. To her surprise many of the envelopes contained dollar bills that people had sent in to help out the new station. People were excited about this strange little box that could pick music and voices up out of the air. Further, they began coming to Chicago and booking rooms in the Drake Hotel in order to "see the broadcasting station." Stahl was their tour hostess along with her other duties.

In 1924 the Chicago *Tribune* purchased the station along with some others and it became WGN, a full-time station. WGN continued to broadcast from the Drake Hotel for many years and Stahl was assigned to handle its public service programming, which included church programs, board of education, stock market reports, university and public school programs. The station achieved some early fame for its broadcasts of the Scopes trial in Dayton, Tennessee, in 1925 and for early presidential election broadcasts.

Experiments with radio broadcasting had resumed in the United States after the wartime ban by the government was lifted in 1919. Hobbyists and engineers built sets and antennae and sat fascinated as they made contact with others many miles away. "Let us know if this signal is reaching you," became a familiar refrain. Newspapers reported radio broadcasting experiments as remarkable new man-made phenomena, but they seemed to be too complex for the average citizen to tinker with.

Westinghouse, with its KDKA-Pittsburgh broadcast of the 1920 Harding-Cox presidential elections realized the commercial advantage in manufacturing radio sets for the average family. This was an idea David Sarnoff had earlier proposed to RCA in 1916 when he predicted a great market potential in producing a "radio music box," but the idea was considered too risky.

Stations sprang up in 1921 and 1922 in many cities. At first the station owners did everything themselves during the few hours of broadcasting, including playing phonograph records, singing or playing musical instruments and making announcements. But it quickly appeared that musicians and singers would come and perform at these new radio stations in return for the publicity such performances brought them. It was a few years before the full potential of advertising products on the air was discovered.

Audiences for radio grew rapidly and studios expanded operations. This provided employment for young men and women, many of them from theatre, music or writing backgrounds and others with no special training but willingness, creativity and imagination that were readily rewarded in this rapidly expanding new industry.

Public Service Broadcasting

Chicago, for example, had 1,300 radio sets when Westinghouse put station KYW on the air in November of 1921 to broadcast the Chicago opera season. By season's end there were 20,000 sets in the city. By the end of 1921 nearly a dozen stations were in the planning stages in Chicago alone, and leading newspapers were buying radio stations and using them to promote their newspapers.

"Women were to a very large extent responsible for public service broadcasting in the early days of radio because of the special aptitude for that work," said William S. Hedges, a Chicago radio pioneer and later vice-president of NBC.

One of these women was Judith Waller, who in 1922 was asked by the Chicago *Daily News* if she would run its newly acquired radio station. Although she knew nothing about radio at the time—she had been an account executive and advertising copywriter—she wanted a career in business and saw this as an opportunity. She became one of radio's distinguished pioneers, retiring as NBC's public affairs representative in 1957 after 35 years in broadcasting.

The Chicago *Daily News* had purchased half interest in the transmitter owned by the Fair Department Store, Waller recalled. At that time the only other station in Chicago was broadcasting mostly popular music, so she decided to open the station's programming with classical music. She talked Sophie Braslau of the Metropolitan Opera, who was appearing with the Chicago Symphony Orchestra, into singing on WGU's first program which was aired April 13, 1922. "I am sure the program was not heard outside the studio of the Fair store," said Waller. "It may have been, but I doubt it."

Within a week the station was closed down to be rebuilt, but Waller had already planned a number of programs. She got KYW, the Westinghouse Electric Company's station in Chicago, to allow them to program for two one-half hours daily "as a *Daily News* program service over the station." In that way she kept the name of the Chicago *Daily News* radio service alive until the new station was built. The station returned to the air on October 1 as WMAQ, and with a stronger transmitter and a velour-draped studio for better acoustics. WMAQ moved from the Fair Store to studios in the La Salle Hotel in 1923.

"In those early days there was no question of advertising on any station. We had no money for programming, and it was a matter of ringing doorbells and getting anybody to come to the station and to broadcast whomever we could lure," Waller recalled. The "lure" was publicity in the Chicago *Daily News.* Waller got music schools, lyceums, Chatauqua agencies and the like to put on programs in exchange for publicity photos and releases about the programs that she wrote for the *Daily News.* Since she and the engineer comprised the entire staff, she also did the announcing.

Soon they plucked a young pianist, Bob Whitney, from his job behind a soda fountain, to serve as pianist. After a little voice training, he also became their first announcer. (He went on to become a symphony orchestra conductor.)

During the first couple of months Waller said she gave little thought to programming. It was a question of getting what you could. Since KYW was spending most of its time broadcasting jazz, she thought her station should provide some other programs. The *Daily News* was a family newspaper, and she began to think of publicizing the various departments of the paper. *Daily News* reporters and columnists did radio programs on women, children, books and current affairs. By 1926 *Daily News* reporters were giving a weekly foreign news report and in 1928 the station introduced a daily news report.

In 1925 Waller made what she thinks was the first trans-Atlantic phone-call broadcast: John Gunther's report on the health of King George V.

What People Want to Hear

WMAQ gradually developed a varied pattern of broadcasting and the station ranked first in popularity and distinguished features in all polls taken between 1928 and 1932.

"I am sure that we were beginning to have a sense and feel of what people wanted to hear, more than just the kind of programming that we are doing instinctively," Waller said. "As the station grew in popularity and power, the *Daily News* was willing to grant us larger sums of money to spend on programs."

WMAQ hired a musical trio, a small orchestra and formed its own drama group, the WMAQ Players. There were programs on farming, religion, language, cooking and homemaking. Waller recorded lectures from the University of Chicago and from Northwestern University classrooms, and developed programs by various community and service organizations such as the YMCA, Chamber of Commerce and the League of Women Voters.

Sports was a growing area of public interest and Waller talked William Wrigley, Jr. into allowing play-by-play broadcasts of Chicago Cubs' home games from Wrigley Field in 1924 or 1925. The Cubs finished fourth that year but with the highest box office receipts of any club in the National League, she said. The next year WMAQ also broadcast White Sox home games, and soon they added Chicago and Northwestern University football games to their growing sports programming.

Waller continued to direct WMAQ's public affairs programming after NBC bought WMAQ in 1931, later becoming the network's public affairs representative. She was honored by the Radio Pioneers in 1956 for her service in radio and television broadcasting in educational and cultural programming and for her "imagination and warm human understanding."

While Waller and Stahl competed in Chicago, women in other cities such as New York, Philadelphia, Boston and St. Louis pioneered programs for women and children, a sphere they were to dominate in radio in the decades ahead. In St. Louis, Ida Bailey Allen launched her first homemaking show in 1922. She moved to New York and in the 1930's was doing hour-long network food programs for NBC that included skits, music, interviews and chefs in action. (She continued broadcasting into the 1960's.)

In Philadelphia, Henriette K. Harrison became the first woman assistant program director at WCAU in 1928 after four years in radio work. She went on to become program director for WINS, a Hearst station in New York, and continued in radio programming and production into the 1960's. Ruth Chilton had her own women's program over WSYR in Syracuse by 1929, after four years' prior radio experience and moved to Philadelphia with her own women's programs in the 1940's, continuing into the early 1960's. Dorothy Gordon, who rose to fame with her New York *Times'* "Youth Forums" in the 1940's, did her first children's radio program in 1926. Martha Crane started her first interview show with WLS-Chicago in 1928 and continued in the 1960's logging thousands of guests, community leaders and celebrities and becoming a Chicago personality herself.

The Problem of Announcing

Women in radio broadcasting in the late 1920's sized up the field as an excellent one for them. There was less discrimination against women because of sex than in most other occupations of the day, they said, and the opportunity to move into creative and responsible positions was good.

One area where women did seem to be handicapped was in announcing, they pointed out. Radio sound reproduction was best with low pitched voices, and when women pitched their voices low it usually sounded forced and unnatural. When they spoke naturally, the high tones became weak, thin and unpleasant over radio.

"The very qualities that make a woman's speaking voice pleasant—its softness, nuances, inflections and medium pitch—are against her in announcing," said Bertha Brainard in 1926 when she was assistant broadcasting manager at WJZ in New York City. Women can and do announce in special instances, she added, but they cannot qualify for the big positions. Their voices are against them.

Natalie Godwin was one of the early exceptions. An announcer for WEAF-New York City in 1923, she recalled her pioneer experiences on the daily morning "Garden Talks" program as hectic and exciting. She arranged for speakers, edited their speeches and gave them the "radio slant." She rehearsed the participants and announced their talks. Some of the speakers came too thoroughly rehearsed and sounded pompous and wooden, she recalled. Godwin once held up a note saying "Cheer up" to a young woman who was reading her light and enthusiastically written talk in a dull monotone. It helped.

> One of my chief difficulties was getting speakers to realize they could not take advantage of a "sold audience." If they

let them down for a moment, their bored listeners were gone with simple turns of the wrist. I tried to impress upon them the need of winning an audience—and keeping it!

Women could easily adapt their own peculiarly feminine talents to this field, said Brainard, especially in research, programming and interviewing for raw material and as hostesses and executives.

One of the most promising executive positions was in program work, Brainard thought. "It is ideally suited to women who have poise and initiative. A woman makes contacts with more ease than a man, and with much more rapidity."

In her own work Brainard sometimes put in 20-hour days, but found the work so fascinating that she didn't mind the long hours. She enjoyed the many stimulating contacts with people in other professions and the constant variety.

Brainard's entry into radio typifies the qualities she praised. A former ambulance driver, hotel manager and journalist, she had listened to station WJZ in Newark, N.J. and decided to try for a job. They wouldn't even let her in. The second time she said that she had come to write a story about the station. Once inside—that was in 1922—she sold her program idea, a weekly drama review of the Broadway shows, called "Broadcasting Broadway."

Brainard began bringing in theatrical celebrities for radio appearances, and later the station let her put on some radio plays. She was placed in charge of the New York office for WJZ when it was opened, and when the main studio moved to New York she became assistant manager of the station. In 1926 when NBC took over WJZ, she became Eastern Program Manager for NBC with instructions to provide interesting broadcasting programs to the millions of men and women and children who tuned in to the 50-plus stations associated with NBC. By 1937 she was one of the five top-salaried women in the nation.

In offering advice to young women considering future careers, Brainard said in 1928 that "the pioneering state of radio gives men and women equal opportunities" and equal pay for equal work. "The more a woman can help gain money for the station, the better she is liked. Radio stations are as willing to accept women as men who can make money for them." What it takes is initiative, original ideas, perseverance and talent.

"Women are a necessity to radio stations," Brainard added, because housewives form the bulk of the audience during the morning and afternoon. Programming for that audience includes features for women on fashion, food, beauty, health, housekeeping, babies, thrift, music, culture and education. Radio executives asked women to do these shows. All over the nation stations and the networks had women's programs or departments by the late 1930's.

✳   ✳   ✳

In 1934, station WOR in New York, for example, auditioned 50 women for the role of Martha Deane, an imaginary character who would continue into the 1970's. Mary Margaret McBride, a University of Missouri journalism school graduate and a youthful veteran of "sob sistering" at the New York *Daily Mail* in the 1920's was selected from the field of applicants because she "had the common touch."

She was to play a simple, wise, kindly old character who devoted herself to her large family and dispensed homely philosophy. Mary Margaret, as she liked to be called, did this for three weeks. Then one day on the air she "killed" grandma and all her fake family, announcing that she herself couldn't cook very well and disliked housekeeping. She "wasn't even a grandmother at all, not a mother, not even married." And she said the show "doesn't sound real because it isn't." She told them she was a newspaper reporter and she wanted to come there every day and tell them about the places she went and the people she met.

From then on McBride was Martha Deane, "columnist of the air," a forthright and warm woman who interviewed men and women from a variety of fields, read recipes, dispensed information and tidbits and advertised an increasing number of products. In one year she covered more than 1,500 subjects from a flea circus to a White House visit. She believed that women got enough advice from experts, so she specialized in bringing them human interest stories and fascinating people, considerably expanding the original concept of the program with resounding success. Her radio job occupied all her days and nights, and soon people understood that she only went to parties and teas when she could work in an interview or story for her show.

Mary Margaret McBride became an institution and she had broken new ground in radio. Early talk shows were scripted so that people would not make embarrassing remarks, but the practice produced drab and stilted conversations. Mary Margaret ad-libbed and, because of her unique talent, she was able to draw people out and almost make them forget that they were on the air. She asked apparently naive questions and guests often told her more than they intended. Celebrities flocked to her program and her influence was enormous. Her success paved the way for countless local and national talk shows in the ensuing years.

McBride did two shows daily and increased the time of each to three-quarters and then a full hour, reaching an audience of millions. In 1940 CBS offered her a network show. She picked a successor, Bessie Beattie, for "Martha Deane" and started her own "Mary Margaret McBride Show"—15 minutes on network. She did not like the reduced format, and within the year had lined up another local hour show with WEAF and rebuilt an audience. ABC put her on network and she closed the show in 1954 after 20 years on radio. She retired to a country farm to write her autobiography and a newspaper column. She was still broadcasting from her Catskill Mountains retirement home for WGHO, a local radio station, with an interview show three times a week until shortly before her death at age 76 in 1976.

* * *

In less than a decade radio had become a highly organized and departmentalized business combining features of theatre, newspaper, magazine and concert hall. In 1925, recalled Margaret Cuthbert, head of NBC's speakers' program department, "we did a little of everything."

In 1934 radio offered a variety of specialized career fields for women: programming, research, hostessing, secretarial, mail, publicity, advertising, continuity, dialogue, talent. Women were advised to get jobs on local stations first—to learn through experience before trying the network. They were encouraged to take any kind of starting job. Answering the mail, working as secretaries, assistants and hostesses or as writers were all open routes to better jobs for those with imagination, resourcefulness and drive.

Career articles and books of 1932, for example, pointed to an impressive array of at least 22 women who held important executive positions in radio at the station and network level, including Brainard and Cuthbert; Madge Tucker and Naomi Mack, creators of popular children's hours; Sallie Belle Cox and Ora Nichols in sound effects; Lucille Singleton, head of CBS auditions. There were a few station managers and several hostesses of women's shows and talk shows, singers, musicians, actresses and writers. Every sizeable advertising agency had a radio staff of men and women. The tradition had been established—women appeal more effectively to other women listeners.

By far the bulk of jobs in broadcasting then as now were routine, secretarial and clerical for women and engineering and technical for men. A 1936 article estimated that a quarter of all people in radio work were women. The same source reported that 600 women were employed at the three networks (National, Columbia and Bamberger-Mutual) and a fifth of them were in what today might be called professional jobs. At NBC, then celebrating its tenth anniversary, there were 600 men and 300 women employees and 200 of those were stenographers, typists and secretaries. Columbia employed 156 women. Although there were only a few women executives, opportunities were considered good because radio was a young and developing field.

Analyzing the Audience

Early women's programs, according to Judith Waller's book, *Radio, The Fifth Estate*, were at first unwanted children. They filled the air until something better came along. Shows devoted to homemaking, music interviews and serial stories, quiz programs and talks were aimed at women's homemaking and social interests.

Social research, especially Paul Lazarsfeld's 1941 study of the daytime radio audience, showed programmers and advertisers that it was composed mostly of women of modest income, tied to the home by families or lack of income for movies, clubs and other entertainment. These women were likely to be lonely and bored, and radio was a magic thing that allowed them to push out horizons and make new companionships. They listened primarily for social contact and entertainment; information and educational needs were far down the list.

Since women spent 80 per cent of the American income, it was not surprising that advertising was an important, if not the most important, element in many of these daytime programs. Sometimes the program was built around an advertising product, such as beauty aids, clothing, or food. Often the person conducting the program wrote and read the ads, a pattern that continued into popular television daytime and evening talk shows.

Despite the popularity of many of these varied shows for homemakers, by 1938 the "soap opera" had conquered the vast daytime audience, as Eric Barnouw pointed out in *A History of Broadcasting*. Researchers discovered that there were actually two daytime audiences. One large group of women listened only to the serials and thought them educational. They took a personal interest in the fictional characters and found them helpful in solving day-to-day problems like those faced by the homemakers, or they could escape into lives of glamour and romance that transported them from their own dreary existence. The other audience, a much smaller one, ignored the serials and listened to a variety of other programs.

In announcing, and particularly in news work, there were still few women as of 1937. Dorothy Thompson, a distinguished foreign correspondent, and Muriel Draper broadcast interpretations of current events in 1936. Isabel Manning Hewson discussed "Petticoat Philosophy" in Philadelphia and Claudia MacDonald interviewed famous women in NBC's

"Woman's Magazine of the Air." Elza Schallert reported films for NBC, Marcia Davenport commented Metropolitan Opera broadcasts for NBC and Ann Hard did word portraits of important people. Louella Parsons had started her Hollywood news and interviews program in 1928.

The first radio news team put together by Paul White for CBS in 1933 did include one woman reporter, Florence Conley from the New York *Journal-American*. Conley obtained an exclusive interview with Doris Duke, the richest girl in the world on her 21st birthday.

✳   ✳   ✳

But Kathryn Cravens was apparently the first woman news commentator on radio, according to her biographer, Gordon McCullough. Her show, "News Through a Woman's Eyes" went on the air in February, 1934, at KMOX in St. Louis. CBS brought her to New York in October, 1936, to continue her show on the network where it was estimated that she reached an audience of two million.

Cravens, born Kathryn Cochran, began her career as an actress and first obtained a few radio parts in St. Louis in 1922. When stock companies were breaking up during the 1930's, she looked to radio for employment. She did sketches and became KMOX's expert on the woman's angle with a 1933 show "Let's Compare Notes," on household hints, fashion, beauty and style. Cravens listened to Edwin C. Hill and Boake Carter doing news commentary and thought, "They seemed to be having so much fun doing exactly what they pleased." She thought she would like to try it.

She saw no women doing news, but she believed that she could add something to the news: the humor, sympathy, drama behind the news. Her manager first told her to stick to acting, but she sold him with a sample program.

Cravens' first news program ran from 10:15 to 10:30 a.m. daily except Sunday, starting February 11, 1934. It was sponsored by a wholesale grocery concern. She quickly learned reporting techniques from a Kansas City *Star* reporter and made a specialty of "sob sister" interviews in which she asked not who, what, where and when, but *how* does it feel . . . to be the mother of a murdered boy . . . to survive a flood . . . to be a notorious shoplifter . . . to be mayor of a great city?

Cravens also started to editorialize. She was pro-airlines in the days when people considered them risky. After she made some positive comments, the airlines offered her free travel. This turned her into a flying reporter. Her $85 a week salary was not enough to cover flying expenses around the nation. By March, 1935, she had gathered a large audience. During one week the station received 3,183 pieces of mail from her listeners. When CBS bought her show in October, 1936, it was reported that her salary was to be $1,000 a week, and the network paid her travel expenses.

Cravens' voice was low, warm and sympathetic, qualities that were ideal for early radio's somewhat primitive equipment. She became a celebrity and made news in her mad whirl of interviewing personalities in and outside New York City. She was on the air every evening at 5:30, but arose at 5:30 a.m. to write her script for the day. The intervening time was filled with interviews, lunches and teas. She did advertising spots for her sponsors, a customary policy on hosted shows. One free offer of a polishing cloth she announced brought in 228,000 responses in less than 6 days, doubling her previous record.

When it was first suggested to Pontiac Motors that they attempt to attract women's interest in their medium price range cars by sponsoring Cravens' show, there were snickers. Afternoon radio had not been used before to sell cars, but the company wanted to reach women, who were the deciding factor in 65 per cent of their sales. They tried Cravens' show and were convinced of her pulling power when women began dropping into the salesrooms with their husbands and casually mentioning the show. They had heard her say, "It's a wonderful car." Her mail reached such proportions that it required four stenographers.

Cravens was frequently called a pioneer in an all-male field, and was praised for "opening the world" to women who were stuck in the small towns. Women wrote to tell her that they appreciated learning about other places and how things looked. Cravens often said she wanted to share with the world the feelings of people and events—from the inspiration of a poet to the sensation of talking with Helen Keller.

In her first year at CBS Cravens flew 50,000 miles. Her program became an all-consuming affair and resulted in the end of her 15-year marriage. Her husband at first had encouraged her career, but later opposed it. In 1937 and 1938 she spoke out against the developing war in Europe. CBS censored her comments against Hitler in February, 1938, and warned her to stop her "pacifist propaganda." She was listed as the only female news commentator in the *Radio Guide* of January, 1938, along with Boake Carter, Gabriel Heatter, Edwin C. Hill and General Hugh Johnson, but her popularity had started to slip.

According to a Los Angeles *Times* article of January, 1938, Dorothy Thompson gathered 68 per cent of the Los Angeles listening audience in an "unspecific category" while Cravens had only 7 per cent. Comments appeared in print criticizing her style as overdrawn and overcolored, with adjectives "piled on too heavily." Talk shows were abundant but music and entertainment programs were attracting larger audiences. On April 8, 1938, her program was dropped and Cravens turned to free-lancing, returning to radio during the 1940's at WNEW where she covered many war-related stories.

Her last sponsored program stressed the women's viewpoint but included no household hints. Cravens attained a high radio audience for independent stations—11 out of every 100 listeners, at a time when soap operas had 36 out of every 100. She publicized war relief, aid to war orphans, and she encouraged better schools in Harlem and joined a radio committee to fight race hatred.

Cravens wanted to cover the war, so when WNEW dropped her contract in 1945, she got herself accredited as a war correspondent and entered Germany after the surrender. Cowles Broadcasting Co. and Mutual gave her assignments. She made interviews with Generals DeGaulle and Eisenhower, among others, and covered the Big Three Conference in July, 1945, the Vidkun Quisling trial in Norway, and interviewed G. B. Shaw and the Pope. By 1945 her pursuit of the news behind the news had taken her to 22 countries, and she called a halt to her journalistic career, although she was a vice-president of the Overseas Press Club in 1956.

*   *   *

When the Martha Deane show again had a vacancy in 1941 it was filled by Marion Taylor, an award-winning newspaper journalist with 11 years of experience with Scripps-Howard's feature syndicate, Newspaper Enterprise Association. She had been women's editor and a foreign correspondent. Her most famous dispatch was from the Berlin Reichstag when Hitler announced that he had sent troops into the Rhineland.

When Taylor auditioned for the Deane spot, she told WOR that she "wouldn't do one household hint." She didn't know how to take spots out of a rug and wasn't going to try to tell anyone else how.

"I don't go in for the woman's angle. Besides, I don't think there's sex in brains, she told an interviewer.

Taylor kept both jobs for eight months because she wasn't sure about radio. With her arrival on the program, the news content and current affairs emphasis was increased. After 28 years and some 10,000 interviews, she admitted that "radio's a nerve-wracking kind of business. After a newspaper interview, you have time to reflect, revise. On radio, there's no hiding—it's live and you're so exposed!"

Colleagues called her the best interviewer on radio and showered her with many awards including the 1968 Broadcast Pioneers Distinguished Service Award.

Doing Your Homework

People often asked Taylor how she made such good interviews. She'd usually respond that she held "conversations" and that she "did her homework." When a person appeared on her program, she felt that it was her obligation to prepare as thoroughly as possible. "I learn all I can about his or her work, achievements, hobbies and personality traits."

An elaborate filing system is useful for gathering this kind of detail. She never talked to authors, actors, or artists until she had thoroughly studied their work. Taylor "is a good listener . . . doesn't try to think of clever lines of response. She creates an intimate atmosphere . . . no audience and no friendly hangers-on." Her guests faced away from the control room to avoid distraction.

Taylor brought controversial subjects to her radio work and wanted guests who would discuss pressing issues in life, politics and culture. She refused to cater to a supposed "woman's angle." She asked,

> What's a woman's angle? Women are people. If a story is good, it's good; if it's bad, it's bad. Women like to think with my guests as well as sometimes cry or laugh with them. If all they wanted was entertainment, they would have tuned me out a good long time ago.

She was, Taylor believed, a reporter with a good radio job. Some of her broadcasts with politicians made news, especially when they were with presidents and mayors. Senator Robert A. Taft made a policy statement on the Korean War during one of her interviews, and New York mayoral candidates appeared regularly on her program.

Taylor's daily routine when she was almost 60 years old started at 6:30 a.m. with newspaper reading. She walked to the studio for a 9:45 a.m. warm-up session with her guest. After the show, she headed for the office where three women handled fan mail, commercials and telephone contacts with guests. There were lunches with new sponsors for product briefings or lunch at her desk while reading. Afternoons included office work, visiting art galleries and three to four screenings a week. By 6:30 p.m. she was at home for dinner with her retired husband who often cooked. Evenings they attended the theatre or read. She had no intention of retiring, she often said, and died of cancer at 65 in 1973 after 32 years in radio.

✳ ✳ ✳

Youngsters were an important segment of the late afternoon audience and in addition to adventure serials, several youth programs that encouraged discussion or intellectual competition developed in the 1940's. One of these was Rachel Stevenson's "Quiz Kids," which ran for 13 years. Bright youngsters contended weekly to outsmart their contemporaries in order to remain on the program week after week. A few stayed on long enough to become engaging personalities, then faded away as newcomers took the spotlight.

Dorothy Gordon's "Youth Forum," which brought together high school or college students and an adult guest to discuss a topical question began on WQXR in 1943 and was still running on WNBC-TV in May, 1970, when she died at age 81. She had directed several radio programs for WEAF, starting in 1924, including the "American School of the Air," "Children's Corner" and "Yesterday's Children," and directed children's programs for the Office of War Information during the war.

Gordon had traveled in pre-war Europe and had seen the indoctrination of youngsters in Italy and Germany. She became convinced that it was important for American youth to learn the meaning of democracy and warned that "we cannot keep our youth in a vacuum on world affairs."

She advocated "Youth Forum" as a platform, under adult guidance, where a flow of ideas about the world and humanity would take place between young people of varying backgrounds. She brought students from 600 schools, including correctional facilities, to discuss current affairs with presidential advisers, novelists, political leaders, educators and others.

Gordon was the moderator. That meant she had to keep the discussion going and make sure there were no lulls. That meant, she thought, that she had to be completely objective, and she read a great deal on both sides of a subject—six to eight newspapers daily. The program brought her the Foster Peabody Award in 1952 "for outstanding service to the teen-age listening audience" and a *McCall's* magazine award in 1951 for outstanding public service.

✻   ✻   ✻

Talks by prominent men and women were considered a part of radio's public service and several women were associated with these programs. One who became best known was Helen

Sioussat, who headed the Talks Department at CBS. She had started in radio as an assistant to Philip H. Lord on his "G-Men" series, digging out facts at the FBI on which he built his scripts. She moved to network in 1936 as an assistant to Edward R. Murrow, the Director of Talks. Murrow was sent to Europe to develop cultural programs there and as of 1938 found himself establishing CBS's crack foreign reporting team that reported World War II to millions of Americans.

Sioussat moved up and when education and talks were divided into separate departments in 1942, she became Head of Talks. She scheduled all speakers for CBS radio and later TV in news, sports and special events. When TV was new she did an extemporaneous TV discussion show for a year on controversial issues called "Table Talks with Helen Sioussat." Otherwise, she rarely spoke on the air herself. Her days were filled with telephone calls arranging program schedules, speakers, editing scripts, negotiating for speakers and keeping on top of current events.

Sioussat became an expert at calming the fears of guests invited to speak and amused her friends and the public with her recollections of TV bloopers and the off-air fears of famous people in a book called *Mikes Don't Bite,* published in 1943. In it, she said that women were "generally more cooperative in preparing for broadcast and seldom arrived at the last minute with untimed scripts."

But "men sound better on radio. Women are inclined to raise the pitch of their voices when talking on a phone and on radio. This is deadly! Men's voices sound good," she said, even when they are afraid. Then they lower their voices rather than raise them. Two women who did have beautiful speaking voices were Jane Cowl, the actress, and Lisa Sergio, WQXR's commentator.

According to Sioussat, the wartime shortage of men opened opportunities for women in all phases of radio. Columbia relaxed its policy with regard to hiring women as assistant directors and producers and in general was employing more women throughout the organization, including three apprentice engineers at WABC, CBS' key outlet in New York.

Sioussat's advice to young women was not to admit that

they knew shorthand; men and women assume that all women are secretaries.

> So, you've got to "show 'em, girls," not by affecting low-heeled shoes and masculine garb or by acting self-important or bossy. If you have the stuff of which executives are made, don't be tactless or step on others' toes or over the boy ahead.

She thought that swaggering females were even more intolerable than swaggering males and advocated a modest and natural behavior that would help win respect for one's abilities rather than demand it. "Men can be your most valuable guides, as well as your powerful foes. In most cases it's up to you to decide," she challenged.

Sioussat believed that women themselves could do much to change the thinking of the males who remarked, "Female executives, Ugh! Deliver me." She was "no defeatist and no feminist," and she believed that women would have to keep on proving their ability in their jobs to each new male that came into the firm and that this was a task they would have to handle with intelligence and patience.

As television expanded, Sioussat's job was enlarged to cover talks for radio and television. In 1950 she said her department might schedule as many as 350 talks for 50 to 60 hours of free time a year, including many important first broadcasts of national meetings and foreign personalities.

✳ ✳ ✳

News reporting on radio had developed slowly and sporadically with resistance from wire services and newspapers that did not own radio stations. By 1933 NBC and CBS had started to develop their own news gathering organizations. Murrow's short-wave broadcast from Vienna on March 13, 1938, describing Hitler's seizure of Austria, and the round-up by CBS correspondents in London, Paris, Berlin, Rome and New York signalled the coming of age of broadcast journalism. The famous CBS reporting team included Murrow, William L. Shirer, Pierre Huss, Edgar Ansel Mowrer, Frank Gervasi, Eric Sevareid, Robert Trout and H. V. Kaltenborn. NBC hired

Dorothy Thompson and Raymond Gram Swing to do commentaries; Mutual put on Quincy Howe.

Radio activity expanded to take on global dimensions including the Soviet Union, Stockholm, Athens, Hungary, Rumania and Asia. CBS' worldwide news staff of 50 correspondents and stringers was headed by Paul W. White whose book, *News on the Air,* described the acute manpower shortage that forced stations to employ women. In stations with union contracts, salaries were equal, he said, and before long the cliché that women had no news judgment was laid to rest.

White said that like all generalizations, "it was unfair." Women became good reporters and were able at rewrite. Among those he trained and praised were: Jane Dealy, Patricia Lochridge, Margaret Miller, Alice Weel and Beth Zimmerschied. They could easily "hold their own in a male-dominated field," he declared. (Weel spent 25 years as a CBS news writer and producer.)

White added that in union newsrooms salaries were the same for men and women, and he believed this was "a constructive force in office morale."

"As long as women understand they are being treated as equals, with the same opportunities as their male colleagues," he said, "they are not apt to request extra privileges such as days off or lighter hours."

Some women White hired had no experience beyond their school of journalism education, but they demonstrated an ability "to hear a news story as they read it." He also thought women had a good effect on the work place—it was less slovenly and there was more serious discussion of work with them around.

✳ ✳ ✳

Pat Lochridge, who came to CBS after working on newspapers in Boston and New York, said the field of news journalism offered a great future for university-trained, news-experienced women. "It's an exciting, interesting, stimulating profession, but the work is long, exacting, nerve-wracking."

She often found herself working 33 hours at a stretch, flying to Washington and returning to New York at 2 a.m. But "a woman reporter's heart belongs to the wire tickers" and when they "jangle a bulletin or flash story, she follows."

Most of the CBS news staff was composed of newspapermen of wide journalistic background, Lochridge observed, and most of them were fairly young. There were four women on the staff during her tenure—Margaret Miller, a former *Time* magazine staffer; Ann Gillis, who had served 10 years with CBS at a local station and as Washington bureau chief of news and special events; Kay Campbell, an English woman who worked with Murrow and had 10 years' air experience.

Lochridge said, "You have to persuade the boss that you can do a better job than a man equally qualified, and he'll have to believe that you as an individual can take care of yourself on a field assignment and that you will not expect any special privileges or immunities."

There were other young women like Lochridge in radio news rooms around the country, but most of their names are as yet unrecorded. Some may have been just out of college, like Ruth Laird, who was doing odd jobs at WHO in Des Moines when two men left in 1942 for the service. She was there and ready, but she still had to convince the news director that she could write the news update. During the war years she wrote the "Washington Roundup" for the morning news as well as a 10-minute woman's viewpoint program each morning.

Becoming an "Established Fact"

Fran Harris moved into news after nearly a decade of doing sponsored shopping and beauty shows for WWJ in Detroit. When one of those programs was cancelled in December, 1942, as the war began to dominate all thoughts and materials, Harris asked to join the news staff.

"You're going to need me as a newscaster," she told the station manager. All the men are going to be off to war."

"The hell I am," he snorted.

"I've got news background," she continued and begged for an audition. And on January 4, the first working day of 1943, she gave her first morning news show at 6:45. The manager let her start while the show's sponsor was in Florida vacationing.

When the sponsor returned, she was an "established fact" and no one had objected. Harris continued in daytime news and interviews until 1964. She asked to try the evening news, and did so two or three times, but she thought she didn't do that very well.

The 1940's were years when things "really opened up for women in radio" and they had a chance to prove what they could do, Harris recalled. Several women served as announcers on the Detroit stations then and no one made a big thing about it. The jobs were available.

Harris got her own show, "Fran Harris Reports," which ran for 21 years. It was a 15-minute daily show of interviews and features that usually ran around the noontime period. It was "great fun interviewing all the people who came to town." There were no recipes on her show, but it was a period during which several women were developing household and recipe interview shows.

Harris originated a number of other shows because, as she put it, "she had a very creative manager and a receptive one." She would suggest an idea, and he'd say, "Go ahead and try it."

Harris received a 1949 Peabody Award for a show on sex offenders. It was run at 10:45 p.m. so that children would not hear it. She also developed a five-minute travel show featuring where to go if you happened to have enough rationed gas. She originated a school safety show, and when television was introduced, she was the originator of several TV programs, too. One of those was the first TV "Traffic Court" program in 1950, and it was copied across the country.

* * *

It was still rare to hear a woman's voice on the news broadcasts from Europe, but Mary Breckenridge and Betty Wason were sending some dispatches for CBS before America got into the war, and Jo Denman and Helen Heitt, Americans living in Europe, sent dispatches during the war years. Breckenridge had been a free-lance photographer in London when war began and she was photographing the British evacuation of children for *Life* magazine when Murrow asked her to broadcast. She had a natural radio voice and a gift for reporting, and covered headline stories all over Europe as she had done earlier as a photojournalist.

Betty Wason, who had some remarkable adventures in battle areas, turned in a splendid performance despite her lack of reporting experience. A Purdue graduate, she had worked in publicity and had done a woman's radio program before she left for Europe, where she wangled a free-lance correspondent's job for Trans-Radio Press Service and for the Indianapolis *Star*.

She reached Sweden shortly after the Nazi invasion of Norway. Her dramatic broadcast of the escape of King Haakon of Norway from the Nazis brought her full-time radio reporting assignments. Wason worked out of Stockholm and made her way alone into war-torn Norway not long after the invasion, to find out what was happening. After watching an air raid in Norway and getting details of nearby battles, she returned with her story, walking the last 10 miles through deep snow on impassable roads.

Wason followed the war south, sending dispatches from Greece and Albania. Her most frightening adventure was in Albania, when Greek authorities did not want her to cover front-line action there. They did not want a woman in the war zone, but they finally allowed her to go at night when the risk was less. With another reporter she was led into the underground quarters on the line where they interviewed officers and troops. In leaving they crossed a no-man's land, a nightmare of land mines, and "hit the dirt" often as shells shrieked overhead and one crashed into a house 30 yards from them.

Wason reported the fall of Athens and was assigned to do special interest features on the occupation. She stayed two months but was only allowed to make two carefully supervised broadcasts, so she concluded that her usefulness as a correspondent was at an end. She had spent a year and a half as a war correspondent and then returned to the United States to lecture and write in 1941.

Communications were vital during the war and the Government urged women to take civilian or military jobs in communications as operators, radio engineers or technicians. Special training courses in electronics were provided for women, such as the one at Purdue University in 1943. At broadcasting stations over a fifth of the qualified engineers had left for military service or defense work.

A governmental news release sang the women's praises: "Women have shown no radio job is too big for them." Employment of women at NBC, for example, rose from 20 to 25 per cent of the total to a third of the staff during five years. Newspaper and magazine articles of this period featured many examples of successful women like Helen Guy who became assistant to the business manager of the program department of the Blue Network after starting at the bottom in 1922 with WJZ in Newark. (Later she was an ABC television saleswoman.)

Irene Kuhn, who was an NBC war correspondent in the Far East, made the first broadcast from Shanghai after the Japanese gave up. She also was the first person to broadcast from liberated Manila. Later she took over as coordinator of NBC's program promotion after a career as reporter-correspondent. There was "production man" Betty Todd, and there were two women who started their own small radio station at Charlotte, North Carolina.

Finding the Women

Despite all this glowing "women can do anything" publicity, it was still a bit tough for men to swallow Jane Tiffany Wagner's history-making idea in 1944. She had been assigned to produce a recruiting show for the women's military services. She outlined a grand scheme to her boss for four shows—one for each of the women's services on a coast-to-coast hookup.

"I think we should do it ourselves, just us girls, without help from you men, an appeal to women by women, O.K.?"

she concluded. The answer was affirmative. The boss sent a message to the men in the department: "Hands off, all you boys, and God bless the girls." The men obeyed, but some still thought it couldn't be done. They often dropped in to shake their heads or swipe a piece of equipment for another show.

"It was high time somebody started something like this," said Wagner to a *World-Telegram* reporter that April. She had worked for a year and a half at NBC after having studied for radio producing at Iowa and at Columbia.

Wagner said her forte was organization. First she had to find the women; they were there—Nancy Osgood, head of women's radio activities in Washington and an experienced director; Priscilla Kent, NBC scriptwriter; Muriel Kennedy, a radio engineer; Marjorie Ochs, a M.I.T. engineer from a Boston studio who had only been with NBC for two days when she was located; the WAVE chorus and an all-girl orchestra directed by 25-year-old Ann Kullmer, which just happened to be rehearsing in New York at the time.

The four half-hour programs went off without a hitch and Wagner's chief, who was head of NBC public services, sent her a telegram, after the first show saying, "You girls may well be proud. I'm proud of you all. It's a beautiful job."

But these women were still pioneers and they knew it. "It'll be a hundred years before there are as many women top executives as men in radio," said Peggy Myles, NBC's copy director doing publicity for the show.

"It will take men a while to get over their surprise that women could put on a network show without them," added director Osgood. "Men gradually become nicer after we do a good job for a while." She spoke from experience, having been in radio since 1927.

Women's Professional Associations Emerge

The wartime friendship and increased numbers of women in radio may account for the appearance in 1942 of their first professional organization, the Association of Women Directors, whose first president was Ruth Chilton. In 1944 the

Women's National Press Club in Washington accepted radio newswomen into membership for the first time, too.

The AWD had 650 members in two years and intended to be a clearing house for the exchange of ideas and techniques, for the innovation and promotion of projects affecting women broadcasters and women listeners. Women had assumed greater duties during wartime, they said, and this first organization of women broadcasters took the profession seriously. They surveyed stations to see how rapidly news releases were arriving and set policies on the use of credit lines on commercial releases. They compiled information on programs, sponsors and background of women broadcasters. They found 131 women's broadcasts were being done by their own members and only 15 of those ran less than 5 days a week.

The National Association of Broadcasters financed the new organization as an adjunct and NAB's director of women's activities directed the group's convention, election of officers and committees. NAB discontinued its women's division in 1950, but helped women form a new independent group, American Women in Radio and Television, Inc. The AWRT held its first meeting in 1951 and had nearly 3,000 members by the 1970's. Their first president was Edythe Meserand, who spent 42 years in radio, 15 of them as a newswriter for WOR in New York.

Meserand left radio to start her own advertising agency. AWRT worked for exchange of ideas, trends and developments in broadcasting and worked for equal status and pay for members and to assist in their professional development. Members represent a wide variety of professional and technical jobs.

A Labor Department roundup of the status of women in radio in 1947, when the wartime boom was over, predicted increasing opportunities for women and men in broadcasting. Women comprised 28 per cent of the total employees in broadcasting as of November, 1946. Although opportunities for artists, writers, announcers, camera and technical and engineering experts were considered most promising, the warning was that such glamour jobs made up not more than a third of the whole.

The advice to young women was to get experience in radio or their special field before trying the networks. Success stories emphasized that point, but showed that there were a number of women on camera and producing and directing programs as well as serving as executives, writers, and in advertising and audience research.

Television was on the horizon and it seemed likely, to a RCA male executive interviewed then, to attract a percentage of women higher than in radio. TV was still too new for the Labor Department to describe all the job possibilities, but it appeared that TV jobs would combine those in radio, film, theatre, variety hall and journalism along with business and technical positions.

Women who had entered radio work during the war were alrei dy on their way up. Bessee Howard of WCAU, Philadelphia, was a commentator on international affairs and had a daily program called "World Panorama," which covered international news and the historical and cultural background of events.

Ann Holden, originator of "Women's Magazine of the Air," a daily half-hour broadcast from KGO in San Francisco, combined interviews of famous people with homemaking and cultural tips in a West Coast version of Mary Margaret McBride; Josephine S. Hennings was a senior script officer in public information for the United Nations; and Jill Jackson was a local sports commentator, one of few women in the country to hold that job.

TV seemed promising, but when Ellen Wadley left her wartime job in radio at the U.S. Air Force station in Wiesbaden and tried to find a similar job in Washington, she found that it was not so easy. She did find a job writing a locally sponsored shopping column for WTOP and then became a CBS staff writer. But a Red Cross scriptwriting job offered much more pay. When she returned from that and a stint at public relations, she became co-producer for CBS' "Face the Nation" in 1963. She also produced "Capitol Cloakroom," and "The Leading Question," and in 1966 or 1967 was promoted to Director of Public Affairs for CBS radio in Washington. That job included producing all CBS radio special events and "Capitol Cloakroom," "Washington Week," and "The Law and You."

Despite the many advances women had made in all phases of radio work during the war, postwar career literature warned ominously that radio had reached its peak and was no longer an expanding industry. Television competition would be keen, because it attracted talent from the movie studios, magazines, radio and theatre. Experience and college were still the qualifications, but women were warned that announcing opportunities were almost entirely male, the only exception being homemaking programs. The reasons: women's voices were poor, hours were irregular and operation of the equipment was difficult.

Compared to the literature of 1944, it seemed that 1950 had an altogether different audience in mind. One 1950's book pointed out enthusiastically that the weather-girl job was a breakthrough for women! This book warned women not to expect to move very readily from the non-talent jobs into better jobs, and that newsmen and news editors were hired from the working press. Some women were hired as script girls, a job that was called "production assistant" when a man held it, said the text. Opportunities were limited; they appeared to be better for women in educational television.

Women's Place in Postwar Radio

With such glum predictions and increasingly negative attitudes about what women could do in broadcasting, it is not surprising to find fewer women in the field in the postwar years. Some found jobs with the United Nations, Radio Free Europe and Voice of America where language and broadcasting skills were needed, but the glamour and pay of commercial broadcasting were lacking.

Occasionally one could hear Flora Lewis on CBS reporting from Guatemala, for example, and Pauline Frederick made her beginning in this period. But women in radio news were extremely rare, almost nonexistent.

The women had been given a place in postwar radio—it

was the women's program or family/children show. There were still several of these programs going as *McCall's* magazine and AWRT found when they awarded women seven Golden Mike awards each year during the 1950's and into the 1960's.

Television competition brought about a rapid change in the structure of radio, starting as early as the late 1950's. Television took over the living room and many of the programs that had been successful on radio were quickly adapted to video. Radio, thanks to the new transistors that made radio lightweight, could go anywhere and the programming turned to all music and some news and chatter. The audience was segmented, different groups of people listened at different times of day, and vertical programming developed. The old-time dramatic scriptwriter disappeared; the continuity writer filled bridges between commercials, news and music. Some women were attracted to these low-paid but rather fun jobs. New format shows like "Nightline" and "Monitor" (1955) gave program coordinators great freedom to develop interviews and program ideas, but although it was frequently a woman who taped the interview and coordinated the show, "their voices were rubbed off the tape" so that an on-mike announcer could ask the questions.

Disc jockey shows were popular with the youthful audience and a few women were attracted to and held these jobs. Sunny Pryor coordinated a show in Detroit in the late 1950's for which she screened some 200 record releases each week and made a sequence for "smooth listening for housewives under 30."

The woman's daytime program was on the way out and female-interest spots were worked into the day's program. Patti Searight, radio program director at WTOP in Washington, D.C., was one of the new women engaged in this kind of job. A graduate of Ohio State, she had done some college writing and took the programming job in 1952, becoming director at age 27. She created program series on a wide range of topics, including mental health, juvenile delinquency, news for children and the like.

Directors and station managers were often prejudiced

against hiring women in the 1950's and some frankly said they "wouldn't want a woman producer in their office . . . women can't stand up to the pressure."

Those women who did find a place in new radio were expected to maintain feminine dignity and respond with good humor to the studio wags. Said CBS network copy chief Naomi Andrews, women are paid low and expected to have tremendous energy and resourcefulness and jump from one thing to another: "It was good for people with grasshopper minds."

Competition with TV spurred radio to new program formats, one of which was the engaging and popular NBC weekend "Monitor," which lasted for 20 years. The 40-hour service broadcast news and interviews from all over the world from Saturday morning until Sunday midnight. With "Monitor" at its start in 1955 was Helen Hall, an experienced radio and TV commentator. Hall started in local radio duing the 1940's in Tampa, Florida. She handled spot news and interviews in the U.S. and overseas, including the East Berlin riots in 1953, for radio "Monitor."

In the 1960's a few established women's programs remained on radio and a few venerable talk shows continued. Dr. Joyce Brothers, noted psychologist and columnist was new, with a regular section on NBC's "Monitor" where she answered questions telephoned in. Helen Hall developed a 10-minute commentary and interview program for WCBS in New York called "One Woman's New York," and Deena Clark ran a popular daily interview program that started in 1961, called "Deena Clark's Moment with . . ." for WRC in Washington, D.C.

Fran Harris was offered the chance to move into management in 1964 and become WWJ's special features coordinator for AM, FM and TV. Other women "were hanging on by their fingernails to keep on-air jobs," she said. She moved into the new job and enjoyed the community service role, She "was too old for TV news," she said; it was felt that the public would not accept her. (She had been the first woman on TV in Detroit in 1946 and had originated several television programs.)

Looking back, Harris said that people frequently called her a "career woman," but she just thought that she "had a good job." And she had been able to combine that with a close family life. Offers to move to the network had not interested her because she preferred to stay in Detroit with her family. "Behind every woman who made it in those early years in broadcasting," she thought, "was someone supporting her at home." For her it was her husband.

It wasn't until the women's liberation movement began in the late 1960's that Harris thought much about discrimination. She knew that she had received lower pay than her male colleagues, but she had always been grateful to have a challenging job. Her promotion made it possible for her to have more impact on the station and her "only regret was that they didn't let (her) do more."

* * *

Marion Stephenson, who became in 1962 the first woman vice-president (radio division) in the history of NBC, was a vigorous champion of professional women. She took note of the declining role women in the U.S. were playing in the postwar years.

"In this country of ours today women are refusing in greater numbers than ever before the opportunities of higher education that are mandatory to keep abreast of this fast-moving, fast-paced world in which we live," she told the Chicago Women's Ad Club in April, 1965.

Stephenson referred to the declining enrollment of women in colleges and graduate school, the absence of women from Federal government and Cabinet posts, the Supreme Court and judiciary. There were only two women in the Senate and eight in the House, she said, less than two per cent of the total membership. "Unless this changes," she warned, "U.S. women will play a declining role in the country's affairs." She was dismayed over this loss of drive and desire on the part of American women to compete for the available executive positions, their failure to acquire the necessary skills to compete effectively, and their unwillingness to make sacrifices that were frequently necessary to compete in the business role.

Stephenson studied business administration at Antioch College and worked with Standard Oil before joining NBC as a budget clerk in the Advertising Department in 1944. She attended NYU's Graduate School of Business at night during her early years with NBC and was promoted to business manager of the Advertising and Promotion Department in 1948, the same year that she received her M.A. In her position as vice-president of the radio division, Stephenson was responsible for financial affairs of the radio network and owned radio stations, and for the network's sales services and station clearances. (She became vice-president and general manager of the NBC Radio Network and in the 1970's was still encouraging women to consider radio and management.)

Staunch Bias

In 1965, broadcast news directors who were surveyed along with newspaper managing editors exhibited staunch bias against women in the radio newsroom with the time-worn reasons: men sounded more authoritative; women couldn't handle the assignments and some of the heavy camera equipment; women let their personal problems affect their jobs.

About 20 per cent of all graduates in university and college journalism boadcast courses in the 1960's were women, and radio only hired 60 to 80 such graduates a year. According to studies made in 1965 by Kathleen Kienzle, only 4.7 per cent of the radio and television newsroom staffs were female.

A 1960 survey by Smith and Harwood estimated that only about 10 per cent of the jobs held by women in radio were non-clerical or non-secretarial, although women held about a quarter of the total full-time broadcast jobs. Salaries for women were far lower than those for men, even in jobs at the high end of the salary scale. The women saw discrimination, but most were satisfied with their jobs.

A decade later, a study of the 1972–1973 radio members of AWRT showed that women were moving into larger markets and achieving better pay and positions. They expressed even more job satisfaction than did those in 1960, but the most satisfied also perceived the most discrimination. This group of women in radio and television blamed much of the discrimination on the sex stereotyping as well as on female insecurity and lack of initiative, creativity and drive. Add that to traditional male chauvinism and the accepted preference for male voices on the air, for the complete picture. These women believed that it was up to the individual to improve the status of women in broadcasting and that women's own qualities were both their greatest assets and obstacles. In the long run they thought things had improved.

A 1974 study of radio station managers said that prospects for women in radio were still dim. More than half of the managers still believed that people disliked the sound of women on the air, despite recent surveys by journalism professor Vernon Stone that refute the old belief. While only a third took a clearly negative attitude toward women in radio, only slightly under 18 per cent clearly favored women.

The Government's analysis of broadcasting as a career field projected some moderate growth in the 1970's (not taking the recession into account) and indicated that radio stations, because they were more numerous, offered more jobs for beginners than did television. But there were still few women announcers, a mere 8 per cent of the total in 1970.

The impact of the women's movement was still to be felt; 1970 figures were too early to reflect any changes resulting from affirmative action hiring programs and license challenges of the 1970's. Women's voices, particularly on local stations and in National Public Radio, were heard once again in news and social commentary and interviews. Women were producing their own programs, spurred on by feminist groups, and a feminist radio network had formed. Women who worked on campus radio stations realized the value of getting a first class operator license that enabled them legally to operate a transmitter and several of the students seeking broadcast careers were getting those licenses so that they would be employable at the small stations.

Anchorpeople and News Directors

NBC decided to expand its radio news treatment in June, 1975, and hired 15 new anchorpersons for its round-the-clock News and Information Service. Five of them were women, brought from radio news or anchor jobs in Boston, New Rochelle, Detroit, Denver and New York City.

By that time National Public Radio's Susan Stamberg was already a well-known anchor on the popular 90-minute "All Things Considered" daily news background and feature program heard over most of NPR's 200 stations. Stamberg, who started in radio in 1962 as a public affairs producer for WAMU-FM in Washington, D.C., came to broadcasting from magazine journalism. She became co-host of "All Things Considered" in 1972.

During the day she writes, tapes and edits her own material, confers with producers about other story ideas and edits material. After a hectic day, she says, the five o'clock opening of the broadcast signals the time when she starts to relax. And her on-air style reflects that. She makes no pretense at being all-knowing. Instead, she asks questions that ordinary people might ask and shares her findings and sometimes her surprise with the audience. She enjoys the immediacy and flexibility of radio, and she thinks the best part of radio is in bringing people together.

A revealing and penetrating insight into the pressures women faced in radio newsrooms of the early 1970's was provided by Tina Press in a speech at the University of Florida in May, 1974.

She told her student audience,

> . . . The only way you are going to get where you are going is by asking yourself what you want, setting your goals, and then working hard . . . The fact that you are a woman will not be denied, but let it not be your excuse for not getting anywhere. It is an asset, but the bottom line is that professional quality will get you farther.

Press started at the bottom of the professional ladder, answering phones, ripping wires, sharpening pencils and making coffee at KCBS-Newsradio in San Francisco after graduation from Stanford where she had worked on the college newspaper.

In order to learn the broadcast business she asked questions of all the reporters and anchormen (all male and over 30 at the time), and they were happy to tell her about their news experiences.

"I was no threat to them," she explained. She ran errands and made sure their pencils were sharpened. "At this point, I did not think of myself as a woman, but as someone in the newsroom who had a lot to learn and could only learn the business from people who were there—all of them men."

News Director Jim Simon was often in the newsroom. He had hired five young women who were bright, enthusiastic and willing to work. He encouraged them with story ideas and extra responsibilities. "He told me that I had two strikes against me: that I was young and that I was a woman. He said I would face lots of problems because most men in the business were not interested in encouraging young people," Press recalled in an interview.

Press wasn't really conscious of discrimination as a reason so few women were working in radio news, she said. She was 22 and it was 1969, "well before our collective consciousness was raised." She assumed that "this was the natural order of things—if there were no women on the air, it must be because none had shown an interest in that job."

She recalled:

> I think my acceptance of a secondary role was fairly typical of a lot of women who are now my age. Those that went through college and entered the work force just before society's collective consciousness was raised never pushed, never made too many claims of accomplishment.
>
> Things just weren't done that way, and I and many others were not sufficiently angry, rebellious, or even, perhaps, aware, to realize that things didn't have to be this way. . . . I had totally accepted society's second-class status for me as a woman. It simply never occurred to me that it could be otherwise . . . Life hadn't been so bad for me up to then. Looking back, however, I can see the dangers of accepting that definition. I'm sure I would have been far more motivated and aggressive had that been accepted behavior, and there had been any tangible goal to reach for then.

Press was promoted from desk assistant to news editor within three months after having filled in a few times in that spot. She made assignments, read wire copy and made decisions about what stories to use and made sure it all got on the air, but at first her stomach betrayed her outward calm. Since then she learned to chew out reporters who missed deadlines and argue with news directors over decisions made during the shift. She found that being nice and using some flattery helped smooth the problems caused by her youthfulness. She respected the professionals she worked for, and gradually she learned to trust her own judgment.

It was not until the summer of 1970 that the chauvinism of a newsroom really became apparent. San Francisco women had organized a demonstration of solidarity, asking women to boycott their jobs and attend a rally. Press was not an activist and she stayed on the job, but she made sure the story got fair treatment. The second impact came when CBS "allowed" women to wear pant suits to work in the fall of 1970. She thought it was rather silly that CBS would create an official dress code for women, but not for men. Press and a woman colleague started clipping articles on the movement and suggested a series—but they were ahead of the time. The idea was considered "very funny."

By the time she was offered a job as manager of News Operations at WCBS all-news radio in New York in November, 1971, she could assess the situation realistically:

> I had three strikes against me—not only was I still young (24), and still a woman, but I was in "The Big Apple." New York City is the place where experienced broadcasters come after working their way up the ladder of small-time cities. Needless to say, I was not very popular, nor was my assignment received with much enthusiasm.

Once again Press had a boss who made a determined effort to treat women in the newsroom with respect and dignity. Sensitive to the obvious problems her presence created, her new general manager (formerly from her San Francisco station) told her he had faith in her ability to do the job and he did what he could to smooth over the antagonisms from experienced and often much older staffers. He was reorganizing the newsroom operation, patterning it on the San Francisco operation. Her job was newly created. In it she outlined procedures for the newsroom and helped set up systems that would work.

Press knew she had been accepted two and a half years later when a number of the "old guard" made a special point of complimenting her *work* at a station party. They admitted their earlier skepticism . . . but they'd been convinced. She got the job done . . . and she wasn't out to ruin them or undercut their professionalism or diminish the quality of the station . . . that in fact she cared a great deal about the success of the station . . . they had misjudged her . . . they accepted her now. Quality and competence were all that mattered to them.

Later, as an executive producer, Press made the decisions as to what goes on the air. She tried to avoid stereotypical or insulting references to women in news stories and to point out offensive references made in conversation. She looked for stories concerning women, knowing that her mostly male colleagues would tend to skip over them.

The desire to be in that greater decision-making position took Press to Philadelphia as assistant news director of WCAU Radio. When that station switched from all-talk to all-news, she was hired to help design the format, hire the staff, and run the 40-person newsroom.

Once again with enlightened male superiors, Press weathered the special pressures of a female executive. There was not only this professional challenge of becoming one of the highest ranking female broadcast news executives, but of becoming a commuting wife. Her husband, a professor at New York University and contributing editor at *MORE* magazine, had commitments in New York, so she lived Monday through Friday in Philadelphia, coming to Manhattan on weekends. After a year and a half of what she describes as exhilarating pressures and responsibilities, she returned to New York permanently, and now writes for the CBS News division.

Young women like Press took over broadcast news directing jobs at an unprecedented speed between 1975 and 1976, reported Vernon Stone in a Radio Television News Directors Association survey. In 1976, 11 women headed commercial TV news operations (compared with 2 in 1972 and 4 in 1975), and 8 per cent of the news directors in commercial radio were women (compared with 4 per cent in 1972).

The young women in their 20's, who made up half the total in 1976, were college graduates, frequently speech and broadcast majors, and they were employed in the larger markets. The "old-timers," women with a median age of 35 and three years' experience, worked in smaller markets. According to Stone's 1975 survey, these "old-timers" were generally satisfied with their jobs and were not interested in moving, for reasons of marriage or geographical preference.

The dean of women news directors was Shirley Bartholomew, 32 years at KRKO (Everett, Washington) and not far behind was Zona B. Davis, news director for 27 years at WCRA (Effingham, Illinois).

Station managers and owners told Stone in 1975 that they still feared that male employees wouldn't accept female bosses, but the women news directors reported little trouble in supervising men or women employees.

Based on his repeated surveys of broadcasting professionals for RTNDA, Stone predicted that the trend toward younger women news directors would continue. As their numbers increase, it seems likely that the old myths and fears will fade, and women and minorities will not constantly be reminded of their novelty status. As Press remarked, "Someday we'll all be people."

· SOURCES CONSULTED ·

Erik Barnouw, *A History of Broadcasting in the U.S.* 3 vols., (New York: Oxford University Press, 1966, 1968, 1970).

Mitchell V. Charnley, *News by Radio* (New York: The Macmillan Co., 1948).

Giraud Chester and Garnet Garrison, *Radio and Television, An Introduction* (New York: Appleton-Century-Crofts, 1956).

Catherine Filene, *Careers for Women* (New York: Houghton Mifflin Co., 1934).

Frances Willard Kerr, *Women in Radio, Illustrated by Biographical Sketches* (Washington, D.C.: U.S. Department of Labor, 1947).

Kathleen Kienzle, "A Study of the Employment Opportunities For Women in Broadcast News," Unpublished M.A., Ohio State University, 1965.

Robert J. Landry, *This Fascinating Radio Business* (New York: The Bobbs-Merrill Co., 1946).

Mary Margaret McBride, *Out of the Air* (New York: Doubleday & Co., 1961).

Gordon Lee McCullough, "News Through a Woman's Eyes," Unpublished M.A. thesis, East Texas State University, 1970.

Lana Naegel, "Women in Radio," unpublished M.A. thesis, University of Wisconsin-Madison, 1971.

Helen Sioussat, *Mikes Don't Bite* (New York: L.B. Fisher, 1943).

Don C. Smith and Kenneth Harwood, "Women in Broadcasting," *Journal of Broadcasting*, Vol. 10, 1966.

Vernon A. Stone, "Attitudes Toward Television Newswomen," *Journal of Broadcasting*, Winter 73–74.

Vernon A. Stone, "Surveys Show Younger Women Becoming News Directors," *RTNDA Communicator*, October, 1976.

Judith C. Weller, *Radio The Fifth Estate* (New York: Houghton Mifflin Co., 1946).

Paul W. White, *News on the Air*, (New York: Harcourt, Brace & Co., 1947).

Interviews by William Hedges with Dorothy Gorden, Myrtle Stahl and Judith Waller at Broadcast Pioneers Library, Washington, D.C.

Interview with Judith Waller, post-World War II (undated) at State Historical Society of Wisconsin, Mass Communications collection.

CBS News library and archives, CBS, New York, N.Y., *Mademoiselle*, career pamphlets, New York, N.Y.

Personal interviews with Pauline Frederick, Fran Harris, Tina Press (courtesy R. R. Rush) and Ellen Wadley, and personal letter to the author from Tina Press.

5

* * *

Newswoman
on Camera

TELEVISION SEEMED A PROMISING FIELD for women in the immediate post-World War II years. Several had moved from radio to TV, where they found jobs at the network or station level as producers, directors, writers, editors, engineers and announcers. But by the mid-1950's, despite the terrific growth in stations and audience, it was evident that the top jobs for women were limited to heading local women's programs for the most part. Talk of women in executive roles, as engineers and running things alongside the men, as they had been doing during the war, ceased.

The familiar prewar pattern had resumed. There was at least one woman on the staff of every television studio, large or small, to "handle the woman's angle." According to the career literature that job included writing, announcing, advertising, interviewing, public relations, and dreaming up shows that would appeal to women or children.

News was almost closed to women. Pauline Frederick joined ABC News full-time in 1948 and for 12 years she was the only woman handling hard news on network radio and TV. At CBS, Alice Weel Bigart moved over from radio in 1948 to write for the "Douglas Edwards With the News" program for 15 years before she moved into production special events and documentaries. (Edwards was the first major radio news-

caster to move to TV—in 1947—and the show began in
August of 1948. Cronkite replaced him in 1962).

At the local level, Dorothy Fuldheim apparently became
television's first news anchorwoman in 1947 at station WEWS-
TV in Cleveland. She had been on the lecture circuit and was
doing local radio commentaries and network radio when she
was offered the anchor job. At age 83, she was still anchoring
the evening news in Cleveland in 1976, along with taping two
daily TV commentaries and hosting a daily live interview program. She has interviewed celebrities all over the world, and
hosted one of the first live variety shows on television. Fuldheim told an interviewer from *Ms.* magazine in 1976 that she
had no intention of retiring early. She said she was in good
health and enjoyed her unique role in a male-dominated profession and youth-oriented society.

Martha Rountree, who originated and moderated "Meet the
Press" from its start in 1947 was associated with newsmaking
events, although she was not a journalist. She sold out her interest in the program to co-founder Lawrence Spivak in 1954
and started her own program, "Press Conference" for NBC in
1956, but it did not last very long.

The bright young women who were television successes in
1945 and 1946—like Dorothy Wootton of WABD ("the only
woman staff announcer at that time"); Josephine Basil ("the
only woman FCC-licensed sound engineer"); Dorothy Math-
ews, script reader; Sally O'Neill, program coordinator; Helen
Rhodes, producer; Jane Clark and Dorothy Martin, video
engineers—were no longer being hailed in the headlines.

Lela Swift, a WCBS associate director in 1948, who would
direct soaps and late night movies for ABC in the 1970's, predicted that "the boom days for women in television had
ended" and she appeared to be correct. Her colleagues, on the
other hand—Beula Jarvis, film acceptance editor for WNBT,
and Frances Buss of CBS, television's first woman director in
1944—envisioned a bright future for women in broadcasting.
Women, they thought, would fill important jobs as writers,
producers, directors, advertising consultants, writers, interviewers and other behind-the-scenes workers. They thought
that women, who had been relegated to women's programs on

radio because of their voices, "appeared destined for a wider future emceeing shows for mixed audiences." Somehow, that just didn't happen.

The numbers of women in broadcasting had reached an all-time high in proportion to males during the war and began to decline. No longer would press releases boast of station staffs that were one-third female, as had CBS and General Electric's Schenectady studio in 1945.

* * *

Male prejudice against women reporting news on the air was one of the first obstacles Pauline Frederick had to overcome. She had majored in political science, taken an advanced degree in international law and reported for the Washington *Star* and *U.S. News*. Her first on-air experience was a series of interviews with wives of diplomats in Washington for NBC. But when she applied for a full-time radio news position, Edward R. Murrow turned her down. In a CBS staff memo from 1946, he said that although she read well and her voice was pleasing, "I would not call her material or manner particularly distinguished." He mentioned a long list of women applicants and "little opportunity to use them," and said her name would not be put very near the top of the list.

Disappointment did not deter Frederick, however, and she supported herself by writing features for the North American Newspaper Alliance and stringing for ABC News in New York City. ABC kept sending her on so-called "women's news," although she argued that there should be no sex in news.

"All news activities are about people and the ability to cover should not be judged by the sex of the reporter but by the reporting ability," Frederick said. She decided that the only way to beat the women's news classification was to dig up articles about the United Nations that no one else got.

A desk editor told her (in secret) that although some officials objected to her being on the air, if she turned in an exclusive story he would have to use her. The men, she recalled, only had to rewrite copy to get on the air. She turned in several scoops, but was kept on as a stringer nevertheless. One editor even told her that she covered news well, "like a man," but she wouldn't be used on the air because a woman's voice "didn't carry authority."

Frederick's chance came one evening in 1948. ABC News had two major stories to cover, a truckers' strike and a foreign ministers' conference and only one regular reporter in the studio. Most of the men had returned to Washington after spending a week at the conference. The network thought there might be violence at the truckers' strike, so they assigned her to the foreign ministers' conference, which she continued to cover for several weeks. That year she became a full-time correspondent for ABC.

Television was still in its infancy in those days, and someone put up a memo in the studio that anyone who wanted to report on TV should sign the list. Frederick did not sign. When one of the other reporters asked her about this she said, "Maybe if enough of you men go to television, there will be a chance around here for me."

She was on television in 1948 in Philadelphia at the first televised political convention because her editors sent her. "But I don't know anything about television," she said when they told her they intended to use her quite a lot at the convention. "That's all right," said the editors reassuringly, "neither do we."

Although Frederick supposed that she was there especially to interview women, wives of political leaders and delegates, on the first pre-convention program she took turns with Elmer Davis in interviewing officials and delegates. She was also the "make-up expert" for women guests, including the wives of Truman, Dewey, Stassen and Douglas. She had asked at Elizabeth Arden's studio for advice on make-up and they said their experience was only with make-up for film. They didn't know anything about make-up for TV. "I hate to think how we all must have looked," she recalled.

Frederick's first regular assignment with ABC was to cover the United Nations, but she also had an early morning radio news program of her own. For this she had to rise at 4 or 4:30 a.m. After the radio show she went to the United Nations to cover the daily activities and interview delegates. She broad-cast from the UN during the day and often returned to the ABC studios to appear on the evening television news. After four years of that she was about worn out. "I never got enough sleep," she said.

The Korean War in 1950 was her first crisis. ABC decided to cover the Security Council meetings completely and Frederick was on air all day and into the night. At first she was to be the leg reporter for another correspondent. But it was soon evident that there was too much to cover and both were put on the air. When the other reporter went on vacation, she was given helpers and she continued in the senior role. She did a lot of filling-in with background and profiles during the periods of consecutive translation.

The response to the ABC coverage was overwhelming. The Boston station called to say it was "the greatest program since 'Stop the Music' " and people took the radio along to the beach in order to keep tuned in for developments. During this six-week period, Pauline Frederick became a familiar name in American households and ABC pioneered a new kind of con-tinuous news coverage.

Her offer from NBC in 1953 was attractive in part because it included her own radio program later in the day. Frederick moved to NBC but the UN was still her assignment. She shared it at first with a colleague, but soon she was *the* UN correspondent for NBC. When crises arose, the network would send someone down to cover for radio and she handled televi-sion. The night the Congo crisis boiled over, for instance, she was on television from 8:30 p.m. until 3:30 a.m. as Secretary General Dag Hammarskjöld asked for authority to send mili-tary aid to the Congo. After covering the Congo, the Hungar-ian and Middle East crises on American television, she had become identified with television as America's only television newswoman, but she continued her radio news work. She was a frequent guest on "Today," as well.

Frederick's reporting earned her the respect and esteem of her colleagues and she was given many awards, including the George Foster Peabody Award in 1955 for her contribution to international understanding. The year before, she had been the first woman to win the Commentator Award from the Alfred I. duPont Radio Awards committee, which cited her for

> . . . avoiding the slickness, automatic orthodoxy and superficial sensationalism characteristic of such news commentary today . . . (and for her) honesty, independence of judgment, a high sense of integrity and personal devotion to the important basic values of our culture.

Frederick won the top award from *McCall's* and AWRT in 1956 for her ingenious reporting and the courage to say what she believed, and was the first woman president of the UN Correspondents' Association.

Although Frederick was the first woman to anchor network radio's convention coverage in 1960, she "wasn't interested in anchoring," she said. "I am essentially a reporter. I like to go out and dig up stories and report them, and personally I don't care about going on the air unless I have something important to say or explain."

News analysis was an important part of Frederick's job as a UN correspondent because events were often complex and involved, and she liked doing news analysis.

* * *

Other women in television at the time were primarily doing women's, youth, community dialogue programs and the like in cities around the country, and *McCall's* and AWRT awarded seven "Golden Mike" awards each year from 1951 and into the 1960's to several of them. There were a few women producers at the networks in 1954, such as Nancy Hanschman Dickerson in Washington, and five directors: Lela Swift, Gloria Monty, Mary Dean Pulver and Joan Woodward at CBS, and Gertrude Tipper at ABC.

At NBC, Doris Ann Scharfenberg managed all the network's religious programs and Pamela Ilott had a similar job at CBS in the 1950's. Dr. Joyce Brothers burst into the spotlight in 1955 as an unlikely expert on boxing on the "$64,000 Question." Producer Mildred Freed Alberg achieved early fame in 1953 for her daring and successful Shakespearean television adaptations on the "Hallmark Hall of Fame," a job she kept for six years before switching to film.

* * *

Mildred B. Zorbaugh was one of the few women to reach a top executive post in broadcasting in the 1950's. She was promoted to vice-president and special assistant to the president of ABC in 1956, and it was thought that she was the first woman to achieve this rank at a major network. She had enrolled in law school after her second child had been born, having developed an interest in the field while she was a secretary for NBC. She returned to the network after graduation from law school and was half of the legal department. Zorbaugh stayed with ABC when it was split from NBC in 1943 and rose to general counsel in 1953.

In making the announcement of her promotion, ABC network President Robert E. Kintner said he took a genuine pride in having a dozen women in top posts at ABC. Many of them had pioneered as women in their jobs and were still pioneers in 1956, but Kintner said "we find that it helps the morale of all women in the organization and makes it easier for us to attract girls right from college" when we promote women to top jobs.

He attributed the women's success to their loyalty to the company, ability to work hard, conscientiousness, excellent judgment and tact. "Of course," he added, "I think these women were outstanding to begin with." He emphasized that men and women should be offered equal opportunities, but that women should be aware of the long hours and hard work required in broadcasting. The day runs from 5 p.m. to 1 a.m., he said, and "that can put a strain on a marriage, if not on a woman."

Several successful women at ABC started as secretaries and had learned the business, moving gradually into important jobs as director of personnel, operations network manager, program director for WABC radio, director of community acceptance and television sales.

Television was expanding its audience and numbers of stations during the mid-1950's. Daytime soap operas, panel and quiz shows and episode films made in Hollywood came to dominate many of the hours, displacing most of the early talk, music and dramatic shows. The panel shows like "What's My Line?," which started in 1950, included women as regular and guest panelists and some became well known in these roles, including Dorothy Kilgallen, Bess Myerson, Arlene Francis, Faye Emerson and Kitty Carlisle. The scandals that exposed some leading quiz shows as rigged had a somewhat sobering effect on these shows and made networks jittery.

Morning shows of news and conversation with cultural and political figures, like the "Today" show built loyal audiences in the 1950's, as did public affairs programs like "Meet the Press," "Face the Nation" and "Capitol Cloakroom."

The "Vast Wastland" Appears

Edward R. Murrow and Fred Friendly's CBS "See It Now," which started in 1951 built a reputation for hardhitting journalistic reporting and the exploration of political and public issues. Controversial topics were scarce and TV network news lasted only 15 minutes in 1961 when FCC Chairman, Newton Minow, called television a "vast wasteland" bereft of socially responsible and serious programs.

A few women worked their way up from secretary to production assistant, field producer, researcher or writer during the 1950's. For a woman bent on television news, commentary or intelligent talk about the interests of the day, the future looked dim indeed.

Each of the networks did send three or four women to cover the political conventions of 1960—a sign of changes in store for the decade to come when about two dozen women would emerge in network-level jobs as reporters, correspondents, producers or assistant producers. Most of these women had been working in local stations or in allied journalistic fields before making network debuts. Aside from Pauline Frederick, however, women generally did not appear on network television news until after their introduction at the 1960 political conventions. During 1963, network evening news was extended to a half hour and that led to larger staffs, including some women.

In 1960 it was occasionally possible to see Aline Mosby reporting from Moscow, Phillis Hepp from Turkey and Athens, and Lee Hall from Cairo and Havana. Executives at all three television networks told a magazine reporter that year that "the picture for women in television news is better than ever before—it is even bright."

Although a few years ago women "were not wanted" in the gathering and presentation of news, the 1960 feeling was that "women brighten up" a news program and also that they had won places on those programs by the merit of "being good reporters."

✳   ✳   ✳

Networks typically looked for men and women with four to five years' experience in newspaper, wire service, radio or television work. By the time she became a CBS Washington correspondent in 1960, Nancy Hanschman Dickerson had spent six years producing current affairs talk shows for CBS including, "The Leading Question" and "Face the Nation." In 1954, Dickerson began to tire of writing speeches. She had things she wanted to say, and she decided that reporting was the best place to do it. But radio and TV news were "closed to women." CBS was looking for a newsman who knew Capitol Hill and could produce political programs. Dickerson was not a man, but she did know Capitol Hill and she got the job.

As a network news correspondent Dickerson was seldom beaten on a story and often praised by her colleagues. She turned in prized scoops, including Senator Eugene McCarthy's plans to challenge President Johnson over his Vietnam policy and the details from President Johnson on his selection of Senator Hubert H. Humphrey as his running mate.

Dickerson got the latter story because she was the first and only correspondent to point out the possible significance of the presence of Mrs. Humphrey as the only Senator's wife at a welcoming reception for Lady Bird Johnson held in Atlantic City some hours before the President announced his decision on a running mate. She buttonholed the President and he gave her the details. "There are just some things that a woman may notice that a man won't; that was one of them," she said.

When Dickerson was given the assignment as correspondent she was told that she would never have to cover women's news, and CBS kept its promise. One executive, who didn't like the idea, asked her please "not to giggle on the air."

She switched to NBC in 1963 and her interviews were often seen on the "Today" show and on the "Huntley-Brinkley Report" as well as on dozens of television specials. She was the only woman in 1963 to have a daily network television news program, "Nancy Dickerson with the News," and she was the first woman in TV to report from the floor of a national political convention. She was also the first woman correspondent to work in the anchor booth with Murrow and Cronkite. In 1970, she took some time out to spend with her family and wrote a book about her experiences called, *Among Those Present*. She returned to broadcasting in the 1970's with her own nationally syndicated programs which she writes, produces and moderates, the most recent of which is "Nancy Dickerson and the New Woman."

Dickerson and her husband were friends of President Johnson and were often called to private dinners with the Presidential family. She became one of Washington's most respected news correspondents and political analysts. Said Arthur Krock, the New York *Times* correspondent in Washington: "Nancy's very industrious and highly intelligent. She's a good objective reporter with the additional gifts of being a very lovely, effective and charming woman."

You can be aggressive and a woman, Dickerson assured an interviewer for the University of Michigan's WUOM program, "Background," in the fall of 1976. "I have asked some of the toughest questions of any reporter," she continued. "That's a reporter's job—to pursue the news, to ask tough questions without any compunctions. You can be forceful, but you don't have to be abrupt or rude."

✳   ✳   ✳

Lisa Howard of ABC, who turned in scoop interviews with Khrushchev and Castro, among others, in the early 1960's (she died in 1965), also was often praised for her beauty. She bristled when the implication was that her looks got her the stories. Howard had been an actress for the soap operas, but she pointed out that she had also written articles for the *Economist* and had been involved in politics for five years before entering television news.

"Sure, I've gotten scoops. But it's not because I'm pretty— it's because I'm determined, aggressive," Howard replied to interviewers. She had been wanting an interview with Nelson Rockefeller, who ducked the press whenever possible, and she found out where he would be for lunch. She showed up with the camera in front of the hotel, and he fled. She caught him at the elevator and he ducked down the stairs, but she met him on the next floor. She got her story and interview on camera. "The men resent me," she concluded, "because I really work at my job."

Howard interviewed Khrushchev when he came to the UN in 1960 by talking her way into the General Assembly session and cornering him after the meeting. She pestered Fidel Castro for nearly a year by mail and message until someone finally arranged for a visa. After four weeks in Cuba, Castro agreed to the interview. She got the first U.S. interview with Mme. Nhu by leaping on a plane and interviewing her in Paris before her departure for America.

✳ ✳ ✳

Nancy Dickerson also had an answer to the glamour tag. She told a fellow reporter:

> There's a notion around that a woman can function successfully as a reporter simply by being feminine and pretty. It's not so. The truth is that men make it so difficult for women to break into the field that the ones who do get in are really very good at their work. I suspect they are far better than most of the men.

She added that in Europe and in the new countries women are heard as newscasters, but in this country "a woman is still associated with nonthinking." That prejudice was even reinforced by the National Press Club's ban on women members, she observed.

Pauline Frederick, who convinced her editors that she could handle serious stories, disliked the network's attempts to turn her into a glamour girl. They told her to change her hair style, take off her glasses, change the type of clothing she wore. "I want to be appreciated not for glamour, but for my work," she said repeatedly.

*   *   *

Through the aggressive journalism of these three broadcast newswomen in the early 1960's it was evident that women's supposed lack of authority should no longer be a valid reason for keeping women off the hard news beats.

Network executives reported that only one in 20 applications for news jobs were from women in 1960, but some of those women did get hired. Peggy Whedon produced ABC's "Issues and Answers," starting in 1960 and she assisted in election coverage with occasional political interviews. Evening network news was expanded to a half hour in 1963, and this created more jobs. Joan Murray, who joined WCBS-TV in 1965, was probably the first black newswoman on a major television station. She contributed to the evening news broadcasts, and appeared on other news and public affairs programs. Murray also co-hosted for two and a half years "Two at One," a news and current events series with Jim Jensen. (She left television to establish her own advertising agency.)

WNBC-TV in New York hired *Newsday* reporter Liz Trotta in 1965 as the first woman on its local news staff. CBS moved Marya McLaughlin, an associate producer in their election unit, to the network news staff in 1966. McLaughlin, who was at that time CBS' only network woman journalist, had worked as an assistant to the election unit in the 1964 presidential campaign and had worked on editorial research in Washington and for the BBC. Trotta had worked for the Associated Press and for the Chicago *Tribune.*

According to the New York *Times* of 1965, the hirings were

part of a trend toward more women in television news that began a year earlier. The WCBS-TV local news staff had three newswomen including Murray. Marlene Sanders, an award-winning television and radio newswoman, had joined ABC News in 1964 where she had her own daily newscast, "Marlene Sanders and News with the Woman's Touch." She had written and produced various programs for WNEW-TV, including "Mike Wallace with the News" and produced and wrote a 90-minute nightly interview and entertainment program, "P.M.," for Westinghouse before taking the ABC News job.

❋   ❋   ❋

Aline Saarinen became an NBC News correspondent in 1964, specializing in cultural and community issues, art specials and moderated WNBC-TV's "For Women Only." Saarinen, whose husband was architect Eero Saarinen, had appeared previously on television and had worked as a managing editor, art editor and New York *Times* critic. Although she, too, was an attractive woman, she had to respond to another kind of impertinent questioning from those who asked her if she got her job at age 47 because of her husband who died in 1962. To this her reply was,

> I would not have been asked by President Johnson to be Ambassador to Finland if I had not been Mrs. Saarinen. And on the other hand, had I been Mrs. Saarinen who had never done anything herself, I also would not have been asked. As for my entrance into TV: 75 per cent for me, 25 per cent for Eero. After all, I had written a book, *The Proud Possessors,* which did very well, and I had been on the *Times,* which is sacred to everyone in television. But I'm not a professional widow.

Saarinen often said she would have liked to be a latter-day Madame de Staël and have a marvelous home frequented by fascinating people and beautiful guests in the manner of the famous Frenchwoman's salon. To her, "For Women Only" was a poor girl's salon. She treated guests as if they were in her own home. She disliked thinking of the program as educational, but it was, especially when she tackled such sensitive issues as homosexuality, abortion, dissidents and the generation gap.

The 1960's also found Judith Crist, movie critic and former *Herald Tribune* reporter, making appearances on television, including weekly appearances on the "Today" show, where she minced no words in her forthright movie criticism. "Today" had already attracted the talents of Barbara Walters, who in 1974 would become co-host on the program. In 1961, however, she was on the staff of writers and made only occasional on-camera appearances. In 1963, after covering President Kennedy's funeral, Walters went on the air regularly and researched, wrote and edited her own special reports and interviewed guests, among them Prince Philip, President Nixon and Henry Kissinger. She was one of three women reporters on Nixon's 1972 China visit.

In the shift from coffee-server to personality on camera, Walters saw the television industry's changing attitudes toward women. "Of course," she told a reporter, "women are competitive, but we're friendlier as a group than the men. I root for Aline Saarinen and the others because I know every success of theirs will open more doors for me."

✳ ✳ ✳

The networks were actually beginning to go out looking for capable women. To many it seemed most important that Pauline Frederick had been the one to break the trail with her intelligent and distinguished UN reporting and demonstrate that women were good reporters, intelligent and capable of working hard under pressure.

It may have been only a slight echo of the wartime years' enthusiasm, but compared to the previous decade the 1960's were years when women made marked gains in television. A dozen or more women took non-camera jobs with the television networks that would lead to some key promotions in the 1970's—including Suzanne Caraher, night news manager for CBS; Margery Baker, associate producer for "CBS Morning News with Hughes Rudd"; Grace M. Diekhaus, producer on

"60 Minutes"; Judy Towers Reemtsma, producer of "In the News" for CBS; Mary O. Yates, coproducer of "Face the Nation;" Virginia Seipt, associate producer in NBC Sports; Cynthia Samuels, CBS assistant foreign editor; Sylvia Westerman, deputy director of CBS News; and Lucy Jarvis, award-winning NBC producer.

Before the decade ended, Liz Trotta was covering the war in Vietnam, Catherine (Cassie) Mackin had joined NBC News, Ponchitta Pierce was a CBS News special correspondent and Joan Richman was producing CBS News coverage of the Apollo 11 moon shot. Richman, who started her career in 1961 clipping newspapers, sat next to Walter Cronkite—but out of camera range—making decisions on when to switch to Houston, when to use film and so on, for all space shots after she joined the CBS special events unit as a researcher-reporter in 1965. (In 1975 she became a sports producer at CBS.)

* * *

Despite a handful of highly talented television newswomen, the truth was that men still thought women were more suited to the lighter topics and prone to be subjective and unauthoritative, charged essayist Marya Mannes in articles in the late 1960's. "Women with the requisite wisdom, experience and presence to communicate with a large public do exist, but who sees them on television in their own right as voices of authority?"

Mannes challenged the double standard that judged male journalists on ability and intelligence, regardless of age or girth, but regards youth and attractiveness as primary qualities for newswomen. How long, she asked, will it be before authoritative women stop "reminding us of our wives or mothers and become people with equally valid views on the affairs of the world?" The issue was to be raised often in the 1970's as the women's liberation movement made news and forced women and men to attend to this social issue.

Women rarely rose beyond middle management in industries, reported a 1969 survey by *Business Week*. A woman starts lower, moves up more slowly and earns less than her male companion; except in unusual circumstances, she will not move into executive positions, the report continued. "And the pattern has changed only slightly in the past 10 years." The picture was true of TV as well. Richard Salant, president of CBS, said:

> It's our own fault—management's—that the networks don't employ more women and that they are frequently assigned to only certain types of stories once they are hired. But women have to fight back. They have to make their presence felt. They must not let their editors or producers segregate them from the general flow of news. They must clamor for general assignment.

A career guide pamphlet published by *Mademoiselle* in 1969 left no illusions: TV journalism and TV producing were still extremely tough fields to break into for a woman because of the "bone-deep male prejudice" that pervaded them.

"We discriminate against women . . . because they don't look like us, act like us or think like us, so we don't want them around in the executive dining room," one film producer told the writer for *Mademoiselle*. He could count the number of women directors on one hand, he said. (It was no change from the number in 1945.) "Women would leave and so why train them?" asked others. "Women are too fragile" to handle the equipment, they added. "A woman cannot be in the position of ultimate boss over men because it is unnatural and because no red-blooded man could take it."

Women already in television were attempting to change these deeply held attitudes, but it wasn't easy. Irina Posner, one of the few female associate producers at CBS News at that time, said she was enthusiastic about her television career. (In 1975 she was producer on the news series "Magazine.") She had outlined the series "Of Black America" and found and shot the much admired school sequence. On location she was usually accompanied by a union film crew, four to six men over 40.

> I feel I'm trespassing in a man's field. They have to treat you as a woman, yet you can't pull the tricks women pull in mixed company. Which role should you play—co-worker or woman?

> Should you let a man help you with your coat or open the door? If so, he may interpret your film directions as an insult to his masculinity because he considers you a woman . . . You have to learn to be an authoritarian and a woman in the classic sense . . . to be known as a good boss and a lady at the same time.

Competition was keen for a relatively small number of jobs at the network level, but educational television where salaries were lower was open to women. Some of the men who worked with ETV had more modern attitudes. One producer who did perceptive, hard-hitting documentaries believed that it took a male and female team to produce these documentaries that interpreted life. He usually hired a woman associate producer for his work, because women "can make a special contribution with their more intuitive approach." This attitude also helped women progress rapidly in ETV.

Joan Cooney achieved prominence with her Children's Television Workshop and its stunning "Sesame Street," through educational television, and Elizabeth ("Liz") Drew, a writer, developed a keen but low-key interviewing technique for her "Thirty Minutes With . . ." for PBS starting in 1971. In a related field, Theodora Sklover directed the "Open Channel" for cable television in Manhattan starting in 1972.

"Serious Attention" to Women's Liberation

American mass media began to give serious attention to something called the women's liberation movement in the spring of 1970 with cover stories by newsmagazines and a gradual turning away from the emphasis on "bra burning" and sniggering tone of much of the early reporting about NOW and other feminist groups that headed the drive for equal treatment and opportunity for women.

The "Today" show marked the 50th anniversary in 1970 of the 19th Amendment to the Constitution that gave women the right to vote by devoting its two-hour program to women with an all-woman cast, featuring five NBC newswomen: Barbara Walters, Pauline Frederick, Aline Saarinen, Liz Trotta and Nancy Dickerson.

The American Women in Radio and Television's New York chapter that fall tuned in on the message from Mary Jean Parson, ABC's associate director for corporate planning to "stop fighting and competing among themselves and become a united force for equality." She urged women in executive positions to fight for equal money for women and equal job opportunities. Those on camera, she said, should produce stories on women who have fought and won battles in their particular fields. In advertising, women should work toward ending the "insidious subjugating sex commercials" that have "ruined us more than any single thing in the country."

Parson, who began her career as an off-Broadway theatre manager, went to ABC-TV in the late 1960's, "at a time when other networks wouldn't even interview women for management positions."

News correspondents in broadcasting are still getting "fluff" assignments, although they have proven they can cover hard news, ABC correspondent Marlene Sanders told the AWRT members. And Joan Murray of WCBS-TV News described the indignities she had suffered as a young, black female reporter from racists, fellow reporters and television viewers. Lucy Jarvis, NBC-TV producer, speaking from the floor, urged the group to redefine its obligations and "make ourselves felt and heard as a strong body and as a professional group."

The determined tone was one that was to characterize the actions of professional media women in the early 1970's, as they resolved, not just to report the progress of women's rights, but to work for equality within their own profession.

Managements made a few important responses as if to acknowledge the talents of women on their staffs. Aline Saarinen was appointed head of the NBC Paris Bureau, the first woman in TV history to become bureau chief. (She died a year later at age 58). Barbara Walters inherited Saarinen's program and renamed it "Not for Women Only," and changed the delivery to suit her own personality. The audience was seated at round tables instead of in rows, and from time to time men were included in the audience, "since many of the subjects are of just as much interest to them as to women," said Walters.

Walters intended to continue updating topics already introduced on the show—birth control and male contraception, for example, and to include topics about the clash of the sexes, the family, church, ethnic groups, TV and children, among others.

Another brief victory was scored in 1971 when Marlene Sanders anchored the ABC Saturday night "Weekend News" for three months during the summer to fill in for an anchorman on temporary Vietnam duty. She had anchored her own daytime ABC television news program for four years and had been the first woman to anchor a network evening newscast for ABC in 1964. The victory was bittersweet. Although the press hailed the event as a breakthrough related to the women's movement, the anchorman returned and Sanders was returned to her regular job, moving later to full-time documentary producer for ABC News.

As Sanders predicted, neither her successful anchoring in 1964 nor again in 1971, made any real changes in network news. No wave of women anchoring network evening news ensued, but a few women were given anchor jobs, usually for the morning or noon news at local stations in several cities. (A few years later ABC put Virginia Sherwood on as a weekend anchor. Liz Trotta had hoped to be considered for an anchor job when Huntley and Brinkley split in 1970.)

"I have the strong feeling," NBC News president Reuven Frank told *Newsweek* that same year, "that audiences are less prepared to accept news from a woman's voice than from a man's."

"They will always come up with some theory about why it cannot work," Sanders said. "I'm not holding my breath."

Anti-Tokenism

Sanders told a 1971 convention of Women in Communications, Inc.:

> Let's look at the record. Out of 42 correspondents at ABC, two are women; at NBC which has a far larger staff, there are four, and at CBS with a very large staff, there is only one, and she is mostly on radio. With all due credit to the net-

work's local outlets in New York, they all have at least one woman, usually black.

She acknowledged her own success and said that the woman's movement had given needed impetus to equality of opportunity for all. "It's simply inexcusable for women to be denied opportunities in broadcast journalism because stations already have one." Women should be encouraged to become qualified and to try for these jobs. And once in, she said, women should work for the right to go anywhere it is necessary to go—including all-male clubs and sports press boxes—to cover the news.

Sanders often told reporters:

> It bothers me that more successful women don't want to be bothered about women's liberation. A lot of them feel they made it on their own, that discrimination didn't keep them out. But there are still things that need to be changed, and I'd like to see them changed.

She often speaks on college campuses, encouraging women to develop their potential and uses her own career, marriage and motherhood as an example of combining all these activities.

Sanders didn't originally start out to be a newscaster; she was headed for a career in TV production. But she landed a job as production assistant on a local TV news show and 10 years later held that job on an interview show called "Night Beat" with Mike Wallace. Wallace conducted in-depth interviews with celebrities from all fields and sent his researchers out to check every quote the subjects had been credited with uttering. His interviews often made headlines, and Sanders learned the news business from pros like Wallace, and she liked it.

Women had indeed "broken into television journalism" by 1971. Each major station had at least one woman on camera; blacks and ethnic minorities were especially popular since stations and networks were under pressure to end discrimination against these categories. The women were called "a new breed" by the press, but essentially they were like their predecessors; they knew they could cover hard news, but they still had to prove it. The difference was that the bosses listened now when women insisted that old-fashioned protectiveness that had for generations kept most women away from "dangerous assignments" should be discarded for a new standard. Women would take care of themselves and assume responsibility for their own risks just as men did.

"I hate fashion stories," exclaimed Connie Chung, who was with WTTG in Washington in 1971. "Give me a tear-gas, rock-throwing riot any time." Their bosses soon learned that these women could take care of themselves and also would bring back their stories. Some news directors learned that although women could be as aggressive as men, "they also had a sympathetic quality, an ability to get right to the human angle," that was particularly effective on television. The movement had given the women both the courage and the backing they had needed to "fight back" and the legal tools against discrimination provided that cutting edge that forced employers to listen and to evaluate women, not as delicate playthings but as professional journalists. On that basis—as ever—they would succeed or fail in the tough competition ahead.

New forms of programming for women began to appear between the soaps and game shows still prominent in daytime TV in 1972, but only one, Dinah Shore's "Dinah's Place," on NBC-TV was network. The others were local, but all were attempting to tackle topics of greater sophistication and intellectuality, and a wider range of topics than had been typical of traditional "women's programs."

These included producer Raysa R. Bonow's Boston WBZ-TV all-woman produced "For Woman Today," which boasted a 20 per cent male audience and did not preach feminist ideology but approached living and new feminist concepts subtly and with a view of what the woman's movement is all about. Others were "Tomorrow's Woman," a syndicated program by Eleanor Riger and directed by Lela Swift; "Woman!" on WCBS-TV, produced by Phillis Adams with Sherrye Henry as hostess; "Everywoman" on WTOP in Washington, and six-year-old "Contact" with Marie Torre at KDKA-TV in Pittsburgh, which used a telephone-in talk format to cover topics running from sex, death and narcotics to women's liberation, cooking and even tennis.

Challenge to the Media

Talk was translated into action as NOW and other feminist groups, first in New York and Washington and then in other cities, charged that television projected a distorted image of women, did not pay sufficient regard to programming for a large segment of its audience and discriminated against women in hiring, pay and promotion policies.

Using the mechanism provided for station license challenges at renewal time, the 1964 Civil Rights Act, Title VII of the Equal Employment Opportunity Act, which prohibits discrimination against minorities or women, and an FCC ruling of December 17, 1971, that required stations to file affirmative action programs with their license renewals, NOW groups began their challenge.

Teams of women amassed statistics, charts and examples to support their claims. Employment of women in the commercial television stations accounted for only 22 per cent of the total in 1971 and 75 per cent of those were in office and clerical jobs, they found. Public television's record was better— women held 28 per cent of the total jobs; about half of the women were in office and clerical positions. Both were lower than the national average of one third of the full-time labor force that was female.

Two license challenges in particular gained a lot of attention. One was against WRC-TV, the local NBC affiliate in Washington, D.C.; the other against WABC-TV, the flagship station in New York for ABC. Not until March, 1975, was any action taken, however, and then the FCC rejected the petition to deny licenses on the discrimination ground charged.

The first challenge was mounted on May 1, 1972, when New York's NOW chapter filed a petition to deny the license renewal of WABC-TV on the ground that it knowingly violated three FCC requirements—ascertainment of the needs and interests of its audience; fairness in presenting controversial issues; and equal opportunity in employment.

The report said, "Much of the discrimination stems from unfair and highly prejudicial stereotypes which are force-fed in a daily barrage by radio and television to millions of men, women and children."

Television portrayed women unfairly and ignored their needs for services and other information. Women at WABC-TV held only 8 per cent of official and managerial jobs, 12 per cent of professional jobs, but 72 per cent of office and clerical jobs, and only 10 per cent of the newsroom positions were held by women—although 23.3 per cent of the total employment at the station was female.

Direct bias against the women's movement was charged and documented with examples of offhand and biased comments made during a variety of programs. The challenge precipitated a series of meetings between management and ABC women and a Women's Action Committee was established at ABC in the fall of 1972.

In Washington, D.C., a discrimination complaint was lodged against WRC-TV, the NBC-owned station, with the city's Human Relations Commission in February, 1971. In October a suit was filed with the EEOC charging discrimination in various categories. Then in September, 1972, ten local women's groups filed a petition to deny NBC its license renewal on the basis of charges similar to those in the ABC suit, plus violations of the fairness doctrine by presenting a biased point of view of women's role in society and ridiculing or withholding information about the women's rights movement. At this station 22 per cent of the jobs were held by women, and 81 per cent were in clerical jobs. No women were in top management positions and there were 3 women among 17 reporters, and only one woman network correspondent of 20. They, too, compiled a list of degrading remarks made by men on the air about women.

Women's groups continued the barrage of challenges and suits, and although no licenses were removed, a good many affirmative action programs were written and some improvements in hiring, pay and promotion procedures made. Station KDKA-TV in Pittsburgh became the first station in the U.S. to enter into an agreement that dealt exclusively with the issues raised by the women's rights movement and problems of women in society in their news and public affairs program-ming—to broaden sports coverage to include women's ath-letics; to eliminate sexist language; and to improve hiring and employment policies for women. Women employees at CBS had won the right to wear pants at the office during working hours early in 1970 when they struck against that unwritten law.

Public and Minority Access

Another interesting action by women's groups in 1973 re-sulted in authorization of an all-woman's cable television channel in Memphis, Tennessee. Women's clubs from NOW to the garden clubs joined to seize the opportunity provided by FCC regulations governing cable TV franchising that at least one channel be set aside for minority groups and one for public access. These women made certain that one channel was committed to women's affairs.

At CBS the message seemed to have been communicated without resort to legal procedures. CBS president Arthur Tay-lor issued a policy memo in February, 1973, stating his inten-tion to "find solutions to the flood of problems identified by the women's movement." He said that CBS policy allowed men and women the same opportunities for employment and promotion within CBS, and that there was a single standard of qualification for employment and for treatment after employ-ment. That same month Marietta Tree was appointed a com-pany director, the second women to hold that post.

Women at CBS thought there was some room for improve-ment and questioned the mechanisms for working out some of the problems. They presented CBS with their grievances that April, pointing out the small numbers of women in certain categories of employment.

Although 42 per cent of the work force at CBS was female in 1970, among the staff of 30 to 40 correspondents there were only 2 women, compared to 5 out of 56 at NBC and 12 out of 44 at ABC. There were no female directors, only one female crew member out of 92, 21 producers out of 126, 3 women film edi-tors out of 64 and 6 news writers out of 25 at CBS.

CBS News president Richard Salant said his "consciousness was raised rather late" but he promised to rectify this dismal situation. CBS embarked on a program of changes that by 1975 included: increased promotions and a general revamping of women's salaries upward; a 6-month maternity and paternity leave program; in-house training programs to aid employees to qualify for promotion; appointment of four directors of women's programs to counsel women on career choices and all employment problems; posting of all new job openings; and a series of consciousness-raising sessions for management designed to change the attitudes of men and women in the work setting.

The seminars stressed that the attitudes most women had toward their jobs grew out of the cultural training and conditions they have been subjected to, that men do the choosing and women wait to be chosen, partly because women are raised not to take the initiative.

Men who had taken the seminars began to make new observations about the outside world, CBS reported, such as the father who suddenly became aware that his talented daughter whom he thought could be a doctor or professor was emulating traditional roles. He and others like him suggested that this seminar material be taught in the public schools.

Cathy Krein, editorial director and associate producer of CBS Special Events unit, said

> Here at CBS News men think nothing of answering a phone and few expect to be waited on. The CBS handbook has eliminated sexist language, several women producers and a second camerawoman have been hired and positions for technicians are beginning to open up, but unions and seniority are problems.

The women's group meets monthly and was working on an on-site day care center, which Krein thinks would be quite workable in the informal atmosphere at CBS News. The women's group started with high energy and good attendance at CBS, she recalled, and it has become hard to keep up the momentum, but:

> We can't sit back now after winning promotions. Women have to realize that when we get where we are going, we will

still have to keep at it until we become the best at that job. If you are a producer, you have to be thinking of going on; you can't stagnate. In this industry there is never an opportunity to relax, and women are starting to gear up that way now. It's extremely competitive and you just have to stay on top of the news, all the time.

I'd like to see it get to the point where the best person is selected for each job, but right now (1975) women have a slight edge.

The experience has had another interesting result, Krein continued,

Women are learning to be supportive and learning to put in a good word for other women when jobs open up. Men have always done that; women are just learning to enjoy the informal strategy. Men are taken aback by our refusal to cat on each other, because we used to be forced to be petty and catty. There is progress, but women won't have made it until they are the presidents, vice-presidents and publishers.

Not surprisingly 1973 brought a series of impressive female promotions at the networks and FCC figures for 1974 showed that commercial television had increased its total employment of women from 22 to 24 per cent since 1971, but in the top level jobs that increase went from 6 to 11 per cent. Public television had increased its total number of women from 28 to 31 per cent and at the top level from 15 to 19 per cent in the four years in which the networks have had to report these employment statistics.

Despite these gains, a 1975 Task Force on Women in Public Broadcasting report criticized the CPB for its treatment of women in programming and employment and asked them to increase the number of women in decision-making positions and to implement fully the equal pay for equal work policy. Women held slightly less than 30 per cent of all jobs in public broadcasting, the study group learned, but were clustered at the bottom, mostly as secretaries.

Attitudes were improving. A 1973 study of television directors and female staffers showed that 89 per cent of the news directors rated women's job performance high and they reported no special problem posed by women on their staffs. Although two-thirds of the women said they had experienced discrimination, bias against them was decreasing, they thought, and three-quarters of them felt that they were being treated equally with men. In a 1972 survey by the same university, the researcher established that 11 per cent of all television news and television-radio news personnel were women, and 8 per cent of radio news staffs were women, a considerable increase from the 4.7 per cent reported in 1965.

Gains were apparent in many areas; women were more visible at the network level. By 1974 CBS and ABC each had 5 and NBC had 8 women correspondents. Four women had been promoted to vice-presidential jobs in 1973 and Eleanor Riger became the first female staff producer for ABC Network Sports and aired a one-hour special on women athletes the following January. Lin Bolen was appointed the first woman director of network daytime programs at NBC. And at CBS, Sylvia Westerman, a former co-producer of "Face the Nation" and a regular part of the political convention production team since 1964, was moved to New York to become the ranking woman in management at CBS News. She is deputy director of news.

Affirmative Action at All Levels

Camerawomen were again seen at the networks, whereas before that only the independent TV producers had hired them, and a few women appeared as technicians, electricians and sound persons and were attempting to join the unions for those crafts. ABC produced a series of five 90-minute dramatic shows using an all-female production team led by producer Jacqueline Babbin. As had been done at least once before on radio during World War II, Babbin managed to appoint an associate producer, two directors, an associate director, production assistants, casting director and sound supervisor who were women. Only the chief executive for the program was a man.

Although NBC was pleased with its affirmative action program which had nearly doubled the percentage of women in executive and managerial positions from 6.5 per cent to 12 per cent in the period between 1971 and 1974 and had increased the percentage of women in professional categories from 16 to

25, the New York City Commission on Human Rights handed down a finding in January, 1975, that said that although there was no indication that NBC had intended practices that limited female employment, the result was that they did have this effect. The report did take note of NBC's measurable gains since 1972. The report covered the years from 1967 to 1974. (ABC had also circulated an affirmative action plan in 1973.)

Negotiations between NBC and the women's group broke down and the women went to court. The Federal Court in New York City ruled that the Women's Committee for Equal Opportunity Employment did represent a class of women at NBC, and the judge urged both sides to negotiate. The women wanted NBC to set goals and timetables and to begin training programs. They were discouraged over management's unwillingness to involve them in planning and discussion sessions on these issues. NBC in the spring of 1976 did hire a woman as vice-president and her job was to come up with an affirmative action plan for NBC. A consulting firm was also hired to re-evaluate women's jobs. But the women's group was still not being involved or reporting regularly to management as at ABC and CBS. In the spring of 1977, NBC settled the suit with a $2 million payment.

$$* \quad * \quad *$$

Women were being taken seriously in program content in 1974 and 1975. Marlene Sanders wrote and produced "Woman's Place," an hour-long special examining the changing role of women in today's society and Barbara Walters and Tom Snyder co-anchored a three-hour special "Of Women and Men," a 1975 study on changing American sexual attitudes.

Women had also moved into more documentary producing. Lucy Jarvis at NBC had been alone in that male field since the early 1960's. Her most famous documentary probably was "The Kremlin" in 1963 and her most recent prize-winning program was "What Price Health?" In 1975 Marlene Sanders and Pam Hill were producing documentaries at ABC, Joan Richman and Meg Osmer were with the "Reasoner Report," and Sylvia Chase was working with Dan Rather's documentary unit. Chase, who co-anchors the CBS-TV "Magazine" daytime news special—which has dealt with special issues including marriage, divorce, financial crises, rape, supermarkets and unnecessary hysterectomies—has all female associate producers on that program but a male executive producer. Chase predicted that few if any men would be producing women's interest shows by 1978.

When Marlene Sanders produced, late in 1975, "Women's Health: A Question of Survival" for ABC's "Closeup" Series, she was able to put together an all-woman crew. "We enjoyed working together; everybody was involved in the story." The program—which dealt with breast cancer, birth control devices and pills and their use, and government regulation—was aired January 5, 1976, and generated a record response of 400 letters, many of which requested repeat showings because the program had been so informative. (The documentary and Sanders won WICI's 1976 Clarion award.)

Later that month ABC promoted Sanders to the highest news executive position held by a woman in broadcasting, vice-president in charge of documentaries. An activist in ABC's woman's group for the preceding four years, Sanders believes that ABC is the most progressive network in terms of dealing with women employees. Much of this recently is due to the work of the woman's group and management's response. The group reports quarterly to management and feels management has responded.

Sanders said, "Women at ABC are involved at all levels of the operation." She explained that, "ingrained male attitudes have been the problem." In an effort to reduce these prejudices, ABC started monthly sensitivity sessions for management in 1977. "Even at ABC, women still have to fight prejudice." Women newscasters still have to be better looking than male newscasters do, but Sanders predicted that as men's attitudes mature on this point, they will hire differently.

She herself has experienced little prejudice, but she also developed enough credentials so that nobody could quarrel with her capabilities or professionalism. In her new job she will be doing the hiring and firing and developing documentary ideas for ABC.

> We have to come up with subjects that television deals with well, something that people care about. . . . we want to do things in the most effective way. We're not going to create instant revolutions, but we do have a lot of influence.

Detroit news director Phil Nye of WXYZ-TV credited women with pioneering specials on rape and vasectomy. "Women's impact has really added to the quality of our news," he said. In New York City alone, in 1974, 16 women covered spot news for local television. At the network level in Washington, D.C., Marilyn Berger, Carole Simpson, Catherine Mackin and Linda Ellerbee at NBC; Lesley Stahl, Marya McLaughlin and Connie Chung at CBS; and Ann Compton and Virginia Sherwood at ABC handled hard news. Other network correspondents were: Liz Trotta, Rebecca Bell, Betty Rollin and Gail Christian at NBC; Ann Medina, Anne Kaestner, Bettina Gregory and Elizabeth Coleman at ABC; and Sylvia Chase and Sharron Lovejoy at CBS.

It must have seemed a long step forward when Betty Furness was invited to NBC to do a consumer column on its local news program in 1974. She looked back ruefully to her 1952 television experience in Westinghouse live commercials during NBC's election coverage. When she tried to land a news reporting job in 1960 no one would hire her. They said it was because of the commercials.

Several years later, Furness realized that there was also another reason: she was a woman. By 1974, however, she had became an expert in consumer affairs, having worked for President Johnson and the state of New York in that capacity, and newswomen were "in." Her program receives about 900 letters a week and each one is answered. Some are used on the air, others furnish ideas for the consumer complaints she investigates and discusses daily on WNBC-TV's two-hour evening news program.

✳ ✳ ✳

Barbara Walters' elevation to co-host on the "Today" show when Frank McGee died "made a great deal of difference to me about how I felt on the program," she told AWRT members in 1974. "I never asked a major question until Frank had asked his . . . and it's also made it easier to get some of the hard-to-get interviews."

Walters explained that when her contract was renewed in 1973 she had asked to be made co-host if a new host was needed. When she saw a news release that NBC was looking for a new host to replace McGee, she reminded them of the new clause in her contract.

Women executives must be determined, not tough or hard or unfeeling, she said, and added that there is a difference in the way women handle things. It took her 40 years, she said, to "get a sense of herself," but she hopes her daughter will have an easier time choosing her life style.

Walters was concerned about her own durability on television. "Men don't have to worry about getting older," she said. But she didn't know how people would feel about her as she grows older. "If I'm not around at 50 you'll know the answer."

Young women often write to her and say that her experience is an example to them. They think, "If Barbara Walters could do it, so can I." To this she replies that eventually they'll learn that it can't be done without hard work. "The women's movement just makes that very steep hill a little easier to climb."

Although Walters made it up the hill before the movement began, she has noticed that the movement has made a real difference in raising the consciousness of news departments in on-air coverage and in creating a general climate of equality.

"I notice that younger people like Jim Hartz have no trouble accepting me as co-host, while an older man like Frank McGee did."

CBS and ABC both flunked their first well-promoted attempts to compete directly with Walters by introducing Sally Quinn and Stephanie Edwards as star personalities to co-host their morning shows in 1974 and 1975. Succeeding women were tried out for these roles with less fanfare. ABC finally hired Margaret Osmer, an experienced TV reporter-producer at CBS, to read the news on "Good Morning America."

In the spring of 1976, however, ABC attracted Barbara Walters away from NBC with a five-year contract to co-anchor the evening news with Harry Reasoner. She was to be American network television's first full-time anchorwoman and television's highest paid journalist at $1 million a year. Her new assignment included the opportunity to produce four prime-time specials each year and occasionally to host ABC's Sunday interview program, "Issues and Answers."

NBC had offered a roughly equivalent salary, it was reported, but apparently no promise of anchoring. Her personality status was expected to bring a larger portion of the audience to ABC News, which had long been third in the ratings for network news, and it capped a season in which ABC came within a hair of being the most watched network. Instant response from several journalists was to belittle Walters for her limited experience in hard news and to scorn her as a "star" while ignoring her demonstrated and often-praised ability as one of television's most skillful interviewers. Once she appeared at the anchor spot and turned in a flawless and professional performance, the grumbling disappeared and the plaudits returned for TV's most well-known newswoman. But problems with her co-anchor surfaced.

*   *   *

Walters' exit from NBC left two choice jobs open. NBC carefully tried out a succession of experienced television newswomen for the "Today" and "Not for Women Only" programs. Local anchorwoman, Jane Pauley, from WMAQ-TV, NBC's Chicago affiliate station, was selected in the fall of 1976 to fill the "Today" job with host Tom Brokaw. She did not get the co-host title.

Pauley had been a TV reporter for only four years, but according to NBC, she stood out as the most popular with viewers during the final trials in competition with Betty Furness, Catherine Mackin, Linda Ellerbee and Betty Rollin. She works hard, is highly articulate, serious but warm, and according to her former boss at WISH-TV in Indianapolis, "On TV she blossoms. She just has that special quality not many people in this business have. You can't define it, it's just there."

The newswomen on the TV screen today, if indeed they are a new breed, have already turned in an impressive record of handling breaking news, partly because they are extremely talented and experienced and partly because they have been give the chance to show what they could do. Michele Clark of CBS (killed in a plane crash) and Catherine Mackin of NBC covered the 1972 political convention. Lesley Stahl of CBS, who worked on the running Watergate story, and Barbara Walters of NBC joined newsmen in reporting and commenting on election returns in 1974. Stahl was the first woman to serve as regional anchor of CBS News as she reported on the key races and issues in the West. Mackin, after a two-year assignment in the California bureau, was in Washington in 1974 doing political reporting and being groomed for the 1976 political convention. In 1976, Stahl covered the West for CBS and Mackin covered the Senate races for NBC. At ABC, Walters was one of three anchors and Ann Compton covered the gubernatorial races during the 1976 presidential election night coverage. By late fall Mackin was anchoring the weekend evening news.

Stahl, who began television reporting in Boston in 1970, said that there has been improvement for women in broadcast news since she started. She enjoys the thrill of deadline pressure as breaking stories like Watergate develop. Her favorite assignments are longer investigative pieces like the one she did about a Philadelphia building that was sinking just as the General Services Administration had predicted. "We women get assigned to any story now, and no one seems to think twice about it." She enjoys that.

When Stahl was assigned to the Watergate story it was apparently a simple robbery and she was helping Daniel Schorr on the story. As events developed, CBS added Frank Graham, but she stayed on the story. She was not the top reporter but she thinks that was because of her inexperience, not because of her sex. On the other hand, she served during the 1974 elections because the network was actively looking for a woman for that job. "To be honest, being a female at CBS has been a real asset for me," she said.

✳ ✳ ✳

Being a newswoman can sometimes also create credibility problems with sources, Connie Chung found out. She had been a reporter with CBS News since 1971 and had covered the House Judiciary Committee hearings on the impeachment of President Nixon in 1974. She had also covered Senator George McGovern's 1972 presidential campaign and was a member of the CBS News team at the Democratic National Convention. She was permanently assigned to cover the new Vice-President, Nelson Rockefeller, which meant dogging his trail wherever he went.

"I lost my innocence about the job of reporting when Rockefeller questioned my credentials," she told a college audience in Ohio in the spring of 1975. "We had asked him frequently if he was going to run for the presidency in 1980." She said she asked him again on Air Force 2 after a meeting. "At first he refused to answer, and just as the camera ran out of film, he said that he would not be a candidate in 1980 because of his age and relationship to President Ford." Chung had the crew reload and turn on the lights again. She asked him to repeat his statement for the camera. Her job was to get the statement on film; "It's no good just having him tell me." "Your field isn't politics," he said. He was annoyed and refused to repeat his remark. She explained that it would be on all the wires, since he had said it for the record and she was the "camera pool" for the trip. "Right then I decided I was in the right profession. I was happy to find out that I had the courage to stand up to him and argue."

Chung said she had become more aggressive since becoming a newswoman, but she still tries to be herself. "Why should I have to change my personality to do the job?" she asked. "There is a difficult dichotomy for women in news—you have to be tough to handle the story, but you also have to look good. The war," she concluded, "has not been won. We still need more victories."

The war didn't deter her, though. Chung enjoys the job and likes being on the air. Although she seems "to be working all the time" and the job has severely cut down her social life, she hopes it will last for some time. She said she was not very interested in anchoring or producing, but she does enjoy appearing on panel shows and would be willing to be a commentator, although she didn't expect that to happen for a long time. (In the fall of 1976 she accepted an anchor spot at KNYT in Los Angeles.)

"I really like being a reporter, covering news and reporting it. And there's some security in not being 'it.' Television news jobs are vulnerable," Chung explained. "You may be 'it' one day and 'not it' the next. I'm not a star and I can easily be sent day after day on stories that end on the cutting room floor." But she added that she also had the freedom to suggest stories and see them through.

People expect women to be competing to be "it" and to some extent, Chung admitted,

> Of course we do compete. But we—Chung, Marya McLaughlin and Lesley Stahl—get along and we are happy when the others do good stories. Marya got the tax story day after day and Lesley was on election night. Sure, I'd have liked to have been there. But their success is good for all of us. It means they think more of the women when they give us assignments like that.

Being a woman hasn't really given her any problems in her job, except at the beginning, Chung said.

> For the first couple of years it was difficult; you have to establish your credibility and build your own confidence. Once you've been around for a while, people recognize you, know your work and respect you. Sometimes being a woman is actually an advantage. In a large group of journalists all the men tend to look alike, and sometimes that distinction of being a woman is enough to catch the interviewee's eye and get your question asked.

Chung said she was not a joiner and not an advocate. She believes firmly in objective journalism as a goal. She has her own private opinions on issues, but she keeps them to herself. She also thinks that she serves the women's cause better by doing her job well than she could if she began pushing the issue, even though she appreciates what the women are doing.

The question of good looks is often raised to newswomen. At first Chung said, she felt that she had to overcome the audience's first reaction of "Look, she's Chinese," but now she thinks they are listening to what she says. When someone asks if female newscasters will be relegated to off-camera work or radio as they age, Chung kids back that "she will be on the air longer than most because Chinese people don't age very fast." Seriously, she adds that her generation of women reporters will last as long as men have in the past because ability becomes more and more important as a reporter reaches middle age.

> If a man is a general assignment correspondent and hasn't attained some sort of star status or specialty by his 40's, he'll languish regardless of his looks and we women will, too.

✳   ✳   ✳

Norma Quarles of WNBC's local New York evening news, "Newscenter 4," agrees that once you're over being the "new kid on the block and they know you can perform, you don't have to prove yourself again." She enjoys working on local news because it "can be very meaningful to the life of the city and can have an important impact." She often has time to develop series and investigative pieces, such as the one on a stripper who had been brutally assaulted and whose assailant had received a light sentence because of the woman's profession. That series won an award.

"The pressure in New York, even on local news, is terrific," she warned, and she was happy that she had gained her experience before the New York offer came along. In the 1960's the stations were under pressure to hire blacks and women, or black women, and. . .

> When we came in, at first we were given powder puff assignments. But the 1960's were also very volatile and education and welfare, which had been placid beats, also became volatile. Schools were in a turmoil, there was Kent State, race riots and welfare mothers' marches.

Quarles covered them all for a Cleveland station. "After that experience, I felt I could do almost any story," she recalled.

Quarles had observed dramatic changes in the newsroom in

her five years at WNBC-TV. At first there was only about one woman per station on the air, and none behind the scenes except secretaries to executives.

> Now there are 8 or 9 on the staff plus women technicians, a director, producer, camerawoman, sound woman, electrician and film editors. At least 8 women are on air regularly on WNBC's "Newscenter 4" two-hour daily evening report, including investigative reporter Liz Trotta.
> There are still few women executives, and although these are dramatic changes, it's very good as long as it doesn't stop there. We need to see a natural growth by women into middle management and executive positions and a willingness on the part of women to accept those jobs.
> Women in these jobs now need to continue to strive, not stagnate . . . and not walk around with self-pity or chips on their shoulders. We'll have to be persistent and take opportunities. There's still a lot of racism and sexism around, but we have to settle for minor victories and fight in the capacity we're in.

Long range career commitment and professional attitudes characterize these successful television newswomen and they also typify the new ones coming along. Lee Thornton, who joined CBS in 1974 after two years in news at a midwest station, has definite plans for the future. She got into television because stations were looking for black women but she also had a doctorate in mass communications and teaching experience in speech. She advised college students:

> Get the basic skills at the local broadcast level before trying to break into the network. Then take any entry job you can get and once inside keep after them to try you out; audition for any openings. You have to be aggressive to get the job you want. You can move up from secretary, but you do have to push.

An Enterprise Story

It was easier to get in when she did than it was two years later, Lee Thornton thought. She was happy that her opportunity came after she had gained some experience. "I never dreamed when I was young that I'd be on the tube . . . on news . . . but I am. And I like what I'm doing; that's my motivation."

Thornton's first network job was reporter-assignment editor, a beginning assignment in which she spent two days a week on the assignment desk and the other three days doing general reporting assignments. She had opportunities to suggest stories and thought the best one she had done so far was an enterprise story about a successful voluntary busing program in Boston that was working, bringing inner city kids to the suburban schools.

> I went to my boss and said, I want to do that story. He let me go out on it. I spent two full days filming. It was the story of Calvin Smith and the apple tree. It was aired November 4, 1974, on the morning news show, "still too much of a feature for the evening."
>
> Calvin Smith was 14 years old and he talked in imagery. We used his images to shape the story . . . his comments over the bus ride and his band practice. He told us "It's wonderful to go on the bus because I can see trees and apples growing." We shot him riding on the bus. He stays after school for band practice and we showed that as we used his words saying "when I go home at night I don't think about the dirty streets and the drug addicts down the street."

Thornton said that this kind of journalism;

> . . . . tells the world what kind of lives people are living and how they meet their challenges. And these stories are remembered. This is a touch that many women have— Charles Kuralt has it, too—good hard news judgment plus human interest. A teriffic combination.
>
> Are we the gentler sex? Innately softer . . . more loving . . . and thank God. But the job of the journalist takes aggressiveness and tenacity, although that does not mean hard-edged rudeness. It also takes audacity, the audacity to ask questions and permission time and again although you know you'll be refused 50 per cent of the time.
>
> And it takes physical health and stamina to meet unbelievable demands such as working six nights a week for six months with two overnights (midnight to 8 a.m.) each week. You have to be a versatile personality, be fast and accurate. At the network level you are not allowed mistakes of fact or it can land you on your *other* career.

Thornton was promoted to a full-time correspondent's position with CBS in Washington, D.C. in 1976.

*　　*　　*

In study after study researchers found that successful TV newswomen entered the profession after a variety of other jobs, and frequently their first jobs in broadcasting were not in news. Melba Tolliver is a good example of this career path. She studied nursing first, but became fascinated with TV and wanted to become a TV researcher. She got a job as a secretary in order to find out about the news business.

Tolliver was a secretary to the network operations manager at ABC when the AFTRA union struck and ABC needed a quick fill-in for Marlene Sanders' "News with the Woman's Touch." Tolliver was asked to do that job, and after the strike she became a trainee at ABC. She returned to New York University for classes in writing and reporting, and in 1967 again sat in for Sanders during another strike.

The second time it wasn't a lark, recalled Tolliver. She felt uncomfortable as a strikebreaker. She also knew enough about TV to know what it took to do a good job. And she wanted to do a good job. In 1968 ABC hired her as a general assignment reporter for their local station. Later she was made co-host of "Like It Is," a weekly public affairs program and co-anchor of the Sunday hour news.

Tolliver enjoyed working on local news because of its close links to the city. But she also liked anchoring. "It gives you the opportunity to make changes and shape the quality and tone of the coverage. And that can be a very rewarding experience," she said.

In 1976 Tolliver was enjoying a professional sabbatical as a National Endowment for the Humanities journalism fellow at the University of Michigan where she was studying American art, history, black and women's studies. She would return to New York, but to a new job at WNBC News.

*　　*　　*

Women and minorities are at a new stage in their development as professional journalists, Tolliver thought as she looked ahead. For years they had been trying to get in and to be as good as their white, male role models. But now that they have been accepted for their own polished, professional journalism, it may be the time to ask if their presence will enlarge the definition of news. Barbara Walters had suggested as much in an unprecedented personal editorial credo on her first night of anchoring at ABC. Walters promised to try to make the news more understandable and to pay special attention to issues like consumer news, women's stories and health, which are of special concern to women and which had often been ignored by network news.

The woman's movement certainly helped open reporting jobs to women in radio and television at a time when TV was expanding, said Nancy Dickerson. In 1976 "we are well beyond tokenism. The movement has given women an opportunity to cover all subjects," she said, "but we will not really have arrived until women are allowed to share in the top decision-making and to do regular political commentary, Shana Alexander's commentaries on CBS's "60 Minutes" are important, she added, but she is not a network employee. "And that makes a lot of difference."

It was unfortunate, Dickerson explained in a WUOM radio interview, that the woman's movement had been misunderstood by many men. "We don't want your toy, whatever it is. All we want is our individuality, our personhood, our ability to live and to be. We are not a threat to you; we just want to do our own thing."

But doing our own thing, she admitted, might seem threatening to male executives because it would mean one more contestant in the high level competition for executive power. "Men are much more willing to admit women as reporters and correspondents than as executives. It will take much longer for them to admit us into the decision-making jobs."

But there was some indication that even this would happen on a greater scale in the future. Both CBS and ABC were conducting regular management training and sensitivity sessions for men and women at the network, thus encouraging men and women to face their particular prejudices and to deal with them and encouraging women to gain the information and competence needed to qualify for management jobs. CBS received a national service award from the Employment Management Association in 1975 for its "far-reaching and multi-faceted effort to expand the opportunities and encourage the aspirations of women and minorities."

And researchers were helping stamp out the myth of women's "lack of credibility" as newscasters by documenting through carefully monitored tests that audiences really thought women were as acceptable, believable and effective as male newscasters. The nightly presence of capable, effective women correspondents and anchors working alongside men and being treated as equals by their male colleagues was effectively removing that old barrier. The League of Women Voters helped things along by selecting Pauline Frederick and Barbara Walters as moderators in two of the 1976 Presidential debates and Elizabeth Drew and Marilyn Berger as reporters.

Pauline Frederick said in 1975 after she had been retired from television for a year, "Women have many more opportunities now than they did when I first came into television. But there is still a considerable distance to go until women have completely equal treatment in hiring, assignments and promotions."

Frederick, who continued to cover the UN for National Public Radio in 1975, was awarded her 20th honorary doctorate and elected to New York's Deadline Club of Sigma Delta Chi (The Society of Professional Journalists) as one of the top 10 journalists in the last 50 years. One other woman, Sylvia Porter, made that list which also included James Reston and Walter Cronkite.

The rumblings of discontent from women in 1972 had been heard and changes had been made. Women had organized, stood up to their managements, used the law to enforce their stands and continued to turn in professional work in their jobs. Things had improved enough to give Marlene Sanders a glimmer of hope:

> Women have found a new camaraderie, and we have all gained from that—in growing confidence and courage . . . We have made this happen ourselves . . . We must continue to work together.

· SOURCES CONSULTED ·

William W. Bowman, "Distaff Journalists: Women as a Minority Group in the News Media," Unpublished Ph.D. dissertation, University of Illinois, 1974.

Columbine, Vol 3, #6, Feb. 1975.

Nancy K. Gray, "Before Barbara Walters There Was Dorothy Fuldheim," *Ms.* December, 1976, pp. 40–45.

Ralph M. Jennings, *Television Station Employment Practices: The Status of Minorities and Women* (New York: United Church of Christ, 1973).

Kathleen Kienzle, "A Study of the Employment Opportunities For Women in Broadcast News," Unpublished M.A., Ohio State University, 1965.

Marya Mannes, "Should Women Only be Seen and Not Heard?" *TV Guide,* Nov. 23, 1968.

"Olivetti Girls Aren't Forever," *Broadcasting,* Aug. 7, 1972.

Marlene Sanders, "An Overnight Success," *Matrix,* Fall, 1971.

Vernon A. Stone, "Attitudes Toward Television Newswomen," *Journal of Broadcasting,* Winter 73–74.

Susan Whittaker and Ron Whittaker, "Relative Effectiveness of Male & Female Newscasters," *Journal of Broadcasting,* Spring, 1976.

WUOM "Background," interview with Nancy Dickerson, October, 1976.

CBS-News Library, CBS, NBC, ABC (information departments), *Mademoiselle* career literature.

Personal interviews with Connie Chung, Pauline Frederick, Betty Furness, Cathy Krein, Norma Quarles, Marlene Sanders, Lesley Stahl, Lee Thornton and Melba Tolliver.

6

* * *

Peopling the Women's Pages

AFTER NEARLY A CENTURY of promoting the idea that "woman's place is in the home," the women's pages of the late 1960's were re-evaluated and so were their audiences.

The women's liberation movement insisted that women be seen as people who were in fact engaged in a whole world of activities, no longer confined only to home and family. Why should the women's pages be limited to fashion, food and homemaking? Men and women were (or should be) interested in family life, health, the quality of goods they consume and the quality of life in and outside the home, went the argument. Then, why not drop the women-only angle and look at people, at human affairs, families and life styles?

Re-evaluating the Women's Pages

These were the ideas behind the changing image of the women's pages in American newspapers. In part these changes were in response to the issues raised by the women's liberation movement; in part these pages had been changing since the 1950's. In a receptive era of social change, some of the old stereotypes about women seemed hopelessly dated by the facts about women of the 1970's, and new names and fresh editorial approaches seemed appropriate.

More than half the adult American women between the ages of 18 and 64 were in the labor force. An increasing proportion of them were over 30; many headed families. Most women worked because they had to, not just to earn "pin money." Women were underpaid, under-utilized and over-educated for the jobs they held, and their jobs often were the least desirable and had the lowest status. More than ever before women were a long-term labor force, a fact made possible by declining birth rates that limited the active child-rearing years to 10 or less for most women.

The woman of 40 who had raised children found herself in an efficient, modern house with little work to do for the 25 active years remaining until legal retirement. She had a dated education or job skill in a youth-oriented market. This emerging social problem made re-training and re-entry in the job market necessary for such women.

Women's pages with their tradition-bound vision of woman as happy housewife/mother/sweetheart were missing the story right under their noses: women were quietly becoming people! But part of the reason the newspapers ignored the change lay in the origin and conception of women's pages. Pages for women appeared first in the big city newspapers of the 1890's when advertisers and editors realized that women controlled most of the dollars spent on consumable goods and advertising was the financial lifeblood for the mass media.

As economist John Kenneth Galbraith said recently, "The decisive contribution of women in the developed industrial society is . . . to facilitate a continuity and more or less unlimited increase in consumption."

The social and political structure, he added, encourages her to take on the role of administrator and overseer of the family's increasing consumption as they rise in status. The woman's pages helped the process along.

By the end of the 1960's, however, some editors were searching for a new identity for their pages. Three approaches emerged in American newspapers of the 1970's. The first, and most progessive, was to re-think the purpose of these pages in a contemporary context. These editors brought out new pages that reflected a wider range of interests and readers—life style, culture, family living and social problems. Their titles: "Style," "View," "Day," "Living Today," in the Washington *Post*, L.A. *Times*, St. Petersburg *Times* and Miami *Herald*, to name a few.

A pioneer in this approach was the Washington *Post* with its 1969 "Style" section, which dropped the "anything about women goes on the women's page" idea and insisted that news stories about women appear in the appropriate news sections of the newspaper. "Style" concentrated on styles of life in and beyond the nation's capital.

A second and earlier approach, and one that was more typical, was to change the title of the section to suggest the newly enlarged outlook and content but also to retain all the standard features of the former women's sections. For most of these newspapers there was little change in staff, whereas the *Post*'s approach also encouraged and attracted male staffers to the section.

A third approach was just to wait and see what would happen. This was more characteristic of small-town dailies and weeklies than of the urban press. But even some of the smaller newspapers included articles on the Equal Rights Amendment and abortion reform in traditional women's pages.

An Associated Press Managing Editor's study of women's pages in 1975 showed that most papers had taken the middle road—printing more leisure-and-life style stories while keeping the basics of the former women's section. The larger circulation papers were most likely to change to life style sections.

Special sections could just as well be used to feature brides, fashion or food as anything else, Grand Rapids (Michigan) *Press* editor Werner Veit suggested at a Mid-America Press Institute seminar in 1975. He had departed from "the traditional order" by producing special sections to serve reader interests—from crafts to bicycling—and then finding advertisers who wanted to be in them.

The things that ought to concern family living sections, Veit said, are "not particular to women." Roughly equal numbers of men are as interested in cooking as women are in sports, he added.

Some newspapers have done away with traditional bridal

stories and now run only paid ads or classified notices; others have condensed the announcements. But most newspapers still view engagements, weddings and club news as part of their public service. In small towns especially these items are some of the best read in the newspaper, and editors are not about to eliminate them. A favored European approach, gathering all family news—births, deaths, engagements, weddings, anniversaries and retirements—on one family page, has not gained acceptance in the U.S.

Tackling New Subject Matter

Changes in the name of women's sections, according to Lindsay Van Gelder, a reporter for the New York *Post*, have all too often meant that the pages get caught in a double bind:

> The name change may liberate the content, but the section is still a dumping ground for anything the male editors consider a "woman's" story. So we get all the serious news stories about the Equal Rights Amendment, rape law changes, back-pay lawsuits and so forth, back among the girdle ads instead of on page one or two or three where they belong.

In an effort to find out if newspapers with these new names were in fact covering more general interest topics and consumer affairs, as critics have suggested they should, one researcher examined a selection of six newspapers in 1973 from different sections of the nation. Although Zena Beth Guenin warned that her results should not be considered absolute, she discovered that the updated sections had expanded their coverage more often by adding entertainment matter than by in-depth, broad-interest articles of the type suggested by contemporary critics of the women's pages.

Some of the more traditional pages, Guenin found—such as the Philadelphia *Bulletin* and the *Arizona Republic*—had covered non-traditional women's page subjects at least as well as the revamped sections. The Los Angeles *Times,* for example, devoted nearly half its section to entertainment and the St. Petersburg *Times,* which covered consumer affairs well, contained a high proportion of entertainment copy. Other papers

examined were the Davenport *Times-Democrat* and Albuquer-
que *Journal.*

A clear trend towards change could be seen by 1973 and
1974 in the Penney-Missouri Awards which had been given
for the best reporting, editing and feature writing in the wom-
en's pages for a decade and a half. Whatever their names,
these pages tackled new subjects and showed a higher quality
of writing and investigative reporting than ever before, said
program director Robert Hosokawa. Traditional topics were
still being covered, he said, "but the fascinating change is in
the nature of the coverage."

Staff writers reported in depth about the cost, quality and
economics of food and they also wrote abut nutrition and
health and truth in packaging, he explained. Fashion writers
covered the new fashion trends and consumer stories about
fabric quality, safety and prices. In recognition of this trend,
the Penney Awards for 1974 added a new category: consumer
reporting.

Hosokawa said, "Today's woman, no less than today's man,
is interested in issues and wants to be informed about social,
political, cultural and economic matters that affect her and her
family."

Colleen Dishon, editor of Features and News Service, which
she formed in 1968 to provide diversified content for the wom-
en's pages, served as a judge in 1973. A women's editor for 15
years, she regarded the varied subject matter and improved
professionalism of these pages as positive additions. She did
not think throwing out women's pages entirely was the right
answer, though.

> I see an unmistakable opportunity for women's pages to
> report in depth the changes in women's world and the prob-
> lems women face. We can use our space to report on discrim-
> ination, women in poverty, infant deaths, politics—all of the
> things that are vital to women and to everyone in society.
> In the flight from fluff, some of the newly-defined sec-
> tions could stand more definition. There is a certain amount
> of faddishness in the new, unrestrained coverage of formerly
> taboo subjects such as gay liberation, rape and abortion.
> Perhaps this is to be expected and in time we will see
> more of the originality and variety that was demonstrated by

some of the contest entries. Exciting changes are going to take place in the middle-size papers. Many are already doing high quality reporting on these pages.

The challenges facing women's editors and their managements in the 1970's were aptly described by Molly Ivins, prize-winning co-editor of the weekly *Texas Observer:*

> I think women's pages are going to have to address themselves to the image of the ideal woman in this country. But right now this image seems to be a big-bosomed blonde who has the whitest wash on the block and no dishpan hands.
>
> Is that what we really want? . . . If we don't want to become like stereotypic males, aggressive and domineering, what kind of human beings do we want to make of ourselves?

The changes in women's pages will have to begin in newspaper offices across the country, she thought, where women still have to fight against being regarded as "second-class citizens" who are unable to cover any story that comes along. Newswomen should be uniting in Guild caucuses around the questions of maternity leave, salary differentials and segregated want ads, she suggested.

> They should be ready to march into the managing editor's office, for example, when a consumer story that criticizes a local advertiser or product has been pulled because it gives offense.
>
> The real tragedy of the garbage currently being published in these papers (she declared in 1971) is that it's so unnecessary. There are so many important things women need to discuss with one another: family life, child rearing, sex education in the schools, why and whether children should attend integrated schools, why Norman Mailer is full of hot air, why children are taught sex differentiation, consumer concerns, job discrimination, why cities aren't habitable—no trees, no parks, no streetlights, no balloon or candy vendors, with their own chants, city ordinances against street vendors, no flower stalls, no outdoor cafes or markets . . .

Similar views were expressed by other women's editors who have led the shift away from traditional women's pages. Sue Hovik, former women's news editor for the Minneapolis *Star*, insisted that her job be abolished and got the paper to begin two new sections, "Taste" and "Variety." Hovik said,

A section devoted to women's news is not consistent with the realities of the 1970's. Women today are interested in and involved in equal rights, social concerns, consumer problems, civic issues, family life and environmental programs, topics facing all of humanity, not just women.

Space, staff and reader interest demand that only the most newsworthy events and programs be reported. I could not think that a club woman would want her organization reported just because it was a woman's group and judged by different standards. If a club event or program is newsworthy, it should face the same criteria for publication—regardless of the sex of its members.

A Background of Benign Neglect

This is quite different from the approach in women's pages of the 1890's which were devised as a means of attracting a new group of potential readers to the newspaper and thus to its advertisements. Coverage of the news of and by women was not the prime function; rather, entertainment, enticements for shoppers and some enlightenment were the goals of these publishers. And the items for these pages were judged by a different set of standards.

As long as the pages attracted readers and did not offend anyone, particularly large advertisers, the pages suffered only from benign neglect. Since the men did not want to bother with such inconsequential material and women were better equipped to speak to other women about matters of house and home, editors quickly made the pages a haven for young women seeking journalistic careers.

This Victorian conception of woman dominated the thinking of society and of newspaper editors in the late nineteenth century. The first woman's movement had, however, made some progress in awakening the public to the unjust position of women as chattel in a democratic society that was supposed to place high regard on the rights of individuals.

Articles on women became a part of the early Sunday newspapers that started during the Civil War. At first these Sunday papers were literary supplements with a news section. After the war the Sunday sections were increased and the papers capitalized on women's and children's interests and sports.

The Philadelphia *Sunday Dispatch*, for example, hired a woman to edit its Woman's Department and she discussed the "woman question" and urged women to become more self-reliant, pleaded for the opening of new fields of employment for women at remunerative wages and demanded full legal protection for married women in their rights to property. The same writer took issue with those who would destroy marriage and break up the family.

It is not absolutely clear who actually started the women's pages in American newspapers, but most researchers agree that Joseph Pulitzer certainly popularized them. As early as 1886 the New York *World* under Pulitzer carried special columns devoted to women's interests. By 1891 a page in the *Sunday World* was devoted to women's fashions and society and after 1894 the *World* ran at least one page daily "For and About Women."

Here women could read about their clubs and social doings of the town and nearby resorts, learn new recipes and tips on beauty care, keep up with the styles from Paris and brush up on their etiquette. But they would also read about unusual women in public affairs, at universities, world conferences and the like.

Two other publications served as models for Pulitzer, said Lorna Watson in her research on the topic. The enormously popular and much copied advice column, "Side Talks With Girls," was started by Edward A. Bok when he became editor of *The Ladies' Home Journal* in 1890. Bok was also the first editor to take women's interests seriously by including articles on successful women, the quality of married life and the importance of music, voice and reading. A short-lived newspaper, the New York *Recorder* (1891–1894) adopted a similar policy with its intention of being "a home paper with a view to pleasing women."

The newspaper soon claimed it had 100,000 women among its readers and its "The Only Woman's Page" carried articles on women's sayings and doings, lives of eminent women, society, domestic economy, fashion, food, gardening, handicraft, child training, shopping, gossip and advice, all of which became standard fare in later women's pages. The *Recorder*'s first woman's page editor was Christine Terhune Herrich, daughter of novelist Marion Harland.

Attempts Toward Improvement

Joseph Pulitzer tried to bring his papers closer to the ordinary people and wanted to reach the entire family. He knew, as did advertisers, that women made the decisions about wearing apparel, household furnishings and items of daily consumption. He also knew that the producers of these mass consumption items for sale in department and chain stores across the nation would find it invaluable to advertise directly to the nation's shoppers. With women's pages he could assure his advertisers that women were reading his papers.

The genius Pulitzer had for attracting audiences and sensing their interests was well displayed in his use of the women's columns. Traditional notions of femininity were adhered to in most of the columns, but the changing progress of women in jobs and professions and their demands for voting and other legal reforms were also reported.

To intellectuals at the turn of the century, however, these women's pages were filled with "glaring drivel," said "The Spectator" in *Outlook* magazine in 1901. "Don't talk to me about the Advancement of Women as long as any newspaper has a Woman's Page," snorted one of his female friends. "The Spectator" examined the contemporary newspapers and agreed that the women's pages were "a hopeless case." He found them an insult to intelligent women, filled as they were with recipes for removing sunburn and freckles, menus for a household of six at 50 cents a day, fashion "dots and doings," sunshine poetry and advice to young mothers. But even "The Spectator" found out that the Woman's Page was read and that advertisements located there commanded high prices.

That left him all the more confused: "The women of America are thought to be the most clever, the most charming, and the most superior of their sex the world over; but while the Woman's Page remains what it is, they can hardly expect the world to believe the claim."

The situation seems to have improved very little by 1912,

according to an article in the *Independent* which goes to great lengths to justify the value of college education for a young woman intending to be a journalist. The author had found two such young college women editing women's pages and believed that because of their college training they had elevated the pages from being "just for housekeepers" and had given them a greater variety.

More young women went to college in the 1920's after women got the vote than ever before, but by and large they said they planned to marry and have families. By mid-decade women's education had adapted to reflect this growing concern by helping them prepare for a home and marriage in domestic science and home engineering courses. Cornell quickly became a center for domestic science and state universities found these courses were very popular with female students. Women's Pages were often renamed Home Pages in the 1920's to reflect the new scientific and professional status of the job. A few women began to appear on journalism school faculties, especially to teach new courses in Home Page Journalism along with magazine and feature writing.

A brief look at women's pages through the twentieth century reflects this ebb and flow of attitudes about women's proper role in society. Until about 1910, the Detroit *News* and the Detroit *Free Press,* for example, ran one column on Sunday and a few daily columns about society and parties and these were intended for the women readers. In 1910 the *News* expanded to an entire page for women and by 1915 that had grown to two pages. Content in these pages was mixed: society and light features, club news, recipes, serialized fiction, advice columns and jokes. During World War I articles appeared about women workers and the war effort. Suffrage was reported and women were encouraged to improve themselves through clubs and other community activities in this era. After about 1930 creative homemaking became an important theme, even though women in this period were freer and had more choices. Homemaking and social roles were the most important topics, but occasionally the conflicts between work and home were discussed.

World War II made a change in the women's pages. New opportunities in jobs, public life and education opened for women as men left to fight in the war. Day after day in the 1943 issues of the Chicago *Tribune,* for example, there were pictures of women pioneering new jobs in business, industry and in the military and earning the respect of society for their contribution to the war effort. Such columns as "White Collar Girl" and Women who Work" ran alongside traditional columns with hints on cooking, fashion, beauty and social news.

A look at the pages of the 1950's and early 1960's shows a return to the more conventional notion of woman as housewife and mother that predominated in those years of postwar peace. Although more women than ever were working, going to college and heading families, this fact went largely unnoticed in the women's pages, even though Betty Friedan challenged sex stereotyping in the ads and women's magazines with her book, *The Feminine Mystique* in 1963.

Some editors encouraged broadening the women's pages in the postwar years, but they were rare. Lee Hills, executive editor of the Miami *Herald* told women's editor Dorothy Jurney in the early 1950's to expand the coverage of women's activities. He said that Miami was changing and growing more cosmopolitan and women had other interests beyond clubs and organizations and homes. "That was too narrow a focus," he maintained. The *Herald*'s women's pages were expanded to include political and social issues and club news was published only when it was newsworthy. The pages carried a large amount of traditional copy including fashion, cooking, grooming and advice, but they also ran Eleanor Roosevelt's column and published a long analysis of the Kinsey Report along with items on equal rights for women and features on professional women.

A nationwide survey of 700 women's page editors in 1970 told the University of Chicago's Center for Policy Study that editors in growing numbers were modifying and abandoning some of the traditional practices on the women's pages and were showing a new thrust toward more news and features that were genuinely relevant to the needs and interests of readers. As a result a group of 40 women's editors from the U.S. and Canada were invited to meet with critics at the Center for a few days in the spring of 1971 to debate the issue.

The Center brought in: Nicholas Von Hoffman, columnist in the Washington *Post* "Style" section; Edwin Diamond, media critic for WTOP-TV; Bryce W. Rucker, deputy director of the School of Journalism at Southern Illinois University; Robert E. Gilka, director of photography for the *National Geographic Magazine;* and Colleen Dishon, former women's editor of the Chicago *Daily News* and Milwaukee *Sentinel* and editor of women's Feature and News Service. Said Dishon:

> The most important story in the women's field in the next decade will be change, and modern women will adopt varied life styles and be involved in the real world. Yet, women's page after women's page is still glued to the old agendas. Fashion and beauty take a disproportionate share of the space.

Von Hoffman laid most of the blame at the doors of the editors and publishers who underbudget these sections so that editors have no choice but "to print the advertisers' lies and press releases" because they are "cheap and fast to slam into print."

> We are beggars in the women's pages, living on payola and freebies, and what's really so bad is that the staff people do it not because they want to, but because they either take the handout or don't get to cover the story.
>
> The result has been that papers have missed the biggest muckraking of the last decade. The reason Ralph Nader and the whole consumer movement has shaped itself the way it has is because the specialized sections of American newspapers didn't break the story; often they have either refused to cover it or have done so with shocking tardiness.
>
> The papers do their worst job on the topics that are most important to people—food, clothing, shelter and health. But the rules for journalism are upside down on the women's page.
>
> A press release on city side is checked and filled-out to make a story before it gets in the paper, but in the women's section it goes right in. Some newspapers tie the department's budget directly to how much advertising it brings in. Many fashion and food editors are allowed to accept free airplane tickets and hotel accommodations from advertisers.

On the other hand, the potential of these women's or life style pages is very great. They do not have to be tied to events. They don't have to tie every story to a newspeg before they can deal with it. They are freed from conventional forms of presentation in writing style and layout. About the only restraint they have is that the material be connected with the lives of their readers and that they be shown why it might matter to them.

Von Hoffman challenged the women's page editors to move away from the idea that women do one set of things and men do another, and to drop their idealized American family image, circa 1927 small town America.

"Wake up your managements to the violations of professional ethics that are going on," he challenged. He recognized the lack of political clout women's pages had in their organizations, so he proposed that the women organize and put out a publication that analyzed performance of their pages. He suggested that they work through their professional associations to give them the needed muscle that each lacked individually in challenging their managing editors.

Since that time several major news organizations have issued strict rules against freebies. In the spring of 1975, the members of the Newspaper Food Editors and Writers Association adopted a strict new code of ethics stressing a separation of editorial and advertising responsibilities and a no-freebies policy. The Newspaper Guild has fought to achieve pay parity in contract renewals in order to remove pay differentials as high as $50 per week between general news reporters and women's page reporters on the same newspaper. Only a few of the non-parity contracts remained in 1975.

Los Angeles *Times* former women's editor and then "View" editor (she was promoted to associate editor in 1975), Jean S. Taylor who did not attend the Chicago meeting took the same challenge directly to the American Society of Newspaper editors (ASNE) in 1971.

What our sections suffer from is lack of affection in high places. We are unloved. We are the pea under the publisher's pillow. . .
Women's pages are what they are because male policymakers will do anything to avoid reading stories directed

> toward women or learning of the issues involving women. And most top editors have no understanding either of their women readers or their women's staffs . . . Editors are among the most enthusiastic protectors of male supremacy in journalism.

She challenged the ASNE to use its collective brainpower to consider the whole issue of women's pages, women's news and women readers in terms of humanity and individuality and potential.

> If half the readers are women and if women are emerging as a consistently more powerful economic and voting force, it would at some point soon appear to be necessary to consider this issue. There should be a re-evaluation of the total approach in handling life style and people stories, with a flow of creative thought between sections and with contributing copy from other staffs.

Taylor proposed that women's staffs be required to write and edit to rigorous city desk standards and that their reporters have experience and background enough to handle stories on consumerism and legislative reform in the areas of pollution, child labor and welfare.

"We will need to be increasingly conscious of the need to tell the truth in whatever we do," Taylor warned. And she asked ASNE editors not to let these changes occur without the intensive look they had given to civil rights and campus unrest, youth, health, war and urban planning.

A pioneer in the movement to re-think the role of women's and feature pages in the newspaper was the Washington *Post*. Its new "Style" section appeared in January, 1969, with the goal of "telling about the private life of Washington and probing the quality of this life—and the kind of things happening elsewhere that affect it."

"Style" was to appeal to "the Washingtonian—male and female, white and black, suburbanite and city-dweller, decision-maker and home-maker," said its first editor, David A. Laventhol.

The new section was a co-equal with news, city life and financial/sports. It appeared daily with subdivisions for society, books, crosswords, bridge, leisure calendar, television and radio, fashion, entertainment and the arts. On Thursdays a food section was added.

Although some early critics called it "mere repackaging" of the former women's pages with the entertainment and other features, "Style" editors believed that it represented a new concept in editing. Laventhol said,

> We were troubled by the narrow range of the women's pages, which were very good women's pages, but which were almost trapped by a defined limitation: many stories, by tradition, had to have a "woman's angle."
>
> Women in news-conscious Washington sensed a certain patronizing quality in "For and About Women," and on some days the women's pages seemed strangely irrelevant as the rest of the world turned. The women's reporting staff at times felt like second-class citizens.
>
> How could the *Post* cope in coverage with the rapidly changing structure and habits of modern life, and at a time when television news was rapidly changing traditional news approaches? More and more, news wasn't the event that just happened—it was the trend that pinpointed a change in the way people lived.
>
> If a newspaper was to exercise its prime function of telling its readers about their world, then it ought to have a vehicle with which to deal regularly with the kind of topics that literally are offbeat in classic newsgathering.

Private Lives and Public Concerns

The *Post*'s solution was a section about people in their private lives, from parties to fashions and kids' problems to music, movies and art exhibitions. The *Post* would group all these features in one section, which would also tackle head-on the exploding problems of a changing society: leisure, youth, consumer affairs and styles of modern life.

Laventhol traveled around the country talking with other newspaper editors who were altering their women's sections, including the Chicago *Daily News,* which had refocused its entire newspaper to a heavy feminine readership, and the Los Angeles *Times'* "Section IV" (later "View") which combined entertainment and women's news and usually featured at least one culture piece, along with society, fashions and family. The

Los Angeles *Times* came closest to the *Post*'s approach, but had not then included the life style concept the *Post* was exploring, Laventhol recalled.

Taking note of "Style's" fifth anniversary in January, 1974, Tom Kendrick, a *Post* assistant managing editor and then editor of "Style," challenged his staff to keep "Style"

> . . . on the leading edge, to stay ahead of the growing number of eager imitators and make "Style" responsive to cultural change. "Style" in the 1970's should be more like a daily magazine in depth and range without sacrificing news and the potential of daily headlines.

"Substance with style," became Kendrick's new motto as he called for a better mix of stories including more commentary, news-edged interviews, timely life styles, focused coverage of the capital's political leaders in social settings, hard news in selected areas, analysis of cultural trends such as new leisure patterns and pressure on the family unit, consumer information oriented toward the family, previews and reviews.

" 'Style' has made a lot of progress," Kendrick said, but there is still "a tough road ahead in making 'Style' match its performance to its potential. We should stop thinking of 'Style' as a soft, feature section that can be ignored or curtailed in a crunch," he emphasized. "The information here directly affects how people spend their leisure time, and that is a third of their lives."

Some of the areas targeted by Kendrick for improvement were: broader issue-oriented coverage of the cultural explosion in the arts; multi-media arts criticism that cuts across traditional lines; social coverage that goes beyond parties and reveals the dimensions of character and political aspects of social leaders; emphasis on more life styles of people outside the political power arena; fashion stories that analyze cost, fabrics, quality and diversity; and increased investigative reporting in several areas, including consumerism.

New Life Style/Family/Feature Pages

"Style" editors believe they have destroyed the old clichés of the women's news pages. The pages are now read by 45 per cent of the male readers, compared to a mere 5 per cent who read "Style's" forerunner. Nearly all of the *Post*'s female readers do read "Style."

But "Style" editors still have to shoot back to the appropriate news desks the occasional items sent to "Style" just because they were about women. "We define news by subject and location, not by sex," said Kendrick. But editors have to keep reinforcing that to avoid slipping back into the old way of thinking of "Style" as a revised women's section.

Until the new definition becomes second-nature in the newsroom, a few stories may "fall in between the chairs," remarked Elsie Carper, herself a former "Style" editor and political reporter, now assistant managing editor handling personnel matters.

> The old women's pages are on the way out. Women planning a career in journalism now should be prepared to write about government and not just about governors' wives. Light feature writing does not prepare one for competition for jobs in the news departments or for sections like "Style."

Men and women like to work on the new life style sections and cityside reporters seek assignments in these sections because they know their articles will be well displayed and read.

"People ask to work in this section," said Dorothy Jurney, then women's editor for the Detroit *Free Press* (later assistant managing editor there and at the Philadelphia *Inquirer*), but the men and women who write the women's news do not want to move.

The new opportunities and responsiblities of editors and reporters on these women's/life style/family pages are expected to improve pay, prestige and job advancement in departments that were traditionally underpaid. With their second-class status gone, Dishon predicted, these department in the future will be exciting places to work. (In 1976, Dishon took charge of the Chicago *Tribune's* "Tempo" section and redesigned it.)

Newsday's "Part II" editor, Richard Estrin, echoed those sentiments at the Penney Awards in 1975 when he explained that he had requested editorship of that new feature section after nearly 20 years of news writing and editing.

> I got a little tired of the here today, gone tomorrow, bang
> this crisis, bang that crisis, then it's gone. I got tired of
> nothing better than yesterday's paper. We're (feature writers
> and editors) the people who take a slower look. We take a
> longer, more careful look . . . What we do has less sensa-
> tion, but what we handle is more enduring. I think what we
> cover is as true today as it was yesterday.

He added that he had found that he could get closer to the
lives of people around him by working in this section and "if
we men let you women monopolize all that, I think we're
crazy."

The section serves both men and women with features and
news articles. It deals with fashions, hobbies, recreation, nature, food, the media and politics and includes specialized
reporting on religion, medicine, science and education. Estrin
says that men and women are interested in these subjects and
believes that categorizing some of this as women's news in the
past "led us into some false beliefs that have never really been
true."

Carol Sutton, the first women to serve as managing editor of
a metropolitan daily newspaper in the United States (the Louisville *Courier-Journal* in 1974) developed her administrative
abilities during a nine-year tenure as the paper's women's editor. She completely revamped the section, including changing
the name from "Women's World" to "Today's Living." She
was among the first to introduce on her prize-winning pages
the subjects of birth control, no-fault divorce, hunger in Appa-
lachia and political interviews. As assistant to the editor and
publisher in 1976 she had started working on developing separate newspaper editions "tailored" to specialized audiences.

"Regardless of what the pages are called, the approach can
be summarized as 'telling readers what they've always wanted
to know—how to lead better lives,' " said Ruth D'Arcy, former
editor of the "Accent on Living" section of the Detroit *News*
and a member of the University of Missouri journalism faculty.

The Penney Awards may be a bellwether of the changes
ahead for women's pages. The contest was originally intended
to promote improved content and to encourage high profes-

sional standards on the women's pages of the past. In its 1974 contest announcement the rules were changed:

> Any full-time reporter may enter stories in the general reporting, consumer affairs reporting, and fashion and clothing reporting categories. Entrants no longer have to be working full-time on a women's section.

The reason—much of the news about women and their families appears "run-of-the-paper these days." The stories still had to be news of interest primarily to women and their families.

As the Miami *Herald*'s "Living Today" editor, Dorothy-Anne Flor said, "I want everyone to read the section," which she called a people's page. "We've graduated women to being people."

· SOURCES CONSULTED ·

William H. Chafe, *The American Woman; Her Changing Social and Political Role, 1920–1970*, (London: Oxford University Press, 1974).

Colleen Dishon, "Women as People on Women's Pages, *Matrix*, Winter 1971–72.

John Kenneth Galbraith, "How the Economy Hangs on Her Apron Strings," *Ms.*, May, 1974.

Zena Beth Guenin, "Women's Pages in Newspapers: Missing Out on Contemporary Content," *Journalism Quarterly*, Spring, 1975.

George Juergens, *Joseph Pulitzer and the New York World*, (Princeton, N.J.: Princeton University Press, 1966).

David Laventhol, "Washington *Post* Thinks STYLE is Stylish," *ASNE Bulletin*, August, 1969.

Alfred M. Lee, *The Daily Newspaper in America*, (New York: Macmillan Co., 1937).

Margaret Mangold, "The Women's Pages: A Reflection of Feminine Progress? 1900–1970," unpublished student paper, Department of Journalism, University of Michigan, 1974.

Valerie Kincade Oppenheimer, "Demographic Influence on Female Employment and the Status of Women," in Joan Huber (ed), *Changing Women in a Changing Society*, (Chicago: University of Chicago Press, 1973).

Penney Press, March 1972, March, September 1973, September 1974.

Suzanne M. Sica, "A Study of the Changes in the Detroit News' Women's Section: 1900–1974," unpublished student paper, Department of Journalism, University of Michigan, 1974.

Jean S. Taylor, "Hell hath . . . just ain't good enough," *ASNE Bulletin*, November, 1971.

University of Chicago Center for Policy Study, *What's Wrong with Women's Pages?* (Chicago, Ill., 1971).

Lindsay Van Gelder, "Women's Pages: You Can't Make News Out of a Silk Purse," *Ms.*, November, 1974.

Lorna Watson, "The New York *Recorder* as a Women's Newspaper 1891–1894," Unpublished M.A. thesis (University of Wisconsin, School of Journalism, 1939).

Personal interviews with Elsie Carper, Tom Kendrick and Dorothy Jurney.

7

* * *

The Feminist Press
Then and Now

UNTIL 1828 when Frances Wright began to edit her New York
Free Enquirer for men and women, there were no reform periodicals published solely by women. In the next few years,
women's periodicals of every conceivable tone and opinion
emerged on the American scene. Most were genteel ladies'
publications, concerned with domestic affairs and social life,
and although a few did have women editors, they avoided
such controversial causes as suffrage and equal rights for
women.

The women's rights convention at Seneca Falls, New York,
in 1848 signaled the official birth of the feminist movement in
the United States. The nineteenth century abolition movement
was a powerful force behind the rise of the women's cause.
Women, while working to free the slaves, became aware of
their own constricted freedom and began their own public
protest against women's political, economic and social sub-
jugation.

The popular, established newspapers provided little or no
encouragement for this budding movement. They were most
likely to scoff or put women in their places as did the New
York *Herald* in an editorial in 1850 saying:

> What do the leaders of the woman's rights convention
> want? They want to vote and hustle with the rowdies at the

polls. They want to be members of Congress, and in the heat
of debate subject themselves to coarse jests and indecent language . . .

The editor found it ridiculous that ladies would like to be
doctors, lawyers, ship captains or generals and could not resist
one final barb. "How funny it would sound in the newspapers
that Lucy Stone, pleading a cause, took suddenly ill in the
pains of parturition and perhaps gave birth to a fine bouncing
boy in court. . . ." The example was considered particularly
cutting because she was unmarried.

Although such editorial comment became less frequent as
the movement grew and some publications ran articles by
feminists, the established press of this period did not provide
adequate channels for the expression of the feminist viewpoint. Only when the movement had grown so large that it
could no longer be ignored did it become "newsworthy."

Abolitionist papers were much more open to the issue, and
they provided the earliest forum for discussion of feminist
ideas. Women were involved in the development and editing
of several abolitionist papers in the 1840's and 1850's including
the *National Anti-Slavery Standard* of New York, the *Boston
Commonwealth* and the *National Era* in Washington, D.C.

Setting the Agenda

The growing conviction of ardent feminists that women, by
uniting, could exercise more power led to efforts to establish
their own papers. There were many of these papers and most
were of short duration and local influence. Although they all
played a role in setting the agenda for early feminist discussion, five were most significant because they were edited by
the movement's leaders and attracted national audiences. As
such they articulated the main ideas of the movement and
reflected its divisions as well as its agreements.

The five leading newspapers were edited by nonprofes-
sionals. None of the women involved in their publication had
a special background or experience as a journalist, and none of
the papers was welcomed into the world of popular journalism
as warmly as the more acceptable sisters, the "ladies' magazines." These were advocacy periodicals, part of a smaller but

tenacious tradition of reform journalism in the United States. The crusading spirit and energy of determined, ambitious reformers who were totally devoted to the cause of women's rights sustained them. These papers were not business ventures, they were essential tools in what their editors saw as a vital crusade for freedom of the American woman and the betterment of American society. Each newspaper developed a style and character very much its own and each was articulate and sophisticated.

Amelia Bloomer's *Lily* (1849–1859) was the first of the early woman's rights papers to survive for any significant length of time. Initiated by a female temperance society, the publication, its editor and readers soon came under the eloquent influence of Elizabeth Cady Stanton. Although the focus of the paper's content subsequently changed from temperance to woman's rights, its circulation remained limited until the controversy concerning "Bloomers" brought it national attention.

Unfortunately for the early woman's cause, the Bloomers joined the frontier movement and went west, leaving the *Lily* behind. If Amelia Bloomer had remained editor of the paper, it is highly probable that it would have lasted longer and enjoyed a more influential life. Before Bloomer gave it up in 1855, the *Lily*'s circulation numbered over 6,000, more than the better known, later *Woman's Journal* or *Revolution* were ever able to achieve. Fresh, lively and well-written, the *Lily* was the most readable of the early feminist publications.

At the age of 21 Amelia Jenks Bloomer had married a younger lawyer who was to become an editor of the *Seneca County Courier* and later postmaster of Seneca Falls, New York. With his encouragement she became deputy postmaster and developed her writing talents by contributing articles to local newspapers. By the late 1840's she had gained a modest reputation for her writing and was actively involved in the temperance cause.

Temperance, Literature and Woman's Rights

When the Ladies Temperance Society of Seneca Falls daringly proposed to initiate the publication of a newspaper devoted to their movement, Bloomer was chosen editor. However, after voting to name the paper the *Lily* and helping with the subscriptions, the organization seems to have lost courage in the venture.

During the first year of the *Lily*'s life the words "Published by a Committee of Ladies" appeared at the top of the front page, but in reality no one but Bloomer took responsibility for the periodical after the first two issues. Working from a small room adjoining the post office, she wrote, contracted printing, read proof and mailed the *Lily*. In time her office became a meeting place for local women to exchange ideas and discuss the latest news from papers and magazines recently arrived in the mail.

Bloomer's claim that the *Lily* was the first paper devoted to the interests of women is open to question, but it certainly was the heartiest pioneer. With a first run of 300 copies issued on January 1, 1849, the eight-page paper announced itself as a Monthly Journal, Devoted to Temperance and Literature." The first pages contained poems and short fictional pieces in three widely spaced columns printed on a large tabloid sheet.

Bloomer and Anna C. Mattison, who withdrew as editor after the second issue, introduced the temperance cause to *Lily* readers, saying:

> It is Woman that speaks through the *Lily*. It is upon an important subject too, that she comes before the public to be heard. Intemperance is the great foe to her peace and happiness. It is that above all, which has filled to the brim the cup of her sorrows, and sent her mourning to the grave.

The paper encouraged women to "throw aside the modest retirement" that became their sex and use their influence in the temperance cause.

The list of *Lily* contributors included such well-known women as Harriet Beecher Stowe, Frances Gage, Antoinette L. Brown, Sarah Grimké, Jane Swisshelm and Elizabeth Cady Stanton. Stanton's thought-provoking articles stimulated discussion of the controversial topic of women's rights. Letters to the editor, items by contributors and even Bloomer's editorials came more and more to concern themselves with this issue. Bloomer had not considered herself a feminist and seldom mentioned the subject, but by the time the Tennessee legislature declared that women had no souls and therefore no right to own property, Bloomer was prepared to vent her anger and loudly:

> If things are coming to such a pass as that indicated by the above decision, we think it high time that women should open their eyes and look where they stand. It is quite time that woman herself should enter the contest.

After this outburst by Bloomer, woman's rights issues became clearly more prominent in the newspaper, and by the fall of 1850 Bloomer was openly advocating suffrage for women. Two years later temperance had been completely over-shadowed by feminist discussion in the *Lily* and the journal's title was altered to read, "Devoted To The Interests of Women." Up to that time the newspaper had a respected though local reputation. It cost 50 cents per year and had a circulation list of about 500.

But the *Lily*'s subsequent support for adoption of a new dress style, later dubbed "Bloomers," was to cause its circulation to soar into the thousands and its pages to turn into a national forum for ideas about women's rights. Bloomer and Stanton were among the first women of Seneca Falls to adopt the costume of long, full Turkish trousers worn under a short, below-the-knee skirt. They had daguerreotypes taken of themselves dressed in the new style and reproduced in the *Lily*. The paper also printed illustrations and detailed instructions for making the trousers. In editorial after editorial they defended themselves, saying that:

> We know that many look upon us as singular—that many frown upon us for daring to do different from the mass; but having experienced the blessings of freedom, we cannot rivet the chains upon ourself again, even to gain the good-will, or to avoid the frowns of slavish conservatives.

The attempted revolution of dress styles was short-lived, but the *Lily* gained lasting benefits. In the face of outrageous public ridicule, the women returned to conventional dress in a matter of months. By 1853 the paper had begun to appear twice every month and its circulation had jumped to over 4,000 and was growing steadily.

In 1854 the Bloomers moved to Ohio, taking the *Lily* with them where its circulation grew to over 6,000. The next year the Bloomers moved further west to Council Bluffs, Iowa, leaving the journal behind. Three hundred miles beyond a railroad, the Council Bluffs area had no facilities for printing or mailing a paper with so large a circulation. The *Lily* was consequently turned over to Mary B. Birdsall, a former head of the "ladies department" of the *Indiana Farmer,* and it was taken to Richmond, Indiana. Bloomer remained a corresponding editor, but her influence on the paper waned and it took on a more literary style and content. Birdsall continued its publication until 1859 as a semi-monthly devoted to "Temperance and the Elevation of Woman."

The *Una* (1853–1856)), which also appeared before the Civil War, differed greatly in style from the *Lily* and from the later papers. Intending to elevate the minds of women, Pauline Wright Davis attempted to attract both the more intellectual and sophisticated readers from the *Lily* and the popular "ladies' magazines." The refined *Una* presented woman's issues in learned, philosophical articles and editorials. But in trying to attract readers from two such diverse groups the *Una* failed. Its intense advocacy of woman's rights prevented competition with magazines such as *Godey's Lady's Book,* whose readers were more interested in the latest Paris fashions.

And the *Una*'s dignified, detached tone was far less exciting to readers than the *Lily*'s spirited, energetic debates and discussions. Consequently the *Una*'s circulation remained small and attracted no great following even within the movement. Later feminist publications followed more in the pattern of the *Lily,* providing their readers with material stimulating to action as well as to thought.

Post-Civil War

After a period of inactivity during the Civil War, the woman's movement was spurred to new growth, in part by Elizabeth Cady Stanton, one of the most influential polemicists of her day. The combined efforts of Stanton, the writer, and Anthony, the organizer, resulted in the *Revolution*

(1868–1871), the first important woman's rights newspaper to appear after the Civil War. Reveling in radical ideas and controversy, the paper appealed to only the most liberal reformers and thinkers of the time. Although it lasted for only a little over two years, it was instrumental in broadening the reputation of Stanton as a writer and in arousing more conservative feminists to action.

The *Revolution* arrived in the midst of a controversy which was to split the woman's movement apart. The adoption of the Fourteenth and Fifteenth Amendments after the war was, in effect, a legal humiliation to the feminists of the era. The Constitution itself had never before contained the word "male." Women had previously been excluded from voting only under state laws. But the Fourteenth Amendment specifically gave "male inhabitants" the right to vote. Later the Fifteenth was added, declaring that the vote should not be denied on the basis of "race, colour, or previous condition of servitude."

The revered Constitution of the United States was thus amended to include the principle of discrimination by sex. As a result, the cause of woman's rights lost ground during this period; women were not merely denied the vote, but it seemed that they would be unable to gain that right in federal elections without a constitutional amendment of their own.

Although adoption of the amendments was a bitter blow to all the women who worked in both the abolitionist and suffrage movements, this issue especially was responsible for a sharp break among feminist leaders. The Elizabeth Stanton/Susan B. Anthony wing of the movement materialized out of disillusionment with the Republican party's handling of their suffrage demands. Many of these women had spent up to 30 years supporting anti-slavery groups, and when the war ended they expected abolitionist backing for female enfranchisement. Such support was not forthcoming. Disappointed, they called for immediate work on a national suffrage amendment as well as broader social reforms.

In contrast, the most conservative members of the movement led by Lucy Stone argued that the Republican leaders had not deliberately betrayed women. Instead they contended that woman's suffrage probably could not have been instituted at that early date, but suffrage for black males had been a real possibility. If woman's suffrage had been attached to the Fourteenth or Fifteenth Amendments, they believed that both causes would have failed.

The conservatives wished to initiate suffrage campaigns to change laws state-by-state. Thus, the two groups clashed on how the goal of woman's right to vote should be approached. Stanton and Anthony founded the *Revolution* in New York City as a platform for the expression of their views, hoping it would become the "guiding star of the enfranchisement of woman."

Supported financially by George Francis Train, one of the wealthiest and most eccentric reformers of his day, 10,000 copies of the first *Revolution* were sent out on January 8, 1868. Parker Pillsbury, who had formerly written for the *Anti-Slavery Standard,* and Stanton were named editors while Anthony served as proprietor and manager. The simply printed masthead declared firmly: "Principle, Not Policy: Justice, Not Favors," while a short, straightforward salutatory explained:

> . . . The enfranchisement of woman is one of the leading ideas that calls this journal into existence. Seeing in its realization, the many necessary changes in our modes of life, we think the *Revolution* a fitting name for a paper that will advocate so radical a reform as this involves in our political, religious and social worlds.

Both men and women would edit the publication, the editor said, and would discuss not just

> . . . masculine and feminine ideas alone, but united thought on all questions of national and individual interest.

With Anthony's special talent for organization and administration put to use in managing the paper and Stanton's often brilliant writing given a free hand in editorializing the newspaper became the mouthpiece of the radical wing of the woman's movement. The paper gave Stanton the opportunity to champion unpopular causes of all varieties. Her numerous articles concerned issues ranging from the problems of working women to marriage reforms; from jury service for women to prison reform; from child care to politics. Her writing was the backbone of the newspaper and her philosophy knew no bounds.

With the *Revolution* Stanton had the chance to develop her views into a cogent argument and to bring it before the public. "As masculine ideas have ruled the race for six thousand years, we especially desire that the *Revolution* shall be the mouth-piece of women," she said. The paper would give the world the feminine thought in politics, religion and social life in its search for truth:

> We declare war to the death on the idea that woman was made for man . . . we proclaim the higher truth that, like man, she was created by God for Individual Moral Responsibility and progress here and forever, and that the physical conditions of her earthly life are not to be taken as a limitation of the evidence of the Divine Intention respecting her as an immortal being.

The initial appearance of the *Revolution* horrified the more conservative members of the woman's movement. The paper's connection of various other social reforms to the woman's cause plus its association with Train, who many considered a charlatan, brought severe criticism from New England reformers. The established press was "in the main cordial," said Stanton, but looked "askance at a political paper edited by a woman. If we had started a *Lily* or *Rosebud* and remained in the region of sentiment, we should have been eulogized to the skies, but here is something dangerous."

The New York *Sunday Times* suggested that Mrs. Stanton should "attend a little more to her domestic duties and a little less to those of the great public." In doing this she "might possibly set a notable example of domestic felicity . . . As for spinsters, we have always said that every woman has a natural and inalienable right to a good husband and a pretty baby."

As time went on the stability of the *Revolution*'s finances became more and more shaken. The imprisonment and subsequent removal of Train from participation with the periodical had left it virtually on its own. The subscription list was relatively small, and the vigorous opinions expressed in its pages appealed only to the most liberal reformers and thinkers of the day. Despite help from Paulina Wright Davis, who had taken Pillsbury's place when he left to pursue other interests in 1870, and loans totaling thousands of dollars from Anthony's family, the *Revolution* was doomed. At the beginning of 1869 circulation numbered about 2,000; by the next year this had grown to 3,000, but it still was not enough to support the paper.

Anthony initially resisted efforts to dispose of the paper, but finally, utterly exhausted, she gave in. Personally responsible for a $10,000 debt for the journal, she turned it over to Laura Curtis Bullard in May, 1870, for the consideration of one dollar. Under Bullard the paper became a more literary and socially-oriented journal, losing much of its controversial content. Although backed by a joint stock company, it still did not prove successful. A year and a half later, it was merged into the New York *Christian Enquirer*.

In the year following the *Revolution*'s appearance, Lucy Stone and her followers organized the *Woman's Journal* (1870–1917), at least in part to counteract the influence of Stanton and Anthony. Published for over 47 years by members of the Stone-Blackwell family, the *Journal* became an institution for the suffrage movement and had an unprecedented life span for women's reform newspapers. It was invaluable in terms of providing communication, encouragement and stability for the suffragists.

The *Woman's Journal* first appeared in 1870, a time when women's participation in business, professional, artistic and political life was growing rapidly. Formal education for females was likewise increasing significantly. Oberlin College, founded in 1833, had opened its doors to students regardless of race, color or sex. Mount Holyoke Seminary started accepting students in 1837; Swarthmore opened as a co-educational college in 1864; the first student enrolled at Vassar in 1865; Smith College was chartered in 1871. In 1870 several women were admitted to state bars as the first female lawyers in America.

Suffrage Issues Out in the Open

Along with this kind of development, additudes toward woman's suffrage were slowly changing. Agitated by conventions, meetings, speeches and newspapers such as the *Revolution*, the issue was being openly and often hotly debated. Increased interest in the subject became apparent politically as national and state legislatures were faced with mounting numbers of petitions supporting enfranchisement. The pro-suffrage faction in these bodies was gradually gaining strength, though it was not yet even approaching majority opinion.

Led by Lucy Stone and Henry Blackwell, her husband, the *Journal* was the conservative feminists' answer to the *Revolution*. The masthead pronounced it as a "weekly newspaper, published every Saturday in Boston and Chicago, devoted to the interests of woman, to her educational, legal and political equality and especially to her right of suffrage."

As such the *Journal* attracted its readers from the more moderate and conservative women's groups. Club women, professionals, writers and the upper- and middle-class women whose primary interest in the movement involved the issue of suffrage were its readership. For these women the *Journal* provided the latest suffrage news, counsel and inspiration. Although most of its readers were centered in the Boston and Chicago areas, its subscribers were scattered from Maine to California and from Canada to the Gulf. As advertised in the first issues, the price of a year's subscription was $3.00, later reduced to $2.50, "invariably in advance."

Founded as a joint stock company, the *Woman's Journal* was incorporated with 200 shares of stock at $50 each. The New England Woman Suffrage Association had urged establishment of such a newspaper. The association bought stock and repeatedly tried to help the paper financially by sharing with its proceeds from suffrage bazaars. At various times in its long career the *Journal* represented other suffrage organizations such as the Massachusetts and later American Woman Suffrage Associations while also serving as a link between smaller organizations nationwide.

Lucy Stone, who had been writing regularly for the paper, officially took over as editor in 1872. Under her influence, the *Journal*'s editorials contrasted rather sharply to those of the *Revolution*. Where the Stanton-Anthony paper was bold, daring and at times rash, the *Journal* was polite and undemand-

ing. It seemed chiefly concerned with supplying its readers
with encouragement to support the suffrage cause. For example, Stone's piece "Lend a Hand," which appeared in 1886,
is much less impelling than any of the *Revolution*'s opinion.
She said:

> The first woman's rights convention in this country was
> held thirty-eight years ago . . . But in looking back over all
> these years, it is marvellous to see how much the condition
> of women has been ameliorated. From less than half-a-dozen
> occupations poorly paid, they have now over two hundred
> better-paid occupations. Then only one college admitted
> women. Now they are welcome in hundreds of colleges.
>   (Public opinion had changed too, and) instead of the idea
> and its advocates being preached against, scouted, derided
> and mobbed, most intelligent people know that woman suf-
> frage is coming . . ."

Stone urged every suffragist to "lend a hand" and make it
come all the sooner.

This type of editorial was very much the norm for the *Journal*. Strong, moving, persuasive opinion was not a hallmark of
the paper, especially when contrasted to the *Revolution* and, at
times, the *Lily*. In many issues more opinion was expressed in
letters to the editor than by the paper itself. And frequently no
editorial comment from Stone or Blackwell appeared at all. For
the most part, the *Journal*'s editorial page contained short articles which greatly encouraged or warned against current
happenings relating to the movement.

At about the same time that Stone took over as editor-in-
chief, the *Journal*'s original capital exhausted itself. In an attempt to remain solvent, it became necessary for the editors to
serve without pay. Contributions were solicited and bazaars
held for the paper's benefit. Gift premiums such as croquet
sets, books and dinnerware were even offered for new subscriptions. The paper managed to continue, nevertheless, and
by January of 1884 its economy was once more stable as it
proudly reported that the *Journal* owes "no man anything except goodwill."

Controlled by the leaders of the conservative wing of the
movement, the paper necessarily reflected their viewpoints.

Little social awareness of issues beyond suffrage was apparent, especially in the early years of the paper. The panic of 1873, followed by a short period of depression, hurt the paper, which struggled to remain stable. Yet the surrounding poverty and unemployment found little expression in the pages of the *Journal*. It consistently maintained its aloofness from general social reforms like the growing labor movement, which it completely ignored. Suffrage was the one great cause of the paper's editors, and by isolating it from other social reforms, the conservatives hoped to reduce the amount of controversy and hysteria surrounding the issue. They desired to keep suffrage respectable at all costs.

Subscribers were initially impressed by the *Journal*. It claimed a circulation of 4,000 in 1872 and by 1877 this had grown to 4,500. The paper's peak circulation sales seem to have come around 1882, when its distribution reached 6,000; after that circulation slowed and steadily decreased until the paper's demise. The *Woman's Journal* was the longest running suffrage paper in the nation. The weekly issue never failed to appear, not even during a period when the printing office burned down. Although it suffered from financial problems at various times, as long as the paper was under the control of Stone and her family, it never went into debt except to its editors.

After Lucy Stone's death in 1893, Blackwell took over as editor along with their daughter Alice Stone Blackwell who did much of the editing. In 1909, when her father died, she became editor and carried on suffrage work as secretary of the National American Woman Suffrage Association (NAWSA). The *Journal* had been adopted by the country's major suffrage organization, NAWSA, in 1889 as its official organ. In 1917, the paper was consolidated with two other suffrage papers, the *Woman Voter* and the *Headquarters News Letter*, and renamed the *Woman Citizen*. It then became the property of the Leslie Commission and died in 1919, about the time New York State voters approved a full suffrage amendment to their constitution.

Under Alice Stone Blackwell, the paper argued enthusiastically for woman's suffrage, and during World War I she said that it was ludicrous for the United States to claim it would make the world safe for democracy when it denied the vote to half of its population, a popular suffrage theme of that time. Giving the vote to women would be a blow to Germany and would strengthen the war effort, she said.

Occasionally a sense of humor was useful in refuting the anti-suffrage charges and Blackwell used it effectively, often in answering claims by the opposition that all suffragists were childless. She said:

> One anti-suffragist got himself into a curious pickle. . . . He berated the alleged unwillingness of suffragists to be mothers, and held up the typical suffragist, Carrie Nation, and as the typical anti, Martha Washington—who lived so long before the suffrage movement that she cannot fairly be claimed either as a suffragist or an anti. Thereupon some better informed person called his attention to the fact that Martha Washington had only four children (by her first husband), while Carrie Nation was the mother of thirteen."

The *Journal* and the movement at the turn of the century rested upon the narrow basis of suffrage support. Other issues concerning women were swept aside in the final drive for enfranchisement, and when suffrage was legally instituted the paper, like the movement itself, lost its reason for being.

All these feminist newspapers suffered from financial strain at one time or another; significantly, the two longest-lived were the *Journal* and the *Women's Tribune*. These were the most moderate of all the publications editorially, and thereby took the least risks of offending people.

The *Woman's Tribune* (1883–1909) did not display the liveliness, originality or intensity of the earlier publications. Its founder, Clara Bewick Colby, was a member of the third generation of feminist leaders, the first group to realize the dream of enfranchisement. She had graduated as the valedictorian of the first class of women from the University of Wisconsin in 1869. After gaining campaign experience in various state suffrage referendums, Colby took over the management of the Nebraska suffrage movement in 1883. That same year she also began publishing the *Tribune* in Beatrice, Nebraska, as a source of suffrage news and information for Western women.

Printed until March, 1909, it was the second longest running newspaper to emerge from the movement.

Perhaps reflecting the times, the *Tribune* lacked the imagination, originality and spirit of the earlier publications. It was an even weaker paper in editorial content than the *Journal*. The body of the paper, however, furnished a complete record of the more important events which occurred in the suffrage movement during its term of publication. Colby's consistent concern that the paper be alert for new ideas and also "prove all things and hold fast to the good," kept the paper timely and informative.

Moving to Washington, D.C. for eight days in the spring of 1888, it acted as the official organ of the International Council on Women, presided over by Stanton and Anthony. After enjoying success with this venture, Colby moved the *Tribune* to the nation's capital on a permanent basis. There it was able to record all Congressional hearings and the latest legislative developments concerning women.

Other Topics Besides Suffrage

By 1898, in order to spur circulation, Colby increased the portion of poetry, fiction and features in the paper. "Perhaps because the suffrage matter in the *Tribune* is taken for granted, it is those features of the paper which do not directly pertain to suffrage that have brought in most words of approval," she explained."

The *Tribune* believed that it was taking the course "most acceptable to the majority of its readers in not devoting the paper wholly to the reform for which it stands first, last and all the time . . ."

Financial problems were a way of life for the paper, which often seemed to have struggled along solely on Colby's sheer determination. Forced to change the paper's frequency and size several times during its lifetime in order to survive, Colby refused to consider a price change because such a large consistency of the paper lay among those who could not afford to pay more.

The *Tribune*'s circulation peaked in 1891 at 13,900 subscribers, and then fell off to 7,500 in 1896, and 5,500 in 1898. Against the advice of friends, Colby's optimism concerning the suffrage movement in Oregon led her to take the *Tribune* to Portland in 1904. But circulation dropped swiftly to 2,000 by 1906 and the paper died in 1909.

During the 1890's many of the pioneers of feminist agitation in the 1840's and 1850's either died or retired from activity. The younger women who took their places displayed a somewhat more conservative ideology. Work on broader feminist reforms was by-passed as they concentrated their energies and resources on gaining the supposed panacea of enfranchisement. Consequently, the newspapers of the later period reflected the movement's more limited interests, and contrasted sharply to the earlier feminist publications.

The women's newspapers of the late nineteenth century were especially important to the woman's movement in terms of providing an additional outlet for feminist activism beyond the usual speechmaking and fund raising. They were essential for communication within the often widely scattered movement, concluded Sally Quick in her careful study of the papers. They also served to promote feminist unity, stability and consciousness as well as furnish a national forum for new ideas and opinions, Quick said.

Communication with the world outside the movement was also essential, for women of this period wielded no direct political power or influence. Unable to vote or run for public office, they could not work effectively to change laws they thought unfair. Their only means of altering conditions lay in the unification of feminist opinion and strength and in the persuasion of the public that the present system of government was unjust. The publication of newspapers worked toward this goal as the periodicals allowed women to reach out toward a larger audience than the lecture circuit could accommodate.

The majority of the newspapers concerned with feminist issues during the earlier 1800's managed to survive for only a few years. The most radical and unconventional were the first casualties. Like the movement from which it sprang, the feminist press advocated ideas far ahead of its time. Along with the movement the feminists and their press had modified their stance and focused at last on the suffrage issue. The established press picked up the main lines of the debate, covering the speeches, conventions and suffrage marches as they became news. At the same time the newspapers provided female professional journalists the opportunity to cover a running news story of growing significance for the twentieth century. After the Nineteenth Amendment was approved in 1920 the era of feminism quietly faded into history. The battle had been won, or so some thought.

Women's participation in public life and in the labor force did increase thereafter, modestly and without the changes in social attitudes that would be necessary before all women could attain independence and a sense of self-identity equal to that of men. This ideal had been fundamental to the feminist movement but was displaced by the emphasis on voting rights.

During the two decades following the passage of woman's suffrage it became clear that the feminists were too disunited to press for such major changes in values and also that society was not likely to change without head-on confrontation. As William H. Chafe explained in his analysis of *The American Woman: Her Changing Social, Economic and Political Role 1920–1970,* the woman's rights movement was "beset by controversy, weakened by lack of widespread support and torn by internecine warfare" and had ceased to exist as a powerful force in American society.

Inequality persisted and even during World War II, when women were lavishly praised for their great efforts in the work force, their participation was regarded as supplemental and temporary. The goal of most young women, college-educated and otherwise, was a husband and a family. The careerist and single woman still were considered atypical, to say the least.

The question of "woman's role" at home and in the world was, however, on the minds of many women during the 1940's and 1950's as an increasing number of them found satisfaction in employment outside the home.

"As the nation entered the decade of the 1960's," said Chafe, "it seemed clar that any solution to the 'woman problem' would entail the creation of new roles for both women and men, rather than the restoration of a rigid division of labor based on sex."

Revival of Feminism

All the elements needed for a revival of feminism came together in America in the 1960's with the emphasis on elimination of prejudice and discrimination, the civil rights movement, student protests and ideological debates over American involvement in the war in Vietnam. Women were involved in the student protests and anti-war movement and supported the black protests for civil rights in demonstrations and through the underground press. By 1968 women had begun to articulate their own grievances and with that came a new feminist press, flowering in such profusion that it nearly defied description.

As before, the feminist movement was a movement of middle class women, most of them college educated and was led by highly articulate spokeswomen like Gloria Steinem, Betty Friedan, and later Congresswomen Bella Abzug and Shirley Chisholm, particularly in the political arena. These women were able to blend just the right amount of social protest, righteous indignation and personality needed for leadership in a mass media-saturated society.

Feminine discontent was focused on the victimization of women by society following World War II and their socialization into one role—wife and mother. The core idea of this feminist movement was the drive for equal opportunity for women to develop identities of their own, and it took the form of revising the laws that governed women's bodies, property and status as well as attacking the formidable problem of changing social attitudes and values. The movement challenged the stereotyping and sexist language that passed along—generation after generation through parents, schools and mass media—the idea that women were "second-class citizens."

Chafe pointed out:

In a very real sense, the woman's movement had gone full cycle. The women who started feminism in the nineteenth century had ideas which were similar in substance, if not in tone, to those of their successors. They too wanted an end to the notion that women should occupy a separate sphere, and they too insisted on every person's right to be a human being first and a man or a woman second.

As a social development the new women's liberation movement embraced numerous splinter groups that emphasized radicalism, politics and lesbianism, for example. The feminist press that grew out of this movement reflected both the central goal of self-realization and the wide-ranging special interests and causes that characterized the span of the new movement.

Women's Liberation and Women's Rights

The movement could be seen as two groups: women's liberation and women's rights, explained Maren L. Carden in *The New Feminist Movement*. The first consisted of small, independent groups scattered throughout the country. These were consciousness-raising groups—ones whose "primary function has involved intimate, personal discussion among the participants," she said.

The second, women's rights, according to Carden, included the larger and more formally organized groups such as National Organization for Women (NOW) and the National Women's Political Caucus (NWPC). These groups worked for reform of women's status by applying legal, social and other pressure on the institutions of society.

National Organization for Women was formed in 1966 by Betty Friedan, whose *Feminine Mystique* in 1963 first sounded the movement's ideological theme. NOW chapters were organized and the group's newsletter *NOW Acts* was first published in 1968 and became quarterly in 1970. A combined magazine/newsletter, this early feminist publication at first reported on the group's conventions and activities and later added regular departments covering a range of women's rights issues, such as education, child care, media, legislation, employment and religion. The legal section in each issue reported on NOW suits against companies and Supreme Court, and other legal decisions and changes affecting women across the country. This section was a helpful guide for NOW chapters in developing their own local action programs, some of which focused on monitoring news media, especially television stations and networks, for program content and employment patterns.

The *Spokeswoman*, an independent monthly newsletter of women's news, began in June, 1970 in Chicago, published by Harvard Business School graduate Susan Davis. It was unique in its comprehensive coverage of news of women's groups and issues from coast to coast with brief items on the latest legislation and legal challenges, news of sex discrimination cases and challenges in the schools and in business and industry, plus items on health, welfare, day care, child care, credit, divorce and abortion laws. It listed new publications, bibiliographies, conferences and conventions and served as a rapid carrier of vital information to a growing nationwide community of women united by a common interest in women's rights. It also carried concise information for those planning legal challenges or discrimination cases.

A little later to arrive on the scene, but also in the women's rights category and destined to become a vital source of information in one specific area was *Media Report to Women*, a newsletter published by Dr. Donna Allen, a Washington, D.C., economist. Brief items digesting the latest legal challenges, agreements, petitions, decisions, rulings and discussions on employment and sex discrimination in the broadcast and print media were contained in this monthly. It also carried short reports of speeches, conferences and opinions by and about media and women, plus news of feminist publications, radio and television programs and new programming by feminists and women's groups.

"Men simply cannot, or do not, see things as women do," explained a *Media Report* article. "We need to speak for ourselves if our media image is to be accurate, but in the meantime we must see that men at least present us fairly."

Most of the subscribers were media women, and *Media Re-*

port tried to help them keep informed on what was going on in media from the women's point of view, what women in media were doing and how other women were working to change the image of women in the media.

Allen began by sending out the publication as a free mimeographed report to any woman interested, but in January, 1974, she expanded to a printed newsletter with a subscription fee of $10 a year ($15 for men until the Equal Rights Amendment is passed).

Allen said,

> Although simple in format, *Media Report* has circulated widely. In doing so it has discovered in the nation a volcano of activity by media women and by society itself. Yet this whole new women's media movement has been almost totally unreported, and the women themselves do not know what is being done. Because women are eager for information, the response to the *Media Report to Women* has been phenomenal.

It was the women's liberation groups that encouraged the greatest proliferation of feminist publications, however, perhaps because these women who were discovering their own identities through "consciousness raising" groups sought to keep in touch with others who shared this excitement, dedication and outrage. Since the establishment press was only vaguely, if at all, aware of the movement in its earliest days, alternative means of communication were once again necessary. The underground press of the 1960's had already demonstrated the ease with which such papers could be put together using the inexpensive and fairly simple photo offset composition method.

Variety in Style, Similarity in Message

Filled with crusading energy, ofttimes outrageous and intentionally shocking illustrations and language, these liberationist publications varied greatly in content, style and technical quality, but they were similar in their messages, which were characterized by imaginative titles such as: *Everywoman, her-self, Prime Time, Lavender Woman* and *Off Our Backs*.

A few, *Woman: A Journal of Liberation* and *Aphra*, a feminist literary publication, both founded in 1969, attained national circulation and recognition perhaps because of the quality of writing in them and the seriousness with which they approached the topics. *Women, A Journal of Liberation*, which resembled a scholarly journal, was published by a collective and by 1972 had a circulation of 15,000. Each quarterly issue featured a theme, such as "Women in History," "Women in Art," "Sexuality," "Women Locked Up" and "Women as Workers under Capitalism." Each issue contained fiction interpretative articles, poetry and art, and staffers reported that their analysis was increasingly Marxist-Socialist.

The first publication to concern itself exclusively with women's rights was the legislative newsletter for women, *Skirting the Capitol*, said Anne Mather in her comprehensive study of the new feminist press published in *Journalism History.* This newsletter, published in Sacramento, California, in 1967 was the work of one woman, Marion Ash, who was opposed to women's liberation, so it is not strictly classified as a feminist publication.

By 1968 there were five publications that could be described as feminist and these included two magazines, *Lilith* (Seattle) and *No More Fun and Games* (Boston) as well as the newsletter *NOW Acts.* The following year there were 30 feminist publications, several of them NOW chapter newsletters.

Women's liberation in the underground press took on a new fervor in 1968 as feminist staffers examined the sexist and male chauvinistic advertisements, photographs, cartoons and articles in the publications they supported. Women staff members and feminist began striking back with demands for reform. The women at *Rat,* an underground publication in New York, protested against the pornography that had been added in the name of the cultural revolution. They told the men that it was an insult to their women colleagues and they also said it wasn't in the nature of things for women to do all the menial jobs.

The women asked to put out the next issue themselves. After that, *Rat* became a women's liberation movement newspaper, produced by women identified with feminism, gay liberation, the Yippies and Weatherwomen, according to the account in *Other Voices.*

Cities and towns with feminist organizations soon had their own newsletters or tabloid newspapers, and in 1970 the mass media took the movement seriously with cover features in the weekly news magazines and television specials. By 1971 it was estimated that there were 227 feminist publications and by 1975 at least 560 plus around 400 local chapter newsletters.

An example of a local feminist publication was *her-self,* a monthly for women in the university town of Ann Arbor, Michigan. It was "created to provide information, timely news and features about what is happening woman-wise in the Ann Arbor community." It was not associated with any organized woman's group and was sold mainly through counter-top sales, although it offered subscriptions.

Published by a group of about 20 regular staffers at any one time (students tended to work on the paper for a while and then graduate or drop out), the staff used group editorial decision making. One or two nights each month all hands were expected to turn out for the pasteup and assembly work. One person was designated to co-ordinate the issue. *her-self* usually focused on specific themes, such as "Women and the Law," "Women and Medicine," "Women and Credit," and was one of the first to write about the potentially dangerous side effects from the use of DES in the popular "morning after pills."

One of the largest women's journals was *Off Our Backs,* published in Washington, D.C. Although it was a local feminist publication, the paper was national in scope and covered movement activities from coast to coast, including conferences and reviews. A monthly, it was still considered the closest thing to a newspaper serving the woman's liberation movement, and made a serious effort to cover all news of interest to women's groups, including reports on organizations, articles on abortion, health, nutrition and the like plus political and social essays richly illustrated with graphics and photographs. The circulation was about 10,000 and the staff had about 10 regulars. *Off Our Backs* wanted to be regarded as spokeswoman and critic of the movement.

National and Specialized Publications

Prime Time, edited by Marjory Collins, illustrates one of many specialized feminist publications. It was designed for an audience of older women in "the prime of life." The editor started *Prime Time,* which attained a national circulation, after she had been phased out of her job because of her age and had to go on welfare to have an operation. "But it was good to get angry," she explained. "Anger either destroys you, or drives you to do something about the situation." She had only told her age to some of her closest friends until at a feminist party she blurted out "I'm 60 years old." Then she burst into tears "partly from relief, but also because I felt there was nothing good about being 60 in America." Her publication is trying to do something about that.

Another direction taken by feminist publications was to emphasize lesbianism or gay liberation. *The Ladder* (1957–1972) claimed the distinction of being the first such publication. Others included *Ain't I a Woman?* by the radical lesbians of Iowa City and *Lavender Woman* of Chicago, to name only a few. The focus in these publications is to confront lesbianism honestly and force others to do the same. Feminism is sometimes a minor theme.

Up From Under illustrated another direction. Started in 1970, *Up From Under* was for the working-class women and featured articles on union women, saleswomen and secretaries with how-to-do-it articles and interviews with working women.

Along with the many publications came a few women printers and booksellers. The best known was Know, Inc., organized by the Pittsburgh chapter of NOW to print articles for free distribution at NOW meetings. The articles were so much in demand that the group decided to sell them to pay the printing costs.

The business grew quickly and was making money by 1971 and moved to a storefront location in 1972. Know, Inc. published a few books, including listings of women's studies courses in American colleges and universities, and numerous pamphlets and offprints including the classics, "Woman as

Nigger," "Why Bright Women Fail" and "Why I Want a Wife."

Another publishing house, the Feminist Press, which started in 1970 specialized in non-sexist classroom books and children's literature that it hoped educators would use in order to "alter what women learn."

The publication that came to speak for the women's liberation movement in all its mutations and on a national scale was *Ms.* "*Ms.* is not just a magazine, it's a state of mind," said its editors. That state of mind is self realization. "No matter what their age or work or life situation, *Ms.* readers have one vital quality: they are women who make changes happen."

The magazine that was introduced as a 44-page supplement in the 1971 year-end issue of *New York* magazine appeared on its own in early 1972. It was pronounced a successful business venture after 16 issues to the amazement of the magazine industry, which had underestimated the widespread nature of the women's liberation movement by focusing more on a few of its attention-grabbing tactics than on what it was telling women and the rest of society. By September, 1973, *Ms.* had a hefty 350,000 circulation and a readership estimated at 1.4 million and was sitting pretty.

Its originator, Gloria Steinem, a journalist who specialized in political issues at *New York,* had become one of the women's liberation movement's most provocative and dazzling leaders. She had warned the nation—as had others—that the press was failing to report what women really wanted to read and that young women in particular were turning away from the establishment press and looking for alternative sources or information.

In *Ms.* they would find that alternative information. Status of the ERA, unemployment among women, credit laws and women, alimony, abortion, child care, day care, welfare, retirement, new life styles, dual-career families, living alone, aging, working class women, retirement—all would be topics for *Ms.*

Ms. used the slick magazine layout and attention-grabbing graphics associated with *New York* and underground publications. It was dedicated to the "liberated female human being who wanted to seize control of her life." The earliest issues were frankly abrasive and emotional, reflecting the mood of the movement at that point. The editors seemed to want to jolt the reader's consciousness through print in the same way a small group of women experienced that sudden release of anger and exhilaration in grasping the reasons for the contradictions in their lives and finding out they could do something about it.

Articles by Steinem and leading figures in the movement as well as by unknowns, photos, poetry, essays, opinion, fiction and straight information filled its pages each month, and standing features like "Lost Women" gave the readers a sense of continuity with the American past as well as a suggested pathway to the future. Women of all ages, shapes and sizes appeared in *Ms.* photographs, in a deliberate attempt to destroy the myth that all American women were young, slim and beautiful. The bitter tone modified occasionally and articles sometimes took on political or social issues in a straightforward and reasoned way. The movement's ideology and fervor remained, but now and then an article was critical of the movement itself. The appeal, despite attempts to draw in all types of women, was still to the middle class, educated woman.

The magazine staff was democratically organized—that is, everyone participated in editorial decisions, read incoming manuscripts and attended staff meetings to plan the issues. Babies were brought along to the office in the spirit of practicing what *Ms.* preached, and the magazine wrote about the pros and cons of this experiment with its usual frankness. The outside media looked on in amazement.

The spirit at *Ms.* was casual but the work still got done. The office was not chaos as some had predicted, and ideas and information flowed in the easy access each staffer had to the other. With publisher Pat Carbine, an experienced and highly regarded professional researcher and editor at *Look* and *McCall's* for nearly 20 years, directing things the publication since 1972 seemed on a successful and prosperous course, attracting 400,000 subscribers by 1975.

One of the feminists' most vigorously fought issues was stereotypical advertising, which set a limited image of what a woman could be or do and contributed to her sense of inferiority. In *Ms.* the editors and staff were careful to reshape the image of women in their advertising. Advertisers regularly are shown the positive and negative comments their ads draw and have been educated to write copy for intelligent, independent women who decide about their purchases and their lives. And the magazine has kept the ratio of ads to editorial matter low because "our readers want and need to communicate with each other."

The establishment media magazines directed toward women modified their contents during the 1970's in order to appeal to some of these same women, and a few magazines were started for women in sports. For a time it appeared that there would be a new national news magazine, *Woman News*, published by Susan Davis in Chicago. After two years of analysis of market and audience the project was shelved because financial support could not be found in a recession economy. Another magazine combining features, news and service, called *Working Woman*, did premier at the end of 1976, and *Savvy* for executive women arrived in 1977.

The woman's liberation movement of the 1970's did not have one voice, but until 1975 an ideological unity pervaded its many voices. Voices continued to speak out for the Equal Rights Amendment which still needed ratification by four states when the United Nations International Women's Year meeting opened in Mexico City in June, 1975.

An International Conference

International Women's Year in 1975 brought together the first such international group to work out a 10-year plan of action to improve the status of women in five major areas: political decision making, educational opportunities, economic opportunities, a different status in civil courts and in all questions of maternity. A thousand delegates, one third of them men, discussed the problems of the world's 2 billion women, 1.4 billion of whom are in developing countries.

The Conference also illustrated the great disparity between women's roles and status in the most and least developed nations. It sent some home with the feeling that just talking together had been an important start and that progress on their 10-year plan could be made. Others thought it a waste of time and regretted that it had diverted energies better used in making improvements at home, such as getting ERA passed in the United States by its 1979 deadline.

The United Nations Commission on the Status of Women proposed a resolution regarding women and media in the fall of 1976. If adopted by all member nations, it would require them to avoid sexist sterotyping in the media, improve the image of women in the media, stop segregating women's news, increase employment of women in the media and conduct wide-scale research on media images and news values.

Feminists in NOW split, and the "radicals" won the leadership late in 1975. The "moderates," including founder Betty Friedan, formed a group called Womansurge to carry on NOW's mainstream philosophy. *Ms.* magazine reflected these tensions with its increased emphasis on lesbianism and working class women. But in July, 1975, it also ran Vivian Gornick's thoughtful rebuke of the doctrinaire party-line attitude that she believed was leading to "mad squabbling" and "charges of revisionism," threatening the progress of feminism. Women's Studies programs at universities followed various paths; some kept up the political emphasis, others toned down politics and insisted on more rigorous research in an effort to convince other scholars of their programs' academic respectability.

Whatever the reason, the urgency and excitement that the movement generated in the early 1970's seemed gone or at least muted in the Bicentennial Year of 1976. The movement had lost momentum, and no one was quite sure whether society's attitudes had been deeply changed or not. Many believed they had and that the new task would be for women to hold the territory gained and move into responsible policy making positions in management.

A new interest in the interrelationships of men and women and how each sex influenced and defined the other's role was being voiced by the end of 1975. Said Natalie Zemon Davis, professor of history, University of California and a distinguished scholar in the field: "The high hope of herstory is that history will one day yield the full dimensions of ourstory."

· SOURCES CONSULTED ·

Maren L. Carden, *The New Feminist Movement*. (Beverly Hills: Russel Sage Publications, 1974).

William H. Chafe, *The American Woman: Her Changing Social, Economic, and Political Role, 1920–1970*. (London: Oxford University Press, 1974).

Everette E. Dennis and William L. Rivers, *Other Voices: The New Journalism in America* (San Francisco: Canfield Press, 1974).

Eleanor Flexner, *Century of Struggle* (Cambridge, Mass.: Harvard University Press, 1959).

Ida Husted Harper, *The Life and Work of Susan B. Anthony* (Indianapolis, Ind.: The Bowen-Merrill Co., 1908), Vol. 1.

Joy Hart, "The Feminist Press Today," Unpublished research, University of Florida, 1974.

Aileen S. Kraditor, *The Ideas of the Woman Suffrage Movement, 1890–1920* (New York: Columbia University Press, 1965).

Anne Mather, "A History of Feminist Periodicals," *Journalism History*, Vols. 1, 2., (Fall, Winter, Spring, 1974–75).

The New Woman's Survival Catalog (New York: Coward, McCann & Geoghegan, Berkley Publishing Corporation, 1973).

Sally Quick, "The Feminist Press: The Ephemeral Spirit," Unpublished honors thesis, University of Michigan, 1974.

Bertha Sterns, "Reform Periodicals and Female Reformers, 1830–1860," *The American Historical Review*, Vol. 37 (July, 1932).

8

* * *

Women Who Teach
the Journalists

ANY WOMAN IN or interested in journalism education, seeking guidance about her role from the literature, would need only a few hours to cover the topic thoroughly. Since the turn of the century there have been about a half dozen career books on women in journalism and thirty or forty articles. There were 10 articles between 1972 and 1974. Seven of those were papers presented at the annual meeting of the national journalism education organization, the Association for Education in Journalism (AEJ), as the women in that organization became aware of their status as educators. Five of the articles appeared in the *Matrix*, the official publication of Women in Communications, Inc. (WICI), formerly Theta Sigma Phi, a national organization for professional media women.

"What should a school of journalism teach women?" asked newspaperwoman Jean James in 1932. "The same thing that it teaches men," she said after listing some of those things. This, of course, was exactly what the schools of journalism were doing, she hastened to add. "So far as this writer is aware, all of them are open on equal terms to men and women."

It is interesting to see that in the 1930's James pointed out a problem for women, which is still a problem: "One frequently hears the remark that since women do a different type of work from men on newspapers, it is foolish for them to take the same courses." (They were talking about women's place on the women's pages, of course.)

James termed this "fallacious" reasoning, pointing out the newspaperwomen of 1932 were not limited to one or two lines of newspaper work and that newspaperwomen could be found in practically every capacity on newspapers.

> No woman who becomes a staff member of the modern newspaper has any reason to believe that she will never be called upon to do anything other than the one task, or manage the one department, to which she was first assigned. Illness of other staff members, vacations, news crises may force her to assume some extra job on her own paper at any time. And then she will be thankful for a general training.

Journalism school training was a must for the female who wanted to go into newspaper work, James said, although males can go to work without any experience. The young woman without it is "at a loss to know what to do."

> It is comparatively easy for a youth with no experience along newspaper lines to drift into newspaper work and make a place for himself as a reporter, department editor or desk man by the rather simple expedient of garnering a place as office boy and learning the ropes from the ground up. For the young woman, this is practically impossible.
>
> Women are not as a rule possessed of as much "nerve" as men, . . . That indefinable something can be cultivated in schools of journalism.

James also wrote that a newspaperwoman, according to some persons, has little use for the technical details of newspaper making, that

> . . . these folk would do away with such courses as tend to give the would-be newspaperwoman an inkling of the mechanical side of the newspaper. They would substitute some classical studies for this practical knowledge and believe in all sincerity that she would be better for it.
>
> We would pity the newspaperwoman when the city editor railed at her for her failure to get a story or berated her for her lack of news style if she could only reply, "But I know my Browning!"
>
> Teach the woman student the essential facts about the art of printing, the composing room, the process of engraving, sterotyping, make-up and the parlance of the news and composing room (not the expletives!).

The women journalists should be trained to write a feature story as distinguished from the straight news story because they are

> . . . frequently called upon to do features and in many cases develop a slant on them that is different from the type of story a man writes.
>
> If, then, these are things that a school of journalism *should* teach its women students, they are, of course, also the things that a school of journalism *can* teach women. No one would dare gainsay that statement!

James was writing in a magazine whose primary audience comprised women journalists, young women who had formed their own organization because the men of Sigma Delta Chi would not accept them. She gives us the impression that journalism schools of the 1930's offered their women students an equal training with men. From other sources we know, for example, that the early journalism students at the University of Michigan in the 1890's published a laboratory paper and that women were included in that practical course. We also know that all of the 13 schools of journalism that existed in 1912 admitted women on an equal basis with men and that the Columbia School of Journalism, endowed by Joseph Pulitzer, would do so when it opened in 1912. We know too, that in the mid-1920's home economics flourished and this fascination with scientific homemaking would extend to journalism schools in the form of journalism courses taught by women in the art of writing for the Home Pages.

Apparently not until 1953 did anyone attempt to find out what these journalism graduates thought about their education. In the aftermath of World War II with its emphasis of getting back to normal, Adelaide H. Jones published a study of women journalism graduates from the 1941–1951 decade. She sampled 13 schools and departments of journalism, and the results appeared in *Journalism Quarterly*.

The article investigated the professional life of the graduate from the standpoint of general employment trends, specific fields of activity, earned income, and the effects of geographical location and marital status on her career.

"The journalism graduate of 1941 lived much more happily

with her husband and family than with her profession," Jones concluded. To Jones this raised a question for journalism educators: "How can the lot of the woman journalist in the working world be improved?"

Her study indicated that journalism educators needed a better understanding of the needs of the woman journalism student and that there should be more consideration of those needs in curricular planning, course counseling and job placement on the part of the institution of higher learning.

"Improvement might come, too," Jones said, "from a more realistic conception of the profession on the part of the student herself. The problem presents a challenge to all concerned with the education of women for journalism."

Twenty years later the same challenge was issued to journalism educators in the form of a paper from some of its women educators at the 1972 AEJ convention in Carbondale, Illinois. Until that time little if any attention was given to women as journalism educators or to the education of women in journalism.

Roberta Applegate paid attention to the issue in 1965 when she left a distinguished professional newspaper career, which included serving as a political reporter for the Associated Press, press secretary to the governor of Michigan and reporter-feature writer-copy editor on a large metropolitan daily. She became an educator at Kansas State University and soon after her article on "Women as Journalism Educators" appeared in the *Matrix.*

Pioneer Women Journalism Educators

Pioneer female journalism educators had for some reason received little attention, she observed. She identified five pioneers: two Helens—Hostetter and Patterson at Kansas State University and the University of Wisconsin respectively—Gretchen Kemp at Indiana University, Frances Grinstead at the University of Missouri and later the University of Kansas, and Grace Ray at the University of Oklahoma. The two Helens "stuck together for moral support" whenever they attended conventions of journalism educators in the 1930's.

They didn't have much trouble finding each other because frequently they were the only women college faculty members present. Patterson was apparently the earliest of the pioneers, having started teaching at the college level in 1923.

Three of these women spent most of their academic lives in the Midwest—Wisconsin, Kansas and Missouri. Helen Patterson Hyde, Helen Hostetter and Frances Grinstead served distinguished careers in both professional journalism and journalism education. They paved the way and served as educator models for countless students, both male and female. These three women were certainly among the first in all categories of "firsts" for women in journalism education.

* * *

Helen Patterson taught journalism and supervised a newspaper at a high school in Pratt, Kansas, in 1917. Her students won national awards with their newspapers nearly every year until 1923. That year she started teaching in the School of Journalism at the University of Wisconsin. Patterson's may have been the second high school journalism course in the United States.

For the first 10 years of her college teaching Patterson thought that there were no other women in journalism education. She was the first woman member of the American Teachers of Journalism. She taught at Wisconsin for 33 years, from 1923 to 1957, where she was an associate professor and head of the magazine article courses. During those years she lectured at many different schools of journalism, engineering, home economics and to several visiting groups. She served as national treasurer of Theta Sigma Phi and sponsored their annual Matrix banquets at Wisconsin and the University of Arizona. She originated several new courses, concentrating primarily on feature article writing, and wrote two textbooks, *Publicity for Organizations* and *Writing and Selling Feature Articles.*

Patterson retired from teaching in 1957 when she married Grant Hyde, a well-known journalism educator and administrator at the University of Wisconsin. After her marriage she continued lecturing at various clubs and universities in the country.

During summer vacations when she was teaching she often worked on newspapers, magazines and in advertising agencies in order to broaden her experience and to gain new ideas. "I never could decide if I liked teaching better than the journalism work I did. I liked them both." she recalled. "In the days when I was right out of college, we were warned not to tell we were journalism school graduates when job-hunting or we wouldn't be hired,"

Patterson received her degree from the University of Kansas and worked as a reporter in newspapers throughout the state. "I was promoted from reporter to city editor on a Kansas daily (first woman editor they'd ever had) in one of my first jobs," she said. Later the publisher of her paper met an old Kansas University professor at a convention and when he came back he told her, "If I'd known you were from a journalism school, I'd never have hired you." But he didn't fire her. She filled that job and went on to other "firsts" in Kansas—first woman wire editor, first woman critic, first woman copy editor. She had also been the first woman editor of her campus newspaper.

"I changed jobs a lot and kept moving around," she said, "because in those days women in journalism were so looked down upon that in order to get a raise, you had to find a better job."

Patterson made use of her own practical experiences by stressing to students the value of analyzing the markets for their free-lance articles and attributed the widespread success of many of her students to this effort. She started a course called "Writing for Homemakers" and encouraged both journalism and home economics students to take it (adding that it may be the first such course in the country). She believed that the women's pages in newspapers and women's magazines were instrumental in raising the standard of living in the United States. Magazine editors regarded her as an expert and she was frequently asked for advice until her death in 1974.

✳   ✳   ✳

Patterson's friend, Helen Hostetter, had pioneering in her blood; hence it was natural that she too should do some pioneering in her own field, journalism. Her grandfather was an Indiana farmer and her father went to Nebraska as a "country doctor." She was graduated from Nebraska State University in 1917 with an A.B. in English literature. After teaching high school English in Nebraska for five years she was assigned a journalism class—to teach seniors to write news stories about high school events for the local weekly. That exposure to printer's ink inspired her to get a journalism degree at Northwestern University in 1926.

Hostetter's first newspaper job was on a Sioux City (Iowa) labor paper founded by pressmen from Des Moines who had lost their strike for higher wages. Typographers' unions of the Midwest invested in the newspaper and three veteran newsmen from Minneapolis-St. Paul made up its hard-core staff members in 1924 when she joined it.

"I was lucky to get my first newspaper experience under such men," Hostetter observed. She was hired as the society editor—although she had vowed that "she'd take in back stairs to scrub" before she'd accept a society editor's job! Soon she was also writing Sunday features. Not long after, she registered with a teacher's agency and landed a job at Mount Union College in Ohio to put out its alumni organ, handle sports publicity and teach the one course in journalism. She stayed two years.

Kansas State College (later University) offered Hostetter a job teaching journalism in 1926. There she was the only woman on the journalism faculty and the only person with the rank of instructor, but the next year she was advanced to assistant professor. After five more years of teaching at KSU she became an associate professor. No sex discrimination as to rank was apparent there, she said.

One of the courses Hostetter taught, starting in 1931, was "Journalism for Women," for those who would write for women's pages and magazines and other special fields for women writers. "The Home Page" course was offered soon thereafter, with the editor of the local weekly offering his newspaper as a laboratory for the course. Later, over cocktails, the editor of the local daily expressed to the head of the journalism department his pique at being "excluded" from that service. Accordingly, the size of the class was doubled and both local papers had "home pages." Next, some of the men students protested discrimination and wanted to take the course which by that time was called "The Home Page." So it lost most of its sex bias.

Among the most popular feature articles over the next several years were those on home building and design. The faculty of the College of Architecture at KSU became advisers for content and the class visited houses being built by the student architects. The class was given the services of a photographer once a week, and had help on gardening articles from the professors in horticulture. The course also motivated Hostetter to take a B.S. in home economics.

She spent her sabbatical leave during 1940–1941 in New York City free-lancing and taking courses. That spring Hostetter was offered the job as editor of the *Journal of Home Economics*, which she held for five years. In 1946 she returned to Kansas State University with a full professorship but, at $3,600, hers was the lowest salary of any holding that rank in the department. (As far as she knew she was the first woman in journalism to hold that rank.

Hostetter taught reporting and writing courses on the same basis as the male professors and continued free-lancing, and wrote two books, *The Wide World of Clothing* and *Country Gentleman Home Handbook*. After she retired in 1964 she continued to write, teach writing courses and handle publicity for a number of organizations.

✳   ✳   ✳

Another pioneer woman journalism teacher, Frances Grinstead, received a B.J. in 1921 and an M.A. in 1928 from the University of Missouri. Before going into journalism education, she was city editor of the Mexico (Missouri) *Intelligencer* for a year. She then became women's feature editor on the Spartanburg (South Carolina) *Journal*.

> It was clear in Spartanburg that Red Cross news, music criticism, school news and other "non-woman news" I had been doing on top of a full day's work as women's feature editor gave me opportunity to do the general writing but not to get recognition for it.

When an opening came along in the city room, they hired a man, although Grinstead had been promised the job when it should arise.

> I've never had any bitterness about it; it was just the way things were, in a part of the country where at that time few college-educated women entered professions until after they passed the age of "spend the day" parties at which they sewed for their hope chests and took afternoon siestas.

Grinstead joined the faculty at the University of Missouri in 1927 as an instructor and after three years became an assistant professor. In 1948 she went to the University of Kansas School of Journalism as an assistant professor and was promoted to associate in 1951, retiring at that rank in 1967.

Grinstead carried on an active writing career while she taught. She was a travel correspondent for the New York *Sun* in 1929. She also wrote for magazines and completed a novel, *The High Road* (Doubleday, Doran). Early in 1945 she resigned from the University of Missouri, intending to spend full time writing. She soon realized, however, how much she enjoyed teaching and needed continued association with young minds. So she joined the University of Kansas faculty, where she specialized in feature and magazine writing classes and also taught "The Newspaper in Society." Part of her work load became a University writers' conference.

> I felt neither that I was ever discriminated against . . . because I was a woman nor ever given preference for that reason. It is possible that an early personal attachment to the "creative" aspects of journalism gave me occasional advantage in being able to progress as I wished—most of my colleagues (men or women) did not seem to yearn to compete in this part of the field.

Her teaching pay was not so satisfactory, but that was true for females generally and for women colleagues, Grinstead recalled. "Perhaps the only discrimination evident . . . was that there were not 'enough' of me. One woman to a faculty total of 15 to 20 men is female underemployment, sure enough!"

Many schools had no women faculty members in journalism, even at the instructional rank, during much of the time she taught, she said, and as late as 1949 or 1950 another department head asked her dean, "How does it feel to have a woman on your faculty?" Her dean said, "She's just like anybody."

Grinstead retired after 35 years of teaching at the university level without ever having been made a full professor. "In all modesty," she commented, "I cannot accept this fact as a fair assessment of performance," but she is proud to have been a part of the university system when there were few women professors. She looked forward to the day when sex distinction would end and she challenged the current crop of women in academic journalism to do something about it. That "is in your part of the history, not mine," she wrote.

When asked to proofread her listing in an honor society's annual roster, some time after she had stopped teaching, Grinstead changed the classification from "retired" to "writer," which is a designation she thought might last a long while. Her paternal grandmother lived to 107 and she expected to continue her writing course and her free-lancing in Sarasota for some time.

AEJ Investigations

When these pioneers were retiring, other women had taken their places, but they were still for the most part in the skills courses, teaching writing and magazine features or public relations as that subject became popular. And they stayed at the lower ranks.

In 1965 Applegate found that 76 women from 56 schools or departments of journalism belonged to the Association for Education in Journalism. Only 7 of them were full professors; 12 were associate professors, 16 assistant professors and 20 instructors. They comprised 7.5 per cent of AEJ membership, but only 9 of them attended the 1965 convention of that group.

Grant M. Hyde, long-time director at the University of Wisconsin School of Journalism, said he felt that his faculty should include at least one woman, because a third and sometimes more of the journalism students were young women.

Part of the reason for the relatively small number of women journalism educators may be due to what a former Kansas State University Journalism Department head said was "the fact that prejudice against women is still present to some degree."

Despite their growing numbers they still evidently did not feel a part of their own professional group, as one of them said in 1970:

> During the AEJ meeting at Berkeley a number of years ago, a report was presented on the sad state of recruitment of blacks into journalism study and into the journalism faculties of universities. Now don't misunderstand me, I agreed with the report. However, many of my colleagues rose to speak out in scandalized tone about this inequity. As they spoke, I looked around the auditorium at the membership in attendance, some 300 to 400 . . . and could find only eight women other than myself.

Who were these women educators? And where were they? That was the motivation for a group of three journalism educators from Kansas State's faculty—Ramona Rush, Carol Oukrop and Sandra Ernst—to look into the matter. Their 50-page report was presented to the AEJ convention in Carbondale, Illinois, in 1972. It was the first of its kind for AEJ and led to the formation of an Ad Hoc Committee on the Status of Women in Journalism Education. Said Rush,

> No one seemed to know how many "qualified" women there were in the potential pool for journalism education. We were concerned, because if the women did exist they were seldom visible at annual meetings of the AEJ, on the pages of its journal, *Journalism Quarterly*, in the university classrooms or in administrative positions in schools or departments.

A search of AEJ annual reports, AEJ annual meeting programs, pages of *Journalsim Quarterly*, American Association of Schools and Departments of Journalism (AASDJ) directories and responses to questionnaires sent to selected female Ph.D. candidates and graduates provided some answers.

In 1970–1971 there were 131 women members of AEJ out of 1,200 total membership, or about 11 per cent. This was a small percentage increase over 1965 but almost a doubling in the number of individuals.

How did women use their memberships in AEJ? Was their participation active or passive? This was the type of information Rush and her team gleaned for their report. It was obvious that few women held major roles in AEJ administration and in its program planning and participation. They did give papers and act as panel members, but not to any great extent. There had never been a female president of AEJ and few were ever part of the official structure of officers and committees.

As contributors to *Journalism Quarterly* from 1960 to 1971, a period when the number of women teaching in journalism had grown impressively, women had only contributed 10 per cent of the "Research in Brief" items and 7 per cent of the major articles.

According to the 1968–1969 and 1971–1972 faculty directories of accredited schools and colleges of journalism, 67 and 73 women, respectively, were employed in journalism education. Women represented about 7 or 8 per cent of the total employed on journalism faculties in institutions of higher educations. In 1971–1972 about 60 per cent of these schools and departments employed at least one woman.

"How many Ph.D. women can you identify in journalism or communications?" Rush asked AEJ officials and department heads. "About 10," was the answer.

If the number of Ph.D. women was indeed that low, then schools and departments of journalism had some justification in claiming that there are few qualified women available for employment in a job market that increasingly requires advanced degrees in addition to media experience, Rush observed. There were, of course, qualified women other than those with doctoral degrees, such as those with master's degrees and professional experience, but they were even less visible to the administrators.

The search by Rush and her colleagues turned up 44 Ph.D.'s and 57 women in process toward the doctorate in universities offering graduate education in journalism or mass communication—a far larger supply than had been supposed. Another study in 1972 found that 10 per cent of the 402 Ph.D.'s in mass communications between 1968 and 1972 were awarded to women.

Of these women with or working toward advanced degrees (doctorates) 73 per cent answered a 1972 survey abut sex discrimination in journalism education. They did not find much evidence of discrimination in admissions, counseling or in aid for the doctoral program. But few of them had ever had any women faculty at the graduate level in journalism as "role models."

"Strange," said one, "I hadn't thought of it, but I had no woman faculty members during my entire graduate program. Very few are members of the graduate faculty on this campus."

Where the women did experience problems was in the conflict between their personal and professional roles, especially in social gatherings with faculty and students.

"The faculty (males) and Ph.D. candidates (males) would gather in a group to talk shop and the wives would gather in another group talking family and children. Where does one go in such a situation? And with what results?" queried one woman student.

Another pointed out the necessity to make very clear to the wives that "you're only interested in their husbands professionally." She added, "Inevitably I spend time at a party listening to the problems of raising a family when I'd rather be talking with the men about professional matters."

Over half of the women agreed that women had to "do more" to earn the respect of their professors and male counterparts in the doctoral program because, "If they were female and young, they were "assumed to be dumb and had to prove themselves to be competent. Men, on the other hand, are automatically assumed to be competent unless proven stupid."

Those who were teaching and studying agreed on three major areas where sex discrimination did occur: promotion in rank, leadership positions and salary. Tenure and lack of travel opportunities were also problems. Only a fourth of them believed there were no problems of sex discrimination in journalism education.

Women educators specializing in broadcast media were surveyed in a 1975 study by Leeda Marting and K. Sue Foley with similar results. The 101 respondents, 39 of whom were teaching assistants, were generally young and low paid, in the lower professional ranks and relatively inexperienced in media work. They showed little participation in academic professional organizations. But most of them agreed that they had experienced discrimination in their work because of their sex and had to work harder than males to prove themselves.

While these investigations of women in journalism were admittedly limited, they did seem to point to questions and conflicts about the role of women in this academic area that deserved further investigation. There were certainly 10 times more women in the potential pool of qualified women for journalism education than many individuals had supposed. One obvious problem was that there had been no central source to identify them or their needs and no concerted effort to bring them into active participation in their own professional organization.

An independent study by Women in Communications, Inc., in 1972 was a first step in locating these women. They found that of 170 schools, 90 had no women and only 48 had one woman on their faculties. WICI resolved to call for an affirmative action program to increase the number of women in communications faculties at American colleges and universities and to remove discrimination in hiring practices and promotion procedures. The study showed a sharp reduction in the percentage of women as one progressed up the ladder to full professorships.

The AEJ Ad Hoc Committee on the Status of Women in Journalism Education gave itself the task of finding answers to some of these questions. A directory was started, a salary survey taken, and studies of the history and attitudes of women educators were made. These were presented at a plenary session at the 1973 convention, the first time the organization had placed an official spotlight on the status of its women members. Some of the findings were discomforting.

Reported Paul Jess of his 60-school survey:

> If you teach journalism in a college or university which
> has a sequence accredited by the American Council on Edu-

cation in Journalism and you are a woman, you tend to be ranked lower, promoted more slowly and paid less than your colleagues who are male.

Women held only 8.64 per cent of the full-time faculty positions and two thirds of them were in the lowest ranks: instructor, lecturer or assistant professor. One third of the males were in these categories.

Young Protestors and Seasoned Objectors

Those women educators who responded to a survey that year (1973) made by Wilma Crumley and Joye Patterson were aware of the discrimination, but they responded in different ways. Half of them were "young protestors" under 40 years of age, untenured and at the assistant professor rank or below. This group felt discrimination strongly in their professional environment and thought salary inequities should not be tolerated. A small group of "seasoned objectors, who were older and enjoyed higher rank, more pay and more experience than the first group, thought things were improving. They championed their own schools for fair treatment but they were still generally concerned about discrimination. A third group of "accommodators," were older and had considerable teaching experience and were generally satisfied.

A fair interpretation of the study was that the young protestors, given the favorable atmosphere of the 1970's and their strong feelings, would be heard from by their deans and administrators, especially after they had examined the salary survey.

Women members at that convention, and there were 54, including several doctoral candidates, for the first time met as a group to get acquainted. The "old boy" system that had operated for decades in academe received a "sister." These women would be helpful when candidates for new positions were being discussed at their schools because they would know some of the potential female candidates. The women decided that they still had more concerns and that the committee ought to be continued. It was.

Leaders of the committee, having had the opportunity to

learn the internal workings of the organizational structure of AEJ for two years, attended the winter meeting where program arrangements were solidified for the annual meeting. When they left, women journalism educators were assured of a substantial showing at the 1974 San Diego convention.

The informal meeting of 1973 was replaced thereafter by a regularly scheduled breakfast "get-acquainted" session and evening committee meeting. Women in Communications, Inc., hosted receptions to bring women educators in contact with professional members in the convention cities.

Visibility for women educators at AEJ conventions among the spouses and women book exhibitors was another problem the women's group solved. Name tags for members would be one color; name tags for guests and spouses another. From San Diego on, AEJ has followed this custom. It gives the women members professional visibility. It has also eliminated those embarassing "Where does your husband teach?" questions by thoughtless males whose first assumption was that the woman was a colleague's spouse.

By the 1974 convention in San Diego a directory of 254 women educators had been published, and it contained the names of 49 women holding doctorates and 48 women in the process of earning that degree.

Matilda Butler-Paisley and Suzanne Pingree re-analyzed earlier studies of doctoral graduates in communication, and found that communication schools had not produced enough women doctorates to sustain an affirmative action program for their own faculties. A greater proportion of women doctorates than men are "lost" to academe in jobs outside the universities.

"When and if communication schools move toward affirmative action in faculty appointments, it is doubtful that more than a token redress of balance can be achieved without preferential admission of doctoral students," they concluded, "a policy that is usually rejected as 'unfair.' "

The numbers of women in journalism takes a funnel shape, said Mary Ann Yodelis and Marion Marzolf in a 1974 study of women at the master's level. It is large at the undergraduate level (women make up about half to 40 percent), of the classes the number decreases at the master's level and is down to about 10 per cent at the doctoral level, they said.

Women in the master's program detected little if any discrimination in academic, social or professional areas, which apparently speaks well for their teachers who are still mostly male. They did have problems with role conflict in classroom and social situations. Three quarters of these women had not had "role models"—women journalism professors—in their graduate schools, but only a third of them thought that they had to "do more" to earn respect of their professors and male counterparts.

Journalism teaching at the college level is mainly a white, male profession in the United States, concluded an American Association of Schools and Departments of Journalism study in the summer of 1975. The study, which examined the Association of Education in Journalism membership directory for 1975, found that of 1,139 members, 960 of those were currently active teachers and of those, 107 or 11.2 per cent were women. No more than 5 to 6 per cent of the teachers were racial minorities. Undergraduate classes at the same time were about 50 per cent female. The study predicted that more qualified female teachers would enter the job market in the decade ahead.

The creation of an ad hoc committee in AEJ in 1972 to deal with the status of women in journalism education was undoubtedly a major milestone in generating research on academic women in the field and in increasing their participation in AEJ. More women attended the sessions and held divisional and national offices in 1974 and 1975 than ever before. Five additional reports on women and journalism were presented in 1974, and the 1975 convention in Canada scheduled two sessions on women, including a special one featuring women in Canadian journalism. Another milestone was reached in 1977 when the University of Kentucky named Ramona R. Rush as its first Dean of the College of Communications. The newly created college comprises the School of Journalism and the Department of Human Communication. As far as can be determined, Dr. Rush is the first woman dean of a college of communications at a major university. Perhaps the most important result of all this activity was that women promised to take on their share of the professional obligations in AEJ, making things a little easier for the women coming along in the future.

· SOURCES CONSULTED ·

Roberta Applegate, "Women as Journalism Educators," *Matrix,* June, 1965.

Matilda Butler-Paisley and Suzanne Pingree, "Women Doctoral Students in Communication," a paper presented at the International Communication Association, New Orleans, April, 1974.

Steven H. Chaffee and Peter Clarke, "Training and Employment of Ph.D.s in Mass Communication," report presented at AEJ, Fort Collins, Colorado, August, 1973.

Wayne A. Danielson and Nwabu Mgbemena, "A Descriptive Study of College and University Teachers of Journalism in the United States," *AASDJ Studies,* 2, August, 1975.

Jean James, "Women in Schools of Journalism," *Matrix,* June, 1932.

Paul Jess, "The Status of Women in Journalism Education—1973," paper presented in AEJ, Fort Collins. Colorado, August, 1973.

Adelaide H. Jones, "Women Journalism Graduates in the 1941–51 Decade," *Journalism Quarterly,* 30, (1953).

Leeda Marting and K. Sue Foley, "Women in Broadcast Education," *Journal of Broadcasting,* 19:1 (Winter 1975).

Marion Marzolf, "The Changing Profile of Women in Academic Journalism and Mass Communication—A Report on the AEJ Directory of Women and Minority Men in Academic Journalism and Mass Communication," a report presented at AEJ, San Diego, California, August, 1974.

Ramona R. Rush, Carol E. Oukrop and Sandra W. Ernst "(More than You Ever Wanted to Know) About Women in Journalism Education," paper presented in AEJ, Carbondale, August, 1972.

Ramona Rush, "Women in Academe: Journalism Education Viewed from the Literature and Other Memorabilia," a paper presented at AEJ, Fort Collins, Colorado, August, 1973.

Mary Ann Yodelis and Marion Marzolf, "The Funnel Effect: Graduate Women in Mass Communication," paper presented at AEJ, San Diego, California, August, 1974.

Personal interviews with Frances Grinstead, Helen Hostetter and Helen Patterson Hyde (all courtesy of R. R. Rush).

9

* * *

View from Europe

THE EDITORS OF Western Germany's highly regarded *Die Zeit* and France's *L'Express* news weeklies in 1972 were women. So were the heads of French television news for the second channel and Finnish television's Swedish channel and a few chief editors of daily urban and provincial newspapers. So, for that matter were the directors of several women's magazines and countless women/family pages and women's broadcast programs. Despite such achievements by several outstanding Western European journalists, the profession could hardly be characterized as "liberated."

As in America, most women journalists in Western Europe clustered in certain jobs: on the pages for women and families, in feature writing, in magazine and book publishing, on family and consumer affairs broadcast programs. There, as in America, only a handful made the managerial and editorial decisions that influence media policy. Women accounted for from 10 to 30 per cent of the media jobs, depending upon the country.

Some Europeans, however, did see women newscasters on their home television screens several years before that innovation appeared in America. In Finland, Norway and Sweden women have been newscasters since the late 1950's and in all these European countries their voices have been heard on radio at least since World War II.

When over a hundred professional newswomen in Sweden, Finland, Norway, Denmark, West Germany, England, France and Belgium were asked in 1972 in a series of interviews if they had equality with men in their professions—equal pay, promotions, opportunities and prestige—many of them quickly answered: "Only on paper."

What they meant was that most of the professional journalist unions had adopted equal pay for equal work provisions in their contracts, but women still often received less pay for equivalent jobs with men. Individual "merit" pay increases, slower promotions and limited professional experience accounted for much of the salary difference. Salary surveys in some countries in the 1970's indicated 10 to 20 per cent pay differences between men and women journalists.

Some of the women were sanguine about it. Happily placed in jobs they enjoyed, fearful of creating a fuss and conscious of the limitations that motherhood and family responsibilities placed on their mobility, they regarded this second-class status as one of the prices of dual-role lives.

Others, however, made a fuss and organized to do something about the situation. Organizations of women journalists in England, Finland and Sweden fought for wage equality and elimination of sex discrimination in their professions. Although most of these women said they were not anxious to participate in "American-style feminist confrontations," they were firmly resolved to bring about change. Their first steps were to bring about union action to study and equalize pay, establish maternity leave, day care facilities and fair pensions for women.

Changes in attitudes about women's role in life outside the home have paralleled similar developments in America. The urban newspapers were first to shift their women's pages from the old-style "children, cooking and clothes" to broader coverage of politics, life styles and social issues of the 1960's. A similar trend occurred in the afternoon radio and television programs directed to the at-home audience—the names indicate the trend: "Family Mirror," "Everyday," "Notebook," "Today's Life," and "Modern Life."

Opportunities for women in journalism in Western Europe increased in the 1960's. More women students were found in the one- and two-year professional journalism schools and increased numbers entered the profession. Although a few women moved into political and economic reporting in several countries, they were still rare, as were crime and sports reporters, foreign correspondents or chief editors who were women.

"Compact Dominance by Men"

A study released in the fall of 1974 by University of Uppsala students, for example, charged Sveriges Radio, Sweden's national radio and television system, with a "compact dominance by men." The study analyzed radio and television newscasts during the winter of 1973–1974 and found on their sample days that men anchored all the news, gave all the opinion-essay segments and nearly all of the news reports. Women reporters appeared for 5.5 minutes compared to 234.5 minutes for men during one sample period and for 63.5 minutes compared to 352.5 minutes for men in the second sample period. Most of the subjects being interviewed were men. In this study they found that women dominated the feature programs—hosting and editing shows about people, styles of life and the family. Men dominated the public affairs programs, in sports, science and entertainment.

The Uppsala study posed this question: "Should Sveriges Radio merely mirror society as it is today, or should it take some of the responsibility for breaking traditional patterns?" The researchers thought that the broadcasters should play an important role in helping women identify with all aspects of society, including politics, sports, science and other traditionally male activities.

The biggest hurdle was changing the attitudes of employers and the women professionals themselves. These attitudes were changing in Western Europe during the early 1970's and the younger woman was looked upon by her colleagues as the hope for the future.

More than a third of the journalists in Finland were women—the highest percentage in the eight countries studied. This is partially explained by Finland's having one of the highest proportions of women in the labor force in Western

Europe. Some 40 per cent of the Finnish women work, compared to 24 to 36 per cent in the other countries studied.

Until 1974 a woman co-edited the country's largest afternoon paper, *Ilta-Sanomat*. Another published Turun *Sanomat*, one of the country's most technically advanced provincial city dailies. World War II brought many Finnish women into journalism because most of the men journalists were at war, explained Maija Liisa Heini, former co-editor of *Ilta-Sanomat*. The women stayed in journalism and the numbers have increased recently as Finland "tears down traditional sex-role barriers," she added.

Sweden had a union membership of 25 per cent women journalists in 1974. A quarter of the staff of *Dagens Nyheter*, the leading liberal daily, are women. Women made up from 14 to 27 per cent of the other Stockholm newspaper staffs, and they appeared frequently on radio and television feature and life style programs. They dominated magazine journalism, as elsewhere, but still tended to be mostly in women/social problem/feature writing specialties.

Sharing the Work

Even though Finland and Sweden both have large proportions of women in their unions of professionally practicing journalists, there were differences between the countries. Finnish women complained that "although they are expected to work alongside their brothers and husbands, they are also expected to do the housework and see to the family." Finland has a long tradition of women working alongside men in agriculture, and when industrial jobs opened in the late nineteenth century, both men and women took them.

Swedish women, on the other hand, led the western world in the sex role debate. The discussion was intense there during the 1960's and as a result there was a good deal of public acceptance of the principle of equality of the sexes and a positive attitude developed toward working wives and mothers. This is not to say that all or even many Swedish men shared equally in bringing up the families and in part-time jobs while families are young, but some young couples did this. Sweden and Finland backed up their working women with large, well run, publicly supported day care centers.

In France, a nation with a long tradition of women in the professions, 2,577 women held professional press cards as of 1974, about 20 per cent of the total. In Paris 23 per cent of the journalists were women.

England ranked fourth in this informal survey with women holding 20 per cent of the journalist union memberships in 1974. This was an increase of about 10 per cent since the early 1960's and much of that increase came from the growing provincial dailies and suburban newspapers where women were particularly welcomed. London daily journalism remained largely a masculine preserve.

In West Germany, Norway and Denmark only about a tenth of the working journalists were women.

Early Journalistic History

Women have a long tradition in western printing. Soon after the invention of moveable type, wives and daughters were pressed into the business, and widows often carried on the work after their husbands died. The earliest women actually to print were the nuns of the Convent of San Jacopo de Ripoli in Florence in the 1470's, but none of their books were preserved. The first book frgm the press of a lay woman, the widow Anna Rügerin of Augsburg, Germany, in 1484 is in the Morgan Library.

Soon after 1500, women in France and the Lowlands were printing under their own names. In Paris, Charlotte Guillard, also a printer's widow, began a career as printer in 1502 that lasted over 50 years and brought her fame all over Europe, according to the research of Dorothy Gies McGuigan.

In England widows who inherited printing shops and carried on the businesses were considered rich matrimonial prizes because they could either retain the place of master printer or marry a freeman of the guild, and that occurred fairly frequently, said McGuigan. Occasionally, women printers also got into trouble with the law for illegal printing, especially when censorship was strict.

A woman, Elizabeth Mallet, is credited with publishing the first English daily newspaper, the *Daily Courant*, on March 11, 1702, in London, but it lasted only a few weeks. "Mercury Women," who hawked and sold the latest news sheets and pamphlets in seventeenth and eighteenth century London streets were also a part of the colorful history of women and the press.

Some women publishers worked along with their husbands and carried on family printing businesses throughout the centuries, but women did not really make much of a mark on daily journalism until the end of the nineteenth century. By that time most daily newspapers in the big cities had one or two of the "lady journalists." Feminism introduced some of the earliest women writers to the public. Women who led the mid-century discussion on "the woman question" found it useful to get their ideas published in the local newspapers, and the editors welcomed this copy. It was not until the 1880's or 1890's, as in America, that women were hired on Western European papers as full-time journalists, and women had achieved some of their emancipation goals by that time.

Women journalists entered the job market at a time when some European urban papers were broadening the content and style of their newspapers in order to appeal to a larger, general audience that included women. Most early female journalists found their jobs in fashion, gossip and feature writing. Some of the early women journalists did stunts and wrote women's-eye views of events, some wrote witty commentary and a few broke into hard news reporting and political coverage or became foreign correspondents.

Tekla Hultin, Finland's first woman Ph.D., was also a pioneer in journalism. She regarded her position in 1893 on *Päiväleti* (later *Helsingin Sanomat*) as a natural extension of her degree in economics. Only later did she reflect on the "unusualness of her employment." Some of the men, she recalled, were afraid of her at first, but the editor encouraged her work. Later she studied law at the Sorbonne in Paris and served as a member of the Finnish Parliament for 15 years.

Denmark's first professional woman journalist was Lulu Lassen. She began full-time work at *Dannebrog* in 1899 and moved to *Politiken* in 1910 where she became widely esteemed in Copenhagen for her intelligent and intelligible medical articles.

The London *Daily News,* a penny morning daily, employed a Mrs. Crawford in 1898 to report political news from Paris. She recalled covering the Paris Commune riots and said she had "no trouble getting through the streets to get her story." She and her correspondent husband often worked at a kitchen table in their apartment accompanied by the noise from their four children. She attributed some of her success to her good health.

One of the most ambitious journalistic efforts of the time was the publication of *Le Fronde,* a daily newspaper, written, edited and printed by Parisian women. Its founder and editor, Marguerite Durand, had taken over her husband's newspaper, *La Presse,* when he entered politics, and later she reported for *Le Figaro.* In covering the 1896 Congress for Women's Rights in Paris she found herself in total sympathy with the claims and demands of the women meeting there. She decided to start a daily newspaper on which women would perform all the tasks and through which they could report and combat the social injustices that all women were suffering.

Le Fronde began publication December 9, 1897, and took a liberal stand on issues of the day. It described itself as a "feminist and feminine newspaper" devoted to the cause of women's right to life, experience and equality. It often ran articles about the condition of women in different countries, but it did not press for Frenchwomen's right to vote because Durand believed that women were not sufficiently educated or free from church domination to vote intelligently.

The paper continued daily for five years, became weekly in 1903 and soon ceased. Durand finally had to admit that she had kept the paper alive as her own private charity, an act of will, during the last years. But she had helped change public attitudes about women and was credited with aiding passage of much needed legislation against exploitation of children and prostitutes and laws for the protection of department store workers.

A daily newspaper by and for women seemed a novel idea

to Alfred Harmsworth, later Lord Northcliffe, when he started one in 1903. His weekly magazines for women had opened up large markets in the 1890's so he thought a daily newspaper for gentlewomen, edited along the same lines would be one more success. The first issue of the *Daily Mirror* sold 400,000 copies, but by the end of the week sales were down below 100,000 and falling. After only three weeks, Harmsworth had the entire staff of "writing women" fired and replaced them with men who were told to turn the paper into an illustrated tabloid.

Although some laughed outright at the idea of women editing a daily paper, Northcliffe's biographers say the paper's failure was his own fault. The *Mirror* was neither a serious journal nor a good woman's weekly magazine. It was not for the "naughty new woman who smoked cigarettes and wanted to vote," but for the bright, home loving ladies. It was filled with scraps of poetry and fluff that Northcliffe believed would appeal to the middle class woman trying to enter Society.

When they didn't buy it, he concluded that "women can't write and don't want to read"—a conclusion "not less erroneous than his belief that they should welcome a daily paper which condescended to their special interests which proclaimed them the inferior sex," observed his biographer.

A London *Times* correspondent in 1914 complained about the lack of serious women's voices in the English general press and in the women's publications, although there were capable women leading the suffrage movement and writing their pamphlets. London "lady" journalists replied that they concentrated on fashion and other requirements of women because Englishwomen were not interested in serious matters.

In France at the same time, according to the Paris correspondent of the London *Times,* there were many women editors, critics and editorial writers on the Paris daily papers and several minor women personalities on the staffs of weekly and daily publications. Feminism seemed to be opening even wider opportunities to women in the French press. Some of the better known women were editors of publications for women which included articles on education and health as well as fashions and homemaking. The Frenchwoman, the writer reminded English readers, had always played an important role in political and financial life as an influence through the Frenchman. Topics dear to the Frenchwoman's pen, according to the correspondent, were those dealing with the struggle against alcoholism, tuberculosis and the lack of maternal education.

By the twentieth century most daily newspapers in European cities had found out what women would read on a daily basis. The papers carried columns of homemaking hints, social tips, fashion and food features. A few women managed to wangle general assignment jobs on the European newspapers.

Stockholm of the 1920's, for example, had a little group of women journalists who worked for the daily newspapers. One, Elin Wägner, later became a Nobel Prize author. They met regularly as an informal club in a favorite downtown restaurant. Celie Brunius, at 90, fondly recalled those days. "We never shared our stories, though. Loyalty to our newspapers came first."

Two world wars gave women a rare opportunity to cover battles and foreign events along with the men. The period is studded with "star reporters" like Barbro Alving who covered the Spanish Civil War for *Dagens Nyheter* in Stockholm. She went on her own, but once she found a way to get into Spain and wired for money, it was sent. "They were afraid I'd get killed," she laughed, "and they didn't want to be responsible." Her dispatches from Spain and later those from the winter War in Finland made her famous and reassured her editors that she could take care of herself.

In the 1930's English journalism textbook writers were urging women to interpret the "new woman" and her fuller life as their particular journalistic specialty. This was a distinct change from similar books of the 1890's that had criticized women for "slipshod work and a light-hearted attitude toward journalism."

Women were to further demonstrate the wide range of their journalistic skills during World War II and its recovery period. Educated women often found jobs in newspapers and magazines in that expanding postwar market in Europe. Some, like Countess Dönhoff, stayed with their new professions and

came to occupy leading positions. A few became star reporters.

On Assignment

Oriana Fallaci, an Italian journalist, exemplified the star reporter remaining in the 1970's. She specialized in candid interviews of the world's celebrated political and cultural leaders
for the magazine *L'Europe*. She became an overnight celebrity
in America with her interviews with Dr. Henry Kissinger,
U.S. Secretary of State, and President Nguyen Van Thieu, of
South Vietnam.

The daughter of an Italian war hero who led the underground movement in Florence, Fallaci was raised on excitement, politics and adventure. She gave up medical school for
journalism and traveled the world on assignments for Italian,
American and other European magazines. She was in Hungary
during the revolution, in Mexico City during the 1968 riots
and several times in Vietnam during the war. Her interviews
bristle with her own as well as the subject's remarks. She gets
things out of her subjects because she's really interested, she
said: "I get in fights and discussions with them, and I yell and
scream and they know I really care."

Some young European women journalists may still dream of
being star reporters, but more typical in the 1970's was the
ambition to be an all-round professional reporter, treated the
same as any male reporter and with the same opportunities.
Women actively worked toward this professional standard,
but they also argued that women should not have to become
"substitute men" or "stunt girls" to achieve this. Women have
different perspectives from men and these are especially valuable in today's world with its important social concerns. The
definition of news, not professional standards, ought to be
changed to include this humanitarian-social concern of women
alongside the more typically masculine emphasis on politics,
economics, wars and disasters, they said.

One possible method of instituting change in the
newsrooms, these young journalists suggested, was for

women to develop the kind of camaraderie male journalists have always had. That would help encourage them to press forward their views and to seek more responsible jobs. Unfortunately, this new group consciousness developed in a period of sluggish economy and shrinking job markets caused by newspaper mergers, rising production and paper costs and media closings, which made the task even more difficult than it would have been in good times.

More and more modern European postwar newspaperwomen pushed out of the traditional slots on the women's pages, resisted offers to edit those pages and followed their college interests into economics, politics and business reporting in the 1960's, but it wasn't easy.

Berit Rollen, who came to her job as press secretary for Sweden's Prime Minister, Olof Palme, from the chief editorship of a weekly business magazine, put it this way:

> Every woman has to fight once to struggle to show that she is strong. If you do not fight, you will be on the women's page or something like that. But once you get the chance to show what you can do, everything is O.K. from there on.

Her own fight was staged after working for two years as an economics writer on Stockholm's *Tidende*. Economics was her subject at the university, and she had become "number two" on the staff by the time the economics editor quit. Rollen asked for the job. They offered her the women's page. She refused. The editors tried for months to fill the economics post, and finally, despite their fears that she could not work with older men as subordinates, gave her the job. She held it four years before moving to the top post on a Swedish weekly business magazine. There are several women economics writers in Sweden, Rollen explained, "because women can compete in journalism, whereas it is still difficult for them in industry."

Parliamentary and General Assignment Reporting

Parliamentary reporting was seen as a good stepping stone to becoming a political analyst, and a few women held these posts in Scandinavia: six in Stockholm, three in Oslo and four in Copenhagen. Their assignments depended very much on their editors' attitudes. A few women in Scandinavia were convinced that "informal quotas" still operated in their newsrooms. Rumors circulated that one paper would not hire any more women for a while because "they have too many now." One editor barred any woman on foreign news "for as long as he was around."

But other Scandinavian editors were enlightened and looked for good reporting wherever it was to be found. "You don't *have* to work on the women's page," said a parliamentary reporter for *Berlingske Tidende* in Copenhagen. "Just let the editors know you want to work in general news and you'll get the chance." She did.

Finland had a long tradition of women in general assignment reporting. Some, like Anni Voipio, entered after World War I. Still free-lancing today, she was a "pioneer" all-round woman reporter and correspondent for the conservative daily, *Uusi Suomi.*

Women's pages never really caught on in Finland, although they appeared from time to time, and women reporters more often have had varied assignments in Finland than elsewhere. They sometimes startled visitors. One American oil tycoon who visited post-World War II Finland refused to hold a news conference when he was met by only women reporters. He demanded to speak to men. Editors refused. When no one attended the second conference, he called the Finnish editors and said:

"O.K. Send me your women. Now that I have been here for two days, I see that in Finland you just have to deal with women everywhere." The Finnish women journalists were ready for that confrontation with expert questions. The American treated them cordially, so the story goes.

The newsrooms in Finland and some of those in Sweden contained a mix of men and women, young and old, instead of the mens' club atmosphere of so many city rooms in Europe and America. But even in Finland women were not always equally valued for their political acumen. At least two Finnish women political analysts (one of them a Communist) have hidden behind male by-lines because they knew their words would carry more weight that way. One was passed over for an editorship after 19 years of outstanding work. Her publisher told her: "Too bad you are not a man; you should have had this job."

A few of the old stereotypes were openly bandied about, even in the city room at *Ilta-Sanomat,* whose co-editor, Maija Liisa Heini, was one of Finland's top women journalists. A male colleague volunteered this observation in passing: "Men do some jobs better and women do other jobs better."

"For instance?" he was asked. "Men are better at covering fires and accidents. They are physically better equipped for it. Women are good at gossip columns. Oh, not because *they* gossip, but because people tell them things more readily," he observed, making a fast exit to the telephone.

No Men on the Women's Pages

The "People and Fashion" page on this tabloid has always been edited by a woman, although the female assistant editor (later city editor), Leena Salminen, at the paper believed it could just as well be done by a man. No man had yet been willing to take the job. She herself had to edit the former women's page for a year, until she pressed her request to cover social issues. "Finnish women are taking an interest in politics," she observed, "and their displeasure over the double standard is growing."

Women edited the cultural pages on Helsingin *Sanomat* and *Uusi Suomi* and reported economic, political and sports news. Some were chief editors and department chiefs, but Finnish male journalists still didn't want to work on family page staffs, said Heini. "The situation is, in my opinion, rather absurd, because many problems of today concerning home, children, family and so on have to be seen as common for both sexes and logically should be solved together."

Women have served as correspondents for European newspapers, as they have for American papers, but this occurred usually in wartime when labor was short. In the early 1970's there were only a few women correspondents, and they were mostly with the wire services. At Stockholm's *Dagens Nyheter*, during the winter of 1972, two women reporters applied for openings as American correspondents. They competed with seven men for the two posts. Men got the jobs, but the editors did send one woman to America on a feature series. The women vowed to keep trying for one of the 11 foreign posts and in 1974 a woman, Disa Håstad, was named to the Moscow post. AFP of France also had a woman correspondent, Anne Wahl, in Moscow at the same time.

The idea that sports reporting is a masculine field remained. Editors were not very impressed by the idea that since women compete in the Olympics and play baseball and soccer, women ought to cover sports events as journalists. That seemed no reason to let women report big-time sports. A Norwegian reporter tried for years to break into the field, but the sportswriters would not admit her to their organization because "women can't go into the dressing room to interview players." Despite her colleagues' resistance, the young woman specialized in sports personality interviews and the athletes didn't object to her reporting.

Some women in Europe were publishers and chief editors of newspapers, news weeklies and magazines. These women said they experienced little discrimination themselves on the way up, but at the same time they understood the problems of today's working woman. Household help was readily available when most of these successful women combined young families and jobs. Even though the problem was "understood" by the more experienced men and women editors, they tended to believe that if a woman wanted to work, she should be able to find a way to manage her obligations. Younger women, however, called this "unrealistic." Men with families did not have such pressures, they pointed out, because society does not recognize family responsibilities as equally shared by husband and wife.

Staff Policies

Women chief executives varied in the staff policies toward women. At *L'Express*, editor-in-chief and co-founder Françoise

Giroud employed more women than most French news publications. A third of the editorial staff was female, she said, "but we don't have enough women political analysts." Countess Marion Dönhoff, editor of Germany's *Die Zeit,* agreed. Giroud predicted a change for the better in the next five years because "young women today are interested in politics."

Many of the young women at *L'Express* began their careers as researchers, just as they do on American news magazines, said Giroud. Often they had not made a career choice when they applied for the job, she explained. The men, on the other hand, had usually done newspaper reporting before they applied and were able to start as news magazine editors or writers.

"Research technique is essential for a news magazine writer," Giroud explained, "and if a researcher grasps the work and is ambitious for a journalistic career, she can and does move up to reporting here." (Giroud accepted the post of minister of women's affairs in 1974 and became secretary of state for cultural affairs in 1976.)

In postwar France, at least three chief editor-publishers took over their deceased husbands' posts. Francine Lazurick, chief of *L'Aurore,* in Paris was one. She and her husband worked together as lawyers first, then on the newspaper. She employed women in all departments, she said, including foreign politics, justice and crime, but had no women assistant night editors. Her staff was about 20 per cent female.

European women held jobs as assistant editors or sub-editors in the 1970's despite the fact that many of these were night jobs. Family women liked the regular hours of editing jobs and in England, according to the journalist union's training officer, women were doing "exceptionally good jobs" on the suburban papers as editors.

Other women were content to remain reporters and ignore career ladder routes via the copy desk to top editing positions. A Norwegian woman said:

> I'm partially responsible myself for staying a reporter. I did not seek out the experience to write headlines and do layouts when I started. The young men did. Then I was of-

fered the chance to write on social and educational issues. I took it and liked it, but had I thought of being an editor, I would have had to press hard against the traditional attitudes to get the experience. Still, I think it would have been possible.

The Axel Springer publications in Hamburg and Berlin employed 1,500 journalists and editors in 1972 and about a fourth of them were women. They were trained in the same program with men, and they worked in all departments. But there were no women chief editors or correspondents at Springer papers.

And only a few were "responsible editors," a term that conveys legal responsibility as well as high management and policy responsibility.

Women on the Springer publications worked mostly on local city news, theatre, music, arts or family/women's pages. They did best on the illustrated weeklies and women's magazines owned by the company, said their training director. Still, he predicted a change in the future because of the young people's increased interest in politics.

Legal News and Top Crime Stories

Dr. Hildegard Damrow, who made a specialty of legal news and top crime stories for Springer's *Hamburger Abendblatt* and *Welt am Sonntag,* said women have the "chance to be equal, but not so many take it." An expert on women and law, divorce laws and women's rights, she suggested that the lack of day care facilities and kindergartens, plus the poor education and minimal training many women had, hold them back in employment. The big social problem facing urban, industrial societies is the "unhappy housewife over 40 with nothing to do," she declared. Retraining and re-entry of these women into the labor force will be one of the main social problems of the coming decades, Damrow predicted.

Le Monde's Nicole Bernheim, an economics writer, spent several years trying to convince her liberal Parisian editors that women's employment, pay and job discrimination were "serious economic news and major social problems." The first time she mentioned women's pay inequities in a story in 1966, she recalled, it was cut from the article. But by 1972 she was expected to write long reports on the subject for the economics page. Women at *Le Monde* in the 1970's reported on foreign politics, science, economics and culture and a new chief editor for the Cultural Department was a woman. A decade earlier there were very few women on Parisian dailies, Bernheim recalled. There had been no wage survey or study of working conditions of French newswomen by their unions as of 1974.

As women and attitudes about them changed in Europe, the women's pages and women's daytime radio and television programs changed to reflect the wider interests of their audiences. Urban women of the 1960's and 1970's had fewer children than earlier in the century, were more apt to be self-supporting and to regard the 5 to 10 years of child care as a "temporary absence" from the work force. This female labor force was increasingly made up of women over 40 with serious career goals and more stable lives than was typical of the early twentieth century single career girl.

The pages that first attracted Victorian homemakers with food, fashion, family and etiquette had to broaden their horizons to keep up with a modern woman who often worked outside the home and knew much about the world beyond her doorstep. The biggest changes occurred on urban dailies; provincial papers still carried more traditional women's pages. The new sections that appeared around the start of the 1970's included: "Family Page" at *Helsingin Sanomat, Berlingske Tidende, Politiken* and *Aftonposten;* "Today's Life" and "Fashion and Home" at *Le Monde;* "Fashion and Home" at *Le Figaro;* "Modern Life" at *Die Zeit;* "Women and Society" at Frankfurter *Rundshau,* and "Society and Family" at *Süddeutsch Zeitung.*

In London the *Observer* went from "Modern Living" in the 1960's to "Hers" and then to "Ego," and still wasn't satisfied. The British newspapers were not completely happy with the family/life style approach for these pages and wavered between traditional and modern approaches. The *Evening Standard,* for example, added a page of fashion for men to balance the women's fashion page. The *Times* had "Look," and for a short time the *Evening News* came out with "London's Eve."

New Approaches to the Women's Pages

Elsewhere the new family pages drew wider audiences and seemed more satisfactory. *Helsingin Sanomat* found that 80 per cent of the men and nearly all the women subscribers read its new "Family Page." This page contained consumer advice, abortion and divorce law reform discussions, school lunch plans for the week, articles on education, child care, child abuse, architecture, the environment, house care, cooking and fashions for all ages. The layout was modern and attractive with only a few articles each day, well illustrated with large photographs and sketches. Writers for these pages believed they had more challenges than they would have had on the traditional women's pages because greater precision and research abilities were demanded for these topics and because the pages received more attention from the chief editors.

Helsingin Sanomat and *Dagens Nyheter* in Stockholm illustrate new approaches to the women's pages. Both tried to keep at least one man regularly on their staffs and sought more. Both specialized in provocative, well-researched articles that stirred up talk around town on issues that touched both men and women.

Dagens Nyheter's "Vardag" (Everyday) staff bombarded Stockholm for six weeks early in 1972 with a "womanpower" series that leveled charge after documented charge of sex discrimination in pay and job opportunities in all kinds of jobs in Sweden, including the newspaper's own publishing house. The series was later released as a book. Chief Editor Börje Dahlqvist himself suggested the series and agreed to assign an experimental team of women and men to handle it.

At about the same time the women journalists at *Dagens Nyheter* (DN) first met as a group to discuss pay, promotion, child care and sex discrimination. These talks gave many of the women their first opportunity to get acquainted because this staff of 250 journalists occupied individual offices in a tall, modern office block, quite unlike the large open city rooms of American newspapers. With this meeting the DN women began to see themselves as a group with common goals and problems. They urged qualified female candidates to try for posts of editorial responsibility as these were announced. Women had not tried hard for top jobs in the past, they said, and women had also been overlooked by editors. *Dagens Nyheter* promoted two women to sub-editorships in the early 1970's.

Women took a greater part in union activity, but there was also a change in attitude by some DN male editors. Several men had working wives or daughters and through divorce a few men had learned first hand about the responsibilities of child care. Such men understood the need for regular hours by those young married employees with families at home. Women at DN and elsewhere praised these positive attitudes of male bosses who encouraged their work and hired men and women strictly on the basis of ability. Such editors made it possible for women to get a fair chance to advance, just as the biased editors helped "keep women in their place."

European broadcasting attracted men and women from print media and theatre. Patterns set for women staffers on the daily newspapers were easily transferred to radio. Separate radio programs for the women at home were counterpart women's pages. Women were believed to be especially suited to handle these broadcast positions but not hard news. Women also found niches in educational radio and on children's programs. In Scandinavia their voices were first heard in radio news broadcasts in the 1950's. And in Finland and Norway, for example, women began work as reporters and newscasters on camera in television newsrooms from the inception of TV in 1957 and 1960 respectively. A woman and man shared the news desk reporting for the first six years of Norwegian television.

Sometimes women newscasters in Europe received emotional criticism from listeners who said women's voices "lacked credibility on serious news events." Some Danes "disliked the accent" of their first television anchorwoman in 1972, and Brussels' French language radio listeners also criticized their first radio newswoman in 1962. In both cases the news staffs backed the newswomen and comments soon ended.

The BBC had women news reporters and newscasters at their regional stations and women writer-editors in the London newsroom, as of 1972, but women were only rarely seen on the evening news in London. When one BBC editor placed a woman on his news team, his own London staff refused to cooperate with her.

West German and Belgian television introduced their first female newscasters in 1972, but France had none, despite Jacqueline Baudrier's appointment in 1969 as director of news on the second TV channel. Women reporters were seen on French news television, but were more frequently seen on women/family/talk shows than on the news reports. There were a few in entertainment and executive positions.

Working Double

Marte Dumon, who had worked in Belgian news radio for 10 years in 1972, has headed the home news for French language radio since 1967. She was the first woman to join the news team in 1961, after finishing the trainee program. Entry to the trainee program was very fair (completely anonymous) but once in, it was more difficult for women to get into the news department than it was for men, she said. There were three on a staff of two dozen and they did all types of news.

> Women have to work double to get the same consideration as men. Society doesn't make it very easy for women. Even if a woman says she wants to work hard, it is not always possible. But it is also a question of mind; women are not very responsibility-oriented. It is not easy for women with a family at home to take on such heavy professional responsibilities. Women have to affirm themselves at the beginning when they are 26 or 27. But that is a difficult time for women as they are apt to have young children at home and extremely demanding jobs. It is a crucial point in their professional development. It is easier for women of 40 and over to devote themselves to a career.

In Finland there were 160 women journalist-editors in broadcasting in 1972 (30 per cent of the staff) and they worked in all departments: news, foreign correspondence, education, social and cultural programs, entertainment, regional and foreign relations. Women entered the executive ranks, but felt "more keenly watched than the men," especially by the press and the public. The head of Swedish language television for Swedish-speaking Finns, Joan Harms, directed the 11 hours a week programmed for this 10 per cent of the Finnish population. The lack of women executives in Finland, she explained, was mainly because women "had not been encouraged to try" and were unsure of their executive ability. Women were not trained for administrative work, but men were.

In Norwegian broadcasting, women tended to work in traditional departments at first, but a new general director in 1962 encouraged women to try all kinds of broadcast reporting. Ten years later there were 90 women in production and writing jobs (about 17 per cent) and 18 women in executive jobs in administration and 29 in the technical services.

Norwegians found women to be good television producers and directors because they were so conscientious and careful with details. On the news staff women rotated assignments with men and whoever was assigned to the news desk for the day read the news wire, put the newscast together, wrote the introductions, inserted actualities (voice-taped inserts) and anchored the program. Five of the 25 reporters were women and all the editors were men, but most of the women were fairly new at the work, which they think accounted for their absence from the editing job.

Norwegian television introduced its first woman political reporter, Guro Rustad, a university student, during the election coverage of 1969 as a part-time reporter. When the regular parliamentary reporter was to be away for eight months, editors looked for a male replacement. Finding none they offered Rustad the job and it became permanent. She did not "think of herself as a pioneer," she said, since there had been women on TV news in Norway for a dozen years. But she did believe she "helped broaden the range of choices open to women reporters."

Funny things still happened to women in such traditionally male jobs. Rustad and two of her female colleagues were momentarily stunned at a news conference when their hosts presented them with flowers, because their 30 male colleagues had long since accepted them as working press. She said,

You have to go through a wall, but once you do, you reach the point where you are no longer upset by the reactions of others to you. It takes self-education and experience as a journalist. Many women give up too soon, or they take refuge in writing in fields where they are considered capable just because of their sex.

Broadcast journalists often pointed out that television is far more difficult work for women than radio work, mainly because the technology is more complicated and the working hours stretch on and on until a show is finished. Tape recorders used for radio were simple to handle, so radio free-lance work often became a way to break into broadcast journalism.

Women were well aware of the limitations imposed by their other jobs as wives and mothers. "We are just not as mobile as men," observed Metta Jansson, Norway's first television anchorwoman. Norwegian women have had equal pay for some time, and yet it is still hard for them to get the top level jobs, she explained. "Men make the highest wages and get the important foreign assignments."

Although Rustad did the same work in Oslo as the mobile teams, she had the feeling of being just "not quite as useful as male colleagues who can run whenever a story breaks." Her stories on social issues and local events were important, she believed, but the public and editors tended to give greater importance to world affairs. Her editors "have never held her back" and she had done all kinds of assignments, she explained, because she had an unprejudiced boss who encouraged her work. Still, if she were to try for an executive post, she would have to think of the effect on her family. "A woman can say, 'this is enough; I am happy here.' A man does not have that freedom. He must try for the top."

Sveriges Radio (SR), Sweden's national radio and television system, experienced a large increase in the female staff over the 1960's. "It was pretty much a man's world here in 1959," recalled one woman. But in the 1970's, women worked in news, current affairs, family and children's departments and the staff elected a woman to serve as their *ombudsman* to the board of directors. But women made their greatest impact at SR in the current affairs department on consumer questions and other social and political issues. Women on this staff said they got equal pay and equal foreign assignments with men, and several were paid more than men because they had more broadcast experience.

Union Work

Women at SR also became more active in union work during the 1960's. Earlier they often used family obligations as an excuse, but "if you really want husbands to take some responsibility at home," one radio journalist explained, "you must give up some of it. If you take all of it on your shoulders, he will never give up his work first to take on some family duties." She and her husband shared work at home and rotated foreign reporting assignments.

The director of this section of SR has favored hiring women so the "women dare come forth," as one of them put it. Two of the programs this group presented were "Family Mirror" and "Time Mirror," both directed by women for the daytime audience. "Family Mirror" began in the 1960's as a typical woman's program, but in five years it had begun to take up social issues. "Time Mirror" handled large social problems facing the modern world.

"Despite the fact that Sweden seems to have a progressive attitude toward working women and the Swedish public approves of working women, it is still difficult to rise beyond a certain level," cautioned Ingrid Lundgren, director of "Time Mirror." "Sweden is just like the rest of society; a woman has to be better and work harder to get to the top," she said. "That may change in the future, but women don't help any themselves by avoiding the subjects that would be useful—economics, social science, politics and management—when they are in college."

In Western Germany where broadcasting was established on a regional basis following World War II, each regional unit made its own program schedule and all included programs for women and the family. One show in Munich attracted attention for its liberal political views and experimental format. "Notizbuch (Notebook) tries to politicize women and improve their critical minds by giving them information and ideas so that they can develop their own opinions," explained its editor. Journalists and editors on this program were allowed to express their own views and listeners report that they want it that way.

"Notebook" editors believed that women "cannot remain as they were before—mainly centered in home and family." They must expand their interests and knowledge to include a profession or job and their public responsibility. Conservative politicians in Bavaria have disagreed with the "Notebook" ideas and politics but let the show run. The hour-long program devotes each day to a different topic: modern family, politics, consumers, education, culture, leisure.

The show began as an attempt to attract young listeners to radio. Innovations by younger staffers and the experience of seasoned colleagues accounted for the success of the show, said director Dr. Lore Walb, who anchored the political hour each week. The show reflected her philosophy of "balancing the interests of the individual with those of society in a democratic way."

Women's Magazines

Women's magazines developed in Europe during the mid-nineteenth century, and early feminist magazines also appeared then, including *La Fronde* in Paris and *Hertha* in Stockholm. The contributors to the feminist publications often wrote in their local daily newspapers about the "woman question." As magazines grew in popularity and variety, women formed increasingly larger parts of the secretarial and research staffs, made contributions as writers and free-lancers and became lady editors," especially at the women's magazines.

That pattern remained in postwar Europe where most magazine staffs are predominantly female. Women often moved into magazines from daily journalism or as first jobs, especially if they were looking for regular hours and creative work. Magazine pay tended to be lower than on newspapers, and was often non-unionized, but it was considered more respectable for young ladies. Men kept the jobs of publisher and chief editor, even on women's magazines, for the most part.

Traditional men's magazines like *Punch* allowed a few women staffers and contributors, but none of these women was ever asked to the weekly *"Punch* table" where writers and editors met to dine and review the future issue. British women journalists finally got their very own *"Punch* table" on Leap Year Day in 1972 when they were invited to participate in writing a special issue of *Punch* devoted to the "new woman." The women attended despite protests from some of their colleagues and they took over an entire issue of *Punch*. The men held their regular *"Punch* table" that week and the British press smirked: "The Judys have not been invited back to the table."

European women's magazines in the 1970's were caught in another familiar dilemma—holding their older audiences and attracting the new, youthful one, too. As in America some magazines mixed content in order to appeal to both, and others split into two publications.

At *Birgitta* in Frankfurt, Peter Brash, the chief editor who began this magazine for young women 15 years ago, was proud of the women who write and edit the magazine. He was one of the first to encourage women journalists in postwar Germany, he said. There were few women chief editors, even of women's magazines, in West Germany, but Paris had several, including one of the most famous, Hélène Lazareff, founder of *Elle*. She directed a staff of 98 women writers on that weekly journal of fashion and culture.

Karel Anthierns, an editor at Editions J. Dupis in Brussels, which published radio, television and women's magazines for Beligum, France and the Netherlands, said he was more pro-women's liberation than many of the women of his staff. He encouraged them to write articles on women's rights and discrimination. In his staff of 86, there were 36 women, 23 of them editors and writers, and they were paid the same as men. He mused about the possibility of encouraging men to "liberate" the secretarial field.

Executive responsibility in any field makes strong demands

on women, as Karin Coyet, chief editor of a popular Swedish weekly, *Året Runt,* explained:

> What seems to distinguish successful women editors from the unsuccessful ones is that these women are willing to sacrifice a lot for the job. They can and do take the full editorial responsibility. They may also be feminine and fuss over their husbands and children, but in a choice between job and home obligations, the job comes first.
>
> The opportunities in magazine work are enormous for women. Good executives and editors are rare. If a woman has a good head and willingness to work, she can climb high. But one must dare to do things. Some women do not want to work; especially they do not want the constant worry of executive jobs.

Managing editor of the magazine for 18 years, Coyet was a logical choice when the chief editor resigned in 1968. Still, she had to give it "careful consideration" before accepting.

Salary Games and Surveys

Most Western European women journalists said they had equal pay in principle. The European journalist unions negotiate minimum wages for all jobs and men and women receive the same minimums. The catch was that in the big cities the journalists' pay is well over the minumum, and in many places men got 10 to 20 per cent more than women, according to studies made in the 1970's.

Despite the suspicions of many newswomen that they were underpaid, only a few tried to find out through union pay surveys, some asked their editors. Such a trip to the editor could result in frustration, however, as one Finnish woman recalled. She was told that she got less because she was single—a man had a family to support. She did not get "too angry" about that until a few years later when another woman, who was divorced and had a child to support, sought a pay raise and was told that "salaries were not awarded on the basis of need but on ability. The argument was turned on its head, always to the disadvantage of women," she declared.

But women were partly to blame for that state of affairs, *Dagens Nyheter* women realized. "We found out that men go out and cultivate other job offers and then go to the boss and say, 'Match it or we will leave.' Women don't play that game very well, if at all," one of the DN journalists said. Women liked their jobs and feared to gamble. Only when a wage survey at DN showed that men received 20 per cent higher wages than women did the women become seriously concerned about discrimination.

Sweden's journalist union started wage surveys in 1966 when the labor movement was engaged in a program to raise the pay of all low-paid workers, The first survey showed that on a national average women journalists received 12.4 per cent less than men in the same salary qualification and in Stockholm the range was greater, $40 to $90 per month. Although women tended to have less experience for their age group than men, the union concluded that a good part of the pay differential could not be explained in any other way than sex bias.

These findings spurred the union to work to raise the pay of the low-salaried journalist and by 1970 there was "apparent equity," although by 1972 the union was already finding some slippage and prepared to move again on that issue. Women, who had not been very active in union work, became more active as they became more numerous in the profession and more aware of job discrimination. During the 1974 negotiations at DN, women staffers picketed inside the building and wore sweatshirts proclaiming their equal pay demands. They made significant progress as a result, they felt.

A Malmö study by Lund University sociologists released in 1971 added further evidence. In this third largest city of Sweden the women journalists had more education than the men, but they lagged far behind in responsible jobs. Women tended to cluster in certain fields (entertainment, home, consumer and feature departments) and averaged $180 less per month than men. Even when they had equal education and experience, women were still paid $75 a month less. The Malmö study was small (179 questioned) but the researchers still concluded that women were subject to discrimination from three sources: women's own attitudes, job expectations and society.

In Norway the journalist union surveyed salaries every two years preceding wage negotiations. Equal pay is a union policy and minimums were the same for men and women, but still Oslo journalists averaged 17 per cent more than those in Norwegian provinces (1970 figures) and women got 11 per cent less than men after adjusting for the longer experience of the men. (The unadjusted figure was 15 per cent.) Norwegian women held 10 per cent of the union membership, but only 5 per cent of the editing or assistant-editor jobs, compared to the group average of 12 per cent.

Several Norwegian women journalists were elected to leadership positions in their local unions, and four held top national office in 1975. The national union meeting that year heard a study on the status of women journalists, presented by two women from the University of Oslo. This added weight to the members' appeals for equal pay and better career possibilities. A group of 20 to 30 women journalists began meeting regularly to debate career issues. Norwegian women journalists looked back on 1975 as a break-through year, and said they were "on the move."

Finland's newspaper journalists had not yet conducted a wage survey by 1974, but magazine journalists there ran a study in 1966 and found that women earned about 20 per cent less than men in all magazine job categories. The staffs were 45 to 55 per cent female, and wages began to rise when these women complained to their editors.

Newspaper women in Finland learned in 1973 that salary differences between men and women at a leading newspaper averaged about $90 per month. Union officials were asked to do something about this in the 1975 negotiations, and a survey for all Finland's newspaper journalists was planned. The Union of Finland's Journalists elected a woman, Elina Simonen, from the women's magazine, *Jaana* as vice-chairman for 1974.

Although women journalists were very active in Finland, competing equally with male colleagues in all fields, "they were not paid equally," said Maija Liisa Heini. But they fought for the principle "equal work, equal pay," and "as far as I understand, the attainment of this principle is not very far in the future."

No special studies have been published on French women journalists by their union, but the union said that its women members "do enjoy equal pay and job status based on individual qualities."

A Cardiff University study of 1972 reported a 17 per cent wage differential between English women and men in journalism. Even before that report was issued, women had forced their union to do something about that state of affairs. At the February, 1972 union meeting a volunteer committee of four women and two men was formed to investigate: equality of opportunity and entrance to the profession and the training scheme; equality of promotion and an end to low pay for women; maternity leave benefits, and abolition of unequal pension schemes.

The committee was to conduct a wage survey and look for instances of discrimination that the union could fight. In the 1950's only about a dozen women attended a typical union convention of 200 or more members, but in 1972, 37 of the 412 delegates were women. Women made up 16.8 per cent of the union membership.

London media women circulated an angry newsletter at that union meeting, charging discrimination in: political, economic, labor and crime reporting and in editorial writing, photography sub- and chief editing. Women may participate in the profession, their publication declared, but they have to "stay out of the deep end of the pool where the real power and decision-making processes go on." This group advocated equal pay and promotion and training policies, maternity leave, day care and nurseries plus flexibility in hours for working parents.

The English journalist training scheme was criticized by the women for an "informal quota" that limited women trainees to about one-fourth the total accepted each year. That policy had developed in the past to fit the current market needs because the training scheme guarantees placement of its people, explained its director, George Viner. But "recently women applicants were so much better qualified than the men that they claimed more and more places, about half of them in 1972." So the "quota" no longer existed, he said.

> An interesting side effect of the trainee program, which
> started in 1963, is that women who have gone through it and

have taken two or three years off to have children are finding
it easy to be rehired when they return to the job market
because of their training and previous experience. Many are
working on suburban papers or small dailies and some are
sub-editors and are doing excellent jobs.

Viner expected that trend to continue.

A further step toward equality was taken by the British government early in 1974. Women's rights reforms were proposed
by the government, including the prohibitions against sex discrimination in employment, education and vocational training. Employment ads would no longer be allowed to specify
the sex of the applicants and existing laws, ostensibly designed to protext women from arduous, dangerous or un-
seemly jobs, would be rescinded. It was "the biggest step toward real equality for men and women that any government
has taken since women got the vote," declared Home Secretary
Robert Carr.

Two new women's rights laws, the Equal Pay Act and the
Sex Discrimination Act, became effective with the start of
1976. These laws promise wages similar to those men receive
for doing similar work and outlaw many forms of discrimination on the job and in other facets of British life.

Publications

Part of the credit for the advance was claimed by groups like
the Women in Media (WIM) group, which had grown to 300
members by 1974 and had worked to promote these women's
rights reforms. WIM set up a writer's cooperative and information pool, and an offshoot group, Women's Lobby, worked
with Women's Liberation Workshop and an older established
suffrage group, The Fawcett Society, to produce a bi-monthly
news report and to set up a research and advisory center for
women. Other sub-groups of WIM examined consumer problems, backed women political candidates and held media technique workshops for women. In August, 1974, Feminist
Books, the first independent women's publishing house in the
United Kingdom, announced its first feminist book.

The women's rights movement in Europe gave rise to several feminist publications in the 1970's as it did in America. A few were crudely mimeographed pamphlets at first. Some circulated to radical-liberal and socialist feminists and others were more interested in women's rights and consciousness raising. Some of the feminist publications included: Britain's *Spare Rib*, Holland's *Opjiz Mak Way*, Belgium's *Et Ta Soeur*, Sweden's *Kvinnobulletin* and Rome's *Effe*, modeled on *Ms.* magazine. Norway's *Sirene*, a late entry to the group, sold out its first 5,000 copies when it appeared at the end of 1973.

An early woman's magazine that intended to get women "out from the four walls of their homes" and encourage them to participate as full citizens and to learn a profession so they would not be unhappy and bored later, was *Frauen*. This northern German publication, edited by Dr. Lore Breuer, an experienced magazine editor, contained news, political comment and articles about women, culture and social problems. It started in 1972 as a pulp paper, newsletter-size publication and grew to a quality paper publication on the order of *Ms.* The circulation included 25 per cent teachers, 10 per cent men and 65 per cent housewives and others.

The ongoing discussion over women's role in life, the idea of sharing family responsibilities with husbands, the demands for day care and equal pay and promotions has had its effect in the European media as in the American press. Efforts for improvement in the status of women journalists, however, were national and as such limited. Little information circulated across the borders about these specialized groups, even though a few cross-national professional organizations existed.

Conditions of employment, education and the status of women varied from nation to nation and from urban to rural within those nations, making it difficult to make comparisons. But it was evident that women's roles, their expectations and self-images were changing in America and in Western Europe in the 1970's on a roughly parallel course. Legislation and professional organizations pushed the countries to eliminate sex discrimination and provide social programs that made it possible for working women to hold dual responsibilities. Day care, maternity and paternity leave, re-entry and re-training programs were being discussed or were underway.

It will be the journalist's job to report these changes search-ingly and thoroughly, providing the information and ideas for public discussion. The woman journalist will face the chal-lenge of reporting the changes in the larger society while working for improvements in her own profession.

A European male editor, speaking for many others, no doubt, asked: "Do women belong in the newsroom?"

The answer is "Yes, and with greater responsibility."

· SOURCES CONSULTED ·

E. A. Bennett, *Journalism for Women: A Practical Guide* (London: John Lane, 1898).

Beatrice Braude, "Marguerite Durand: Journalistic Mother of Us All," *Ms.*, March, 1973.

Asa Briggs, *The History of Broadcasting in the U.K.*, (London, Oxford University Press, 1965).

Myfanwy I. Crawshay, *Journalism for Women* (London: Fleet Publications, 1932).

Paul Ferris, *The House of Northcliffe* (New York: World Publishing, 1972.)

Michael Fogarty, Robert and Rhona Rappaport, *Women in Top Jobs* (London, 1967).

Hamilton Fyfe, *Northcliffe, An Intimate Biography* (New York: Macmillan Co., 1930).

Jan Johannesson and Lars Söderström, *Dagstidningsjournalister i Malmö* (Lund: Lunds Universitet, 1971).

Birgitta Johansson, "En kompakt dominans af män," *Hertha*, No. 4, 1974.

Journalisthögskolan, *Journalistkåren i Sverige* (Stockholm: Almqvist & Wiksell, 1970).

Dorothy Gies (McGuigan), "Women as Printers," *Publishers Weekly*, October 5, 1940.

Norsk Journalistlag, *Salary Reports*, 1969, 1970, Oslo.

Report of the Committee on the Position of Women in Finnish Society (Helsinki: Government Printing Centre, 1973).

Evelyne Sullerot, *Women, Society and Change* (New York: McGraw-Hill Book Co., 1971).

Anita Werner, *Norsk Journalister* (Oslo: Universitetsforlaget, 1966).

Women in Media, "Women in Journalism Report," National Union of Journalists, England, April, 1972.

Personal interviews with 112 journalists in eight Western European countries and with officers of the journalist unions in those countries (West Germany, Great Britain, Belgium, France, Norway, Sweden, Denmark and Finland).

* * *

Index